Essential Demographic Methods

ESSENTIAL

DEMOGRAPHIC

METHODS

KENNETH W. WACHTER

HARVARD UNVERSITY PRESS
Cambridge, Massachusetts
London, England
2014

Library of Congress Cataloging-in-Publication Data

Wachter, Kenneth W.
  Essential demographic methods / Kenneth W. Wachter.
    pages   cm
  Includes bibliographical references and index.
  ISBN 978-0-674-04557-6 (alk. paper)
  1. Demography—Statistical methods.   2. Demography—Mathematical
models.   3. Population—Statistical methods.   4. Population—Mathematical
models.   5. Population forecasting—Statistical methods.   6. Population
forecasting—Mathematical models.   I. Title.
  HB849.4W33 2014
  304.6072′3—dc23   2013034550

For Bernadette

Contents

Figures and Tables

Figures

Tables

Preface

This book has grown out of courses in demographic methods that I have taught at the University of California, Berkeley, over the past thirty-five years. Students range from freshmen to pre-docs, and they bring a wide range of backgrounds to my courses. I have tried to make the book accessible to those new to quantitative analysis, but also to keep it interesting to those with prior training in mathematics and social sciences. Graduate-level material and any calculus are confined to sections marked with a star (*).

One of the attractions of demographic methods is the opportunity to develop or refresh quantitative skills and overcome math anxiety while studying subjects of direct human and personal interest. For my courses there are no official prerequisites. Fluency with high-school mathematics is an advantage. The calculus used in the starred sections is explained along the way.

Studying demographic methods means, above all, drawing analogies and exploring examples. It thus provides opportunities to enjoy snippets from our cultural heritage along the way. In this book, the reader will come across a personal sampling of favorite passages and occasional excursions into metaphor.

I am indebted to the many students who have helped me develop this book, and especially to my outstanding Graduate Student Instructors Robert Chung, Debbie Blackwell, Bill Chu, Josh Goldstein, Laura Hill, Jie Huang, Aaron Gullickson, Bryan Sykes, Sarah Zureick, Maggie Frye,

Romesh Silva, and Sarah Bradley; and to Mike Anderson and Hans-Peter Kohler and again to Robert Chung as Visiting Professors; and to Carl Mason and Carl Boe. They have given generous advice. My editor at Harvard University Press, Michael Aronson, has helped at every stage; it has been a privilege to work with him. I thank Paul Anagnostopoulos and his team at Windfall Software for their careful efforts in production. I am grateful to my mentors Peter Laslett and Gene Hammel; to my friend George Merriam, who died as this book was nearing completion; to the Berkeley Department of Demography and my fellow faculty members, who have nurtured formal demography; and above all to my wife, Bernadette, for her loving support.

Essential Demographic Methods

Introduction

Why Study Demography?

As children, our earliest steps forward in awareness take us into demography, as we number our birthdays, put numbers on the ages of people around us, number the others in our family, our town, our country, and our planet, as we learn that the years we will have to live are numbered.

As adults, we cope with a world whose problems and opportunities are shaped by demography. Low growth rates and high growth rates form the backdrop to the contrasts between rich nations and poor nations, peace and conflict, environmental protection and degradation that form the stuff of each evening's news. The expanding proportion of elderly in developed societies challenges the social insurance and welfare systems. Reduced fertility is part and parcel of the transformation of gender roles reshaping social consciousness. Migratory movement puts strains on social cohesion. The transformations of marriage and family come to dominate political debate. Longer average lifespans give many of us new flexibility in planning out our life's fulfillments.

It is one thing to speculate freely about such trends, as all of us do. It is another to gain precise information about their extent so that definite numerical comparisons become possible. The science of demography has grown up over the last several centuries out of efforts to make measurements of population and lifecourse in consistent and meaningful ways. As such, it is an example, one of the best, of mathematics at work on the world.

Some of the readers of this book may, conceivably, have been born to be demographers. Demography is an attractive career, and this book provides a foundation for a professional career in demography. But others come to this subject, not because they plan to stay with it, but because of its intrinsic intellectual appeal. Demography is the quintessential quantitative social science. It bears something of the same relationship to other social sciences that physics bears to other natural sciences. Economics, statistics, and sociology have all grown up in tandem with demography. Of all the sciences of human behavior, demography is the one where it is easiest to count. The earliest statistics, in the book of Numbers in the *Bible* and the catalogue of ships in the *Iliad*, were demographic statistics.

There are three main reasons for the centrality of demography. First is the simplicity of the units of analysis. In sociology and psychology and many other fields it is difficult to settle on the right conceptual units for quantification. In demography, what to count, in the first instance, is obvious—men and women, households, families, old folks, young folks, babies, corpses. There is little fuzziness about the basic units. Second, demographic processes, especially fertility and mortality, are fundamentally more regular and law-like than many other aspects of behavior. Demographic models are closer to the phenomena themselves than models in other disciplines, with more hope of real predictive content. Third, demography relies heavily on all the other sciences that bear on human motivation and response, and it reaches out to them, having an area of study in common with each of them. It is interdisciplinary in fact, not merely in aspiration.

Measurements and Models

In this book we switch back and forth constantly between measures and models. When we study a calculation to measure something, we shall always have a model in mind or in the background. A measurement is more than a number computed in a specified way. As we use the term, a measurement is a number which has a role in a predictive or explanatory model. Consider some examples of things people measure—the probability of rain, the population growth rate, the distance from the earth to the sun. All these are concepts which look natural enough on the surface. On closer examination, it becomes less obvious what one means or what one ought to measure. Take the distance to the sun, from here to up there. For a precise measurement, problems arise. The sun is farther away in summer than in winter. Should we measure from the surface or the middle of the earth? What is the middle of our slightly pear-shaped planet? However, suppose we want to specify the distance from earth to sun in the context of Kepler's laws for planetary motion. Then the right thing to measure is the maximum distance from the center of gravity of the earth to the center of gravity of the sun, because this is the distance involved in formulas for the motion of the earth around the sun. To know what we want to measure, we need a model which shows us how we are going to make use of the measurements for prediction or explanation.

Just the same is true of our first concept, the concept of a "growth rate" for a population. To know what to measure, we need a model within which our measurement has sense. The model for "exponential population growth" found in Chapter 1 is the simplest demographic model. It is a model introduced for defining population growth rates in a meaningful way.

Sources of Demographic Knowledge

Defining appropriate measures is important. Having sources of information from which to calculate them is important too. Demographic information comes principally from four kinds of sources, censuses, vital records, surveys, and ethnographic observations.

Censuses are the oldest, most demanding, and most important source of demographic information. They go back to Biblical times; King David took a census and according to the book of Kings was punished by God for doing so. The Roman and Chinese Empires both took periodic censuses which today supply some of our best knowledge about ancient times. In the United States the Census is established by Article I of the Constitution, and censuses are taken every 10 years by law.

Vital records are the second main source for demographers. All modern governments register births, deaths, and marriages and collect and tabulate totals from these records.

Sample surveys have become more and more important as statistical science has developed. The U.S. has a wide-ranging Federal Statistical System, including periodic surveys like the Current Population Survey and surveys like the Health and Retirement Study which are "longitudinal" in the sense that they follow the same people over time. Since 1984, building on earlier World Fertility Surveys, coordinated surveys called Demographic and Health Surveys or "DHS" have been taken around the world under the auspices of the U.S. Agency for International Development.

Ethnographic observations are the fourth source, including information gathered from open-ended interviews or from systematic notes from "participant observers". Demographers are coming to recognize the necessity of going behind the standardized information that censuses, vital records, and surveys provide and probing the complexity of personal strategies and motivations.

Structure of This Book

We begin with two chapters on the most basic concepts of demography, exponential growth and the distinction between cohorts and periods. A cohort is a group of individuals, like those born in a certain year, followed through time as they age together. All members of a cohort have the same age at the same time. If we look at a population in a period or interval of time, different members of the population will have different ages at the same time. Demographic measures are conceptually simpler when they pertain to cohorts. But they are more useful when they pertain to periods. In this book cohort measures come first, for mortality in Chapter 3 and fertility in Chapter 4. There is a discussion of population projection in Chapter 5, and then we return to period measures, this time taking fertility first in Chapter 6 and mortality next in Chapters 7 and 8. Chapter 9 is devoted to marriage and family demography. The mathematical theory called Stable Population Theory helps demographers think about the distribution of population by age, with all its economic, political, and social implications. It appears in Chapter 10. Chapter 11 turns to migration and to the analysis of patterns of location, the subject of spatial demography. We look backward and forward in Chapter 12. Appendix A documents sources of data, and Appendix B collects useful formulas for ready reference.

Stars on sections and exercises indicate advanced, graduate-level material with some use of calculus, which is not needed in other sections of the book.

1

Exponential Growth

1.1 The Balancing Equation

The most basic demographic equation is the "Balancing Equation". The Balancing Equation for the world as a whole from 2010 to 2011 takes the form

$$K(2010) + B(2010) - D(2010) = K(2011)$$

Here, $K(2010)$ is the world population at the start of 2010, $B(2010)$ are the births *during* 2010, $D(2010)$ are the deaths during 2010, and $K(2011)$ is the population at the start of 2011. The letter "K" is traditionally used for population instead of "P", to avoid confusion with probability, which also starts with p. Estimated values for the numbers that go into the balancing equation for 2010 are shown in Table 1.1. Sources for this table and later tables are listed with abbreviations found in Appendix A.

The world population is a "closed population". The only way to enter is by being born. The only way to exit is by dying. The general form of the Balancing Equation for a closed population is

$$K(t + n) = K(t) + B(t) - D(t)$$

As before, $K(t)$ is the size of the population at time t, n is the length of a period like 1 year or 10 years, and $B(t)$ and $D(t)$ are the births and deaths *during* the period from t to $t + n$.

Table 1.1   The world population 2010 to 2011

Population 1 January 2010	6,851 million
+ Births 2010	+140 million
− Deaths 2010	−57 million
= Population 1 January 2011	6,934 million

Source: Population Data Sheet of the Population
Reference Bureau (PRB) for 2010.

The Balancing Equation for national or regional populations is more
complicated, because such populations also change through migration. The
U.S. Census Bureau keeps track of the nation's population by age, sex, and
race from decade to decade with a refinement of the Balancing Equation
called "Demographic Analysis" with a capital "D" and capital "A". The
Bureau's Balancing Equation includes several kinds of migration. In much
of this book, however, we shall be studying models for closed populations.
This is a simplification that help us to understand basic concepts more easily.
But no one should imagine that most national or local populations are at
all close to being closed.

World population reached 7 billion during 2011. Seven billion, in American English, is seven thousand million. It is written with a 7 followed by
nine zeros, or $7 * 10^9$. Computers have popularized words for large numbers based on Greek prefixes: *kilo* for thousands (10^3), *mega* for millions
(10^6), *giga* for billions (10^9), and *tera* for trillions (10^{12}). Going further, we
have *peta* for 10^{15}, *exa* for 10^{18}, and *zetta* for 10^{21}. In this terminology, the
world contains 7 gigapersons.

Large numbers like these are needed when we study global resources and
the impact of humans on the environment of our planet. For instance, the
total world consumption of power is now around 15 terawatts. Running
a laptop computer consumes about 100 watts, like a 100-watt lightbulb.
Dividing 15 terawatts by 7 gigapeople gives $(15 * 10^{12})/(7 * 10^9) = 2.1 *
10^3$ watts, or about 2 kilowatts of power per person being consumed when
we average across all the people on the globe.

An important pattern can be seen when we consider a closed population
and combine the Balancing Equation for this year with the Balancing
Equation for next year. We let the present year correspond to $t = 0$ and
let our interval be $n = 1$ year long. The assumption of closure gives us

$$K(1) = K(0) + [B(0) - D(0)]$$

The square parentheses are inserted to point out that we are decomposing next year's population "stock" into this year's "stock" plus this year's "flow". Of course, the sizes of the flows are very much dependent on the size of the stock. More people mean more births and deaths. We rewrite the same equation in a form which separates out the elements which vary a lot from case to case and time to time from those that vary less. We do so by multiplying and dividing the right-hand side by the starting population $K(0)$. Multiplying and dividing by the same thing leaves the equation unchanged:

$$K(1) = K(0) \left(1 + \frac{B(0)}{K(0)} - \frac{D(0)}{K(0)} \right)$$

The same equation for the following year is

$$K(2) = K(1) \left(1 + \frac{B(1)}{K(1)} - \frac{D(1)}{K(1)} \right)$$

Here, $K(1)$ means the population at the start of year 1, but $B(1)$ and $D(1)$ mean the births and deaths in the whole of year 1, from time $t = 1.0000$ to $t = 1.999999 \ldots$. Substituting for $K(1)$ in this equation and moving $K(0)$ to the end gives

$$K(2) = \left(1 + \frac{B(1)}{K(1)} - \frac{D(1)}{K(1)} \right) \left(1 + \frac{B(0)}{K(0)} - \frac{D(0)}{K(0)} \right) K(0)$$

The important thing about this equation is that we go from a starting population to a later population by using *multiplication*. The obvious fact that B/K and D/K are less directly dependent on K than B and D themselves makes population growth appear as a multiplicative process. Multiplicative growth is sometimes called "geometric" growth; *geo* and *metric* come from Greek roots for "earth" and "measure". Ancient Greeks and Egyptians multiplied by laying out two lengths as the sides of a rectangle and measuring the area of ground. The name "geometric growth" applies for growth through whole time intervals. When fractions of intervals are also involved, we make use of the exponential function, as we shall see, and geometric growth is then called "exponential" growth.

Our equations are most interesting in the simple case when the ratios B/K and D/K are not changing, or at least not changing much. Then we can drop the time labels on the ratios. Let

$$A = 1 + \frac{B}{K} - \frac{D}{K}$$

Our equations take the form

$$K(1) = A \ K(0)$$
$$K(2) = A^2 K(0)$$
$$K(3) = A^3 K(0)$$
$$\vdots$$
$$K(T) = A^T K(0)$$

At the start of the new millenium in 2000, or "Y2K", world population had just passed 6 billion. One estimate was 6.048 billion, with births exceeding deaths by about 75 million during the year. These estimates made A equal to $1 + B/K - D/K = 1 + 75/6,048$, or about 1.0124. Letting $t = 0$ stand for the year 2000, and assuming roughly constant levels for the ratios of births and deaths to total population, our formula predicts the following populations in billions:

$$K(0) = 1.0124^0 * 6.048 = 6.048$$
$$K(1) = 1.0124^1 * 6.048 = 6.123$$
$$K(2) = 1.0124^2 * 6.048 = 6.199$$
$$K(3) = 1.0124^3 * 6.048 = 6.276$$
$$\vdots$$
$$K(10) = 1.0124^{10} * 6.048 = 6.841$$

As it turns out, the prediction for $K(10)$ is not far from the population estimate for 2010 in Table 1.1. By 2012, the prediction for $K(12)$ reaches

7.012 billion. Despite hefty uncertainties about true population numbers and despite actual changes in the supposedly constant value of A, our formula gives a fairly realistic picture of overall population growth. It is sobering that a billion people have been added to the human head count in so short a time as a dozen years.

1.2 The Growth Rate *R*

The Balancing Equation for a closed population led in the last section to an equation for population growth,

$$K(T) = A^T K(0)$$

Built into this equation is the assumption that the ratio of births to population size $B(t)/K(t)$ and the ratio of deaths to population size $D(t)/K(t)$ are not changing enough to matter over the period from $t = 0$ to $t = T$. (We generally use small "t" to stand for time in general, and capital "T" to stand for a particular time like the end of a period.)

When births exceed deaths, A is bigger than 1, and the population is increasing. Keeping the same value of A from year to year, a graph of $K(t)$ as a function of t would look like Figure 1.1.

Not only is the population $K(t)$ increasing with time, but the amount of increase in population per unit time is also increasing; the graph gets steeper as it gets higher. The two triangles in the picture highlight this steepening. They have the same base, but the right-hand triangle has much greater height. The amount of increase per unit time is the slope of the graph. While we often measure a rate by the slope of a graph, we cannot very well measure the growth rate of the population by the slope of the graph of $K(t)$ versus t, because that slope does not stay fixed. It keeps changing even when the demographic quantities B/K and D/K are unchanging. We need a measure of growth which stays fixed when B/K and D/K are fixed.

The solution is to take logarithms of $K(t)$. Taking logarithms is the usual way of converting multiplication into addition. When B/K and D/K are unchanging, the graph of log $K(t)$ versus t has constant slope. In other words, the graph is a straight line. Taking logarithms converts the curve of Figure 1.1 into the straight line in Figure 1.2.

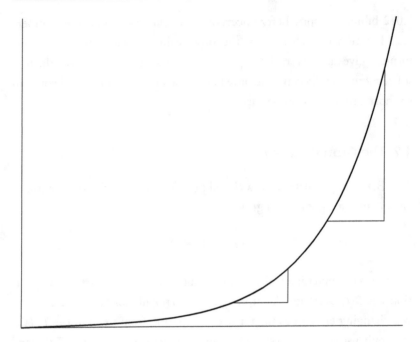

Figure 1.1 $K(t)$ with ever-changing slope

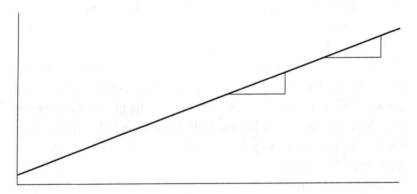

Figure 1.2   Log $K(t)$ with constant slope

In symbols, taking logarithms converts the equation

$$K(t) = A^t K(0)$$

into the equation

$$\log(K(t)) = \log(K(0)) + \log(A)\,t$$

This is a *linear* equation. It has the form $Y = a + bX$ if we write Y in for $\log(K(T))$ and X for time t. The intercept a where the graph crosses the vertical axis is $\log(K(0))$, and the slope b is $\log(A)$. We call this slope R. It is our measure of population growth.

The value of R for world population in 2010, based on Table 1.1, is $\log(1 + (140 - 57)/6{,}851) = 0.012042$, or about 12 per thousand per year in round numbers. The value for 2000 was also about 12 per thousand. It is a statistic worth keeping in mind.

> World population has been growing at a rate of about 12 per thousand per year since the turn of the millenium in 2000.

We always use logarithms to the base $e = 2.71828\ldots$. These are "natural logarithms". For consistency with computer languages, we write "log" for natural logarithm rather than "ln", which is an old notation. On hand calculators, however, the correct button for the natural logarithm log is often labeled "ln". The number "e" is the choice for A which makes the slope of the graph of $K(t)$ equal 1 when $t = 0$ and $K(0) = 1$; this is the mathematical definition of "e".

The key concept here is to measure growth on a *logarithmic* scale. As we shall see, growth on a logarithmic scale is the same as proportional growth. When the logarithm increases by some amount, the population size increases by some proportion of itself. We state this idea in the form of a definition:

> The population **growth rate** R is the slope of the graph of the logarithm of population size over time. It is the proportional rate of change in population size.

This definition gives us a measure of growth which is unchanging when the ratios of births and deaths to population size are unchanging, and only changes when the ratios change.

The slope of any graph is equal to the "rise" over the "run". The "rise" is the vertical increase corresponding to a given "run" along the horizontal axis. When we calculate the growth rate from time $t = 0$ to time $t = T$, the run is the length of the interval, $T - 0$ or T, and the rise is the increase in $\log(K(t))$. The slope is the quotient:

$$R = \frac{\log(K(T)) - \log(K(0))}{T - 0}$$

Using rules for differences of logarithms, we see that this expression is the same as an expression with a ratio of population sizes inside the logarithm:

$$R = \frac{1}{T} \log\left(\frac{K(T)}{K(0)}\right)$$

If we are measuring growth between two times t_1 and t_2, we have another version of the same formula:

$$R = \frac{\log(K(t_2)) - \log(K(t_1))}{t_2 - t_1}$$

Any one of these versions of the formula can be used to calculate a rate of population growth.

For a contrast to present-day growth rates, we can calculate R for earlier periods, like the long period between the start of agriculture around 8000 B.C. and the birth of Christ. Guesses at populations for these epochs, 5 million and 250 million, are given later in the chapter, in Table 1.4. We calculate the growth rate R to be

$$R = (1/8{,}000) \log(250/5) = 0.000489$$

This value is less than 1 per thousand per year. The units (millions of people) on 250 and 5 cancel when we take their ratio, while the units on 8,000—that is, years—in the denominator give us a measure *per year*.

If we average the growth rates for two successive years—say, this year (t goes from 0 to 1) and next year (t goes from 1 to 2)—we end up with the overall growth rate for the 2-year period from $t = 0$ to $t = 2$:

$$\frac{R_0 + R_1}{2} = \frac{1}{2}\left(\log\left(\frac{K(1)}{K(0)}\right) + \log\left(\frac{K(2)}{K(1)}\right)\right)$$

$$= \frac{1}{2}\left(\log\left(\frac{K(1)}{K(0)}\frac{K(2)}{K(1)}\right)\right) = \frac{1}{2}\left(\log\left(\frac{K(2)}{K(0)}\right)\right)$$

This property of our formula for growth is convenient. Knowledge of intermediate populations gives us no extra information when we seek the average growth rate between the start and the end of a long period.

The version of our formula for R with the ratio $K(T)/K(0)$ can be written

$$R = \frac{1}{T} \log \left(1 + \frac{K(T) - K(0)}{K(0)} \right)$$

When T is close to zero, a mathematical approximation for the logarithm, explained in Section 1.5, turns this equation into

$$R \approx \frac{K(T) - K(0)}{T} \frac{1}{K(0)}$$

The squiggly symbol $\approx$ means "approximately equal". The first factor is the slope of K, the rise over the run, and we divide it by the size of K at $t = 0$, telling us how big the slope is, as a proportion of the size. This proportional rate of change turns out, as promised, to be the same as R. We can think of R either as the slope of the logarithm of population size or as the proportional rate of change in population size.

The world's growth rate is believed to have peaked between midyear 1962 and midyear 1964 when the world population as registered on the "World Clock" maintained by the U.S. Census Bureau grew from 3,136,556,092 to 3,277,192,099. This peak growth rate is calculated in the same fashion:

$$R = (1/2) \log(3{,}277{,}192{,}099/3{,}136{,}556{,}092) = 0.021931$$

Of course no one knows the population down to the nearest person, or even down to the nearest 50 million or so. Population totals for countries are thought to be accurate only within 2% or 3% at best. It is sometimes useful, however, to quote totals down to the last unit, to make it easier to pinpoint the numbers' source. As for growth rates, demographers usually quote growth rates in parts per thousand per year. A demographer who says that the world's growth rate peaked at "22" means it peaked at "22 per thousand per year".

1.3 The Exponential Curve

We return now from our discussion of growth rates to our formula for the population over time in the case when the ratios of births and deaths to population remain constant.

$$K(t) = A^t K(0)$$

We rewrite this formula in the form

$$K(t) = e^{Rt} K(0) = \exp(Rt) K(0)$$

Here Rt is the "exponent" of the number "e". We are raising the number "e" to the power Rt, and another notation for this quantity is $\exp(Rt)$, the "exponential function" of Rt. The exponential function is the inverse function for natural logarithms. That is to say, for any x or y,

$$e^{\log(x)} = \exp(\log(x)) = x \quad \text{and} \quad \log(e^y) = \log(\exp(y)) = y$$

We know from our linear equation that $\log(A)$ is R, so we have

$$A = e^{\log(A)} = e^R \quad \text{and} \quad A^t = (e^R)^t = e^{Rt} = \exp(Rt)$$

These facts about logarithms show us that our equation with A and our equation with e are the same equation. The graph of $\exp(Rt)$ as a function of t is called the "exponential curve", the continuous-time version of the curve for geometric growth. It is important to become familiar with its shape. The shape depends on whether R is greater than, equal to, or less than zero, as shown in Figure 1.3. If the ratios B/K and D/K remain unchanged, the population either grows faster and faster beyond all bounds, stays the same, or heads toward zero steeply at first and more gradually later. The most common case is the case in the top panel when births exceed deaths and $R > 0$. This is the case of exponential growth that leads many people to feel alarm at the future prospects for humanity on the planet.

Our formula for exponential growth treats the growth rate R as a constant. To apply it in practice, we break up any long period of time into shorter intervals within which the growth rate does stay more or less constant and proceed step by step. The graph of the logarithm of population size becomes a series of straight-line pieces. In each step we "run" forward

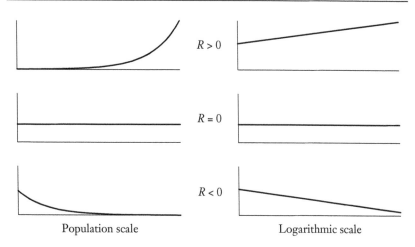

$R > 0$

$R = 0$

$R < 0$

Population scale   Logarithmic scale

Figure 1.3 Trajectories of exponential growth

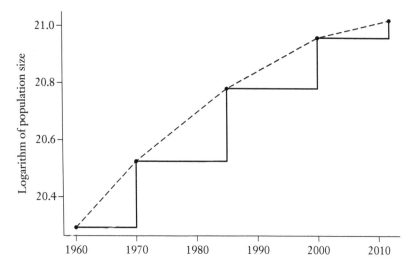

Figure 1.4 Rise and run: China's log-population

in time by some amount n, and our graph has a corresponding "rise" equal to n times R. The value of R at the step is the growth rate at that step, the current slope of the logarithm of $K(t)$, which we know has to equal the rise over the run.

The process is like going up a staircase. Figure 1.4 shows such a "staircase plot" for China, the country with the largest population in the world. The calculation of populations from growth rates is illustrated in Table 1.2. Input

Table 1.2   Growth rates in China

Date	n	R	Rn	$\log(K)$	$K(t)$
1960	10	0.0232	0.2320	20.2935	0.651
1970	15	0.0170	0.2550	20.5255	0.821
1985	15	0.0117	0.1755	20.7805	1.059
2000	12	0.0052	0.0624	20.9560	1.262

Source: Census Bureau IDB (2012).

data are found in the first three columns (before the bar). Results are found in the last three columns. One other datum is required, the initial value $\log K(1960) = 20.2935$, the height at the bottom of the stairs. As we have said, abbreviations for sources are found in Appendix A.

At the first step, to go from 1960 to 1970, we have a run of $n = 10$ years, and we calculate a rise of $Rn = 0.0232 * 10 = 0.2320$. Log population climbs to $20.2935 + 0.2320 = 20.5255$, implying $K(1970) = \exp(20.5255) = 0.821 * 10^9$. The next run of 15 years brings a rise of $0.0170 * 15$, and so forth. An estimate for 2012 is not shown but can be calculated. It comes out a little lower than the estimate from a different source in Table 2.1 in Chapter 2, reminding us that all population estimates are somewhat uncertain. In the figure and the table we see how the slope R has decreased interval by interval in the wake of China's energetic program of family limitation, including a "One Child Policy" introduced after 1978, modified in practice in recent decades. We also see how even moderate slopes continue to drive substantial multiplicative growth.

On the logarithmic scale, our formula for growth at each step involves simple addition:

$$\log K(t+n) = \log K(t) + Rn$$

We convert back to counts by applying the exponential function, which brings us back to multiplication:

$$K(t+n) = K(t)\, e^{Rn}$$

1.4 Models and Parameters

Exponential growth is a model for population size as a function of time. It is the first of many formal models studied in this book, and it provides an opportunity to introduce our terminology and approach and the ingredients that models share.

Every model is a model for some quantity. We call the quantity that takes the lead in the analysis the **leader** or, in the case of model lifetables, the **leading column.** The choice of leader is the first ingredient of a model. With exponential growth, the leader is population size $K(t)$. Other quantities can often be expressed in terms of the leader and the model can tell us about them too. Examples might be slope or acceleration in population size. But the leader is at the forefront of study.

Our second ingredient is the model **formula.** It expresses the leader as a function of some variable or variables, often time or age. With exponential growth, we can write the formula in a version which uses the symbol C for starting population size:

$$K(t) = C \, e^{Rt}$$

The third ingredient is a set of **parameters.** Parameters are values which fix the choice of a particular case to which the model applies from among all the cases covered by the formula. Our formula for exponential growth, as written, has two parameters, the starting size C and the growth rate R. Starting points and growth rates differ from case to case, whereas the functional form of the posited relationship between $K(t)$ and t remains the same. Parameter values may be chosen by intuition, in order to answer "What if?" questions, or they may be chosen to fit empirical data.

A fourth ingredient of some models is a set of constants, often depending on age or time or place, which enter into the formula and help determine what different cases have in common. They define a kind of backbone or spine for a model, and we call them **spines.** (This name is not in general use.) Our model for exponential growth has no spines, but spines are an essential part of most model lifetables.

Every time we encounter a model, we need to learn how to do two things:

- to work **forward** from parameters to model predictions;
- to work **backward** from observations to parameter values.

Our model for exponential growth has many applications, not only to people but to entities like neutrons or transistors on a computer chip. Transistors offer a case by which to illustrate how we work forward and how

Table 1.3   Fitting Moore's Law

Chip	Date	$K(t)$	X	Y	$X * X$	$X * Y$
Intel 4004	1971	$2.3 * 10^3$	0	7.741	0	0.000
Intel 8086	1978	$2.9 * 10^4$	7	10.275	49	71.925
Pentium	1993	$3.1 * 10^6$	22	14.947	484	328.832
SPARC T3	2010	$1.0 * 10^9$	39	29.723	1521	808.207
Sum	—	—	68	53.686	2054	1,208.965
Mean	—	—	17	13.421	513.5	302.241

Source: Wikipedia articles on individual chips (May 2013).

we work backward. The exponential model for transistors is called Moore's Law, named for Gordon Moore, a founder of the Intel Corporation. $K(t)$ represents the size of the "population" of transistors fitting onto one chip. Time $t = 0$ is 1971, when the Intel 4004 chip squeezed in $C = K(0) = 2,300$ transistors. An early guess at the parameter R was $\log(2)/2 = 0.347$.

Working forward, we start with R and C and predict $K(t)$. For 2015, we have $t = 2015 - 1971 = 44$.

$$K(44) = C \, e^{Rt} = (2,300) * e^{(0.037)(44)} = 9.6 * 10^9$$

If Moore's Law continues to hold, nearly 10 billion transistors should fit on a chip in 2015.

Working backward, we start with historical information and estimate values for R and C. Data points are given in the column labeled $K(t)$ in Table 1.3. Up to this point we have been calculating R from starting and ending populations. Now we introduce the statistical method of linear regression, which is well suited to estimating parameters in demographic models treated in later chapters.

Linear regression can be applied when the formula defining a model can be turned into an equation for a straight line using some transformation. With exponential growth, we know that taking logarithms, transforming $K(t)$ into $Y = \log(K(t))$, and writing $X = t$ gives us an equation for a straight line $Y = \log(C) + (R)(X)$ with slope R and intercept $\log(C)$. Linear regression fits a straight line by the method of "least squares", that is, by finding the values for slope and intercept that imply the smallest sum of squared differences between observed values of Y and values of Y predicted from the formula. Theory is explained in courses on statistics. Here, we simply treat linear regression as a recipe. We illustrate it in Table 1.3. The column labeled X gives time since 1971 for the horizontal or "X" axis on a graph. The column labeled Y gives $\log(K(t))$, the outcome for the vertical or "Y" axis. The column labeled $X * X$ is the product of X times itself, which could also be written X^2, and the column labeled $X * Y$ is the product of X and Y. Our "cookbook" recipe tells us to calculate slope and intercept from the following formulas:

$$\text{slope} = \frac{\text{mean}(X * Y) - \text{mean}(X) * \text{mean}(Y)}{\text{mean}(X * X) - \text{mean}(X) * \text{mean}(X)}$$

$$\text{intercept} = \text{mean}(Y) - (\text{slope}) * \text{mean}(X)$$

Plugging in means from the table, we find

$$\text{slope} = \frac{302.2412 - (17) * (13.42147)}{513.5 - (17) * (17)} = \frac{74.07615}{224.5} = 0.330$$

$$\text{intercept} = 13.42147 - (0.330) * (17) = 7.812144$$

The slope gives us our estimate for R—namely, 0.330 per year—close to the early guess. Since the intercept is $\log(C)$, our estimate of C is $\exp(7.812114) = 2,470$, close to our data point for $K(0)$. This approach to the estimation of parameters will be called into service many times.

* 1.5 Taylor Series

The multiplicative property of population growth can matter a great deal over the long term, but over the short term growth can look very nearly additive. The calculated populations $K(0), K(1), \ldots K(10)$ in the example in Section 1.1 were obtained by multiplication, but if we had simply added 80 million each year, we would have come out with nearly the same populations. How short is "short-term"? How long does it take for the multiplicative property to become important?

We can find answers to this question and to other questions about exponentially growing populations using differential calculus to produce approximations known as Taylor series. Our exponential function e^{Rt} has the following Taylor series:

$$e^{Rt} = 1 + \frac{Rt}{1} + \frac{R^2 t^2}{(2)(1)} + \frac{R^3 t^3}{(3)(2)(1)} + \frac{R^4 t^4}{(4)(3)(2)(1)} + \cdots$$

The numerators contain powers of Rt, and the denominators contain factorials, that is, descending products of numbers, often written $1!$, $2!$, $3!$, etc.

When the product Rt is small, only the first few terms are big enough to matter.

The first term in the expansion is a constant. The second term is linear; if t goes up by 1, the term goes up by the addition of the amount R. The third term shows the first multiplicative effect. The third term will be as much as, say, 10% of the second term if $(1/10)Rt \leq (1/2)R^2t^2$ or $t \geq 1/(5R)$. That gives us a rough rule of thumb. For a population like Brazil today, if we care about 10% precision, the multiplicative effect becomes important within $1/(5 * 0.011)$ years, or about 18 years.

For a second application of Taylor series, consider the competing effects of multiplicative growth and declining growth rates. According to U.S. Census Bureau estimates, world population growth rates have declined in every year since 1986, on average by about $s = 0.000372$ per year. Taking $t = 0$ to be 1986, the estimate for $R(0)$ is 0.017305. Using a linear approximation for the changes in R, we have $R(t) = R(0) - st$ for the growth rate *in* year t, or $R(0) - (1/2)st$ for the *average* growth rate between 0 and t. We have seen that the overall growth rate over a period is the same as the average growth rate in the period. So we can plug in $(R(0) - (1/2)st)t$ in place of Rt in our Taylor series for e^{Rt}:

$$e^{Rt} = 1 + R(0)t - (1/2)st^2 + (1/2)(R(0)t - (1/2)st^2)^2 \ldots$$

$$\approx 1 + R(0)t + (1/2)(R(0)^2 - s)t^2 \ldots$$

$$= 1 + (0.017305)t - (0.000036)t^2 \ldots$$

We see that the declines in the growth rate are wiping out the effects of multiplicative growth and actually changing the term in t^2 to a small negative. For most of history, changes in growth rates reinforced the multiplicative effects, but in recent years they have been counteracting them.

In this respect, the United States differs from the world as a whole. Changes in growth rates have been less important than multiplicative effects for a long time. Between the two censuses of 1990 and 2000, U.S. population grew at a rate of about $(1/10)\log(281.4/248.7)$, or about 12.35 per thousand per year, which is close to its overall growth rate of 13.09 per thousand over the whole twentieth century. The U.S. population is far from closed; it has the highest net immigration of any large country in the world. ("Net" immigration means immigrants minus emigrants, those coming in minus those going out.) However, as long as the ratio of net immigrants to starting population in each period is relatively stable, like the ratios B/K and D/K, our argument leading to the multiplicative formula for population growth remains valid, as it does in the U.S. case. The U.S. Census count in 1900 was nearly 76 million. Six terms from our Taylor series with $R = 0.013$ would give

$$76 * (1.000 + 1.300 + 0.845 + 0.366 + 0.119 + 0.031) = 278$$

That is an excellent approximation to the 281 million of the official 2000 Census count.

For understanding Taylor series, it is helpful to go over some facts from calculus about the exponential function. We concentrate on the case when R equals 1. Any case can be transformed into this case by reckoning time in units of $1/R$. For instance, if R is 0.010 per year, as in Brazil, then R is 1 per century. If R is 0.025, as in Nigeria, then R is 1 per 40-year interval. With $R = 1$, the exponential function is $\exp(t)$, which is the same as the number e raised to the tth power, e^t.

What is the number e? As we have mentioned, e is the choice for A that makes the initial slope of the population curve A^t, that is, the slope at $t = 0$, come out to be 1. When $A = 1$, the slope is zero, and when A is big, say, 3 or more, the initial slope is bigger than 1. In between 1 and 3 we find e, actually equal to $2.718282 \ldots$.

At values of t different from zero, the slope of e^t is given by the rise $e^{t+n} - e^t$ over the run n as n goes to zero. That equals $e^t(e^n - 1)/n$, which is e^t times the slope at $t = 0$—that is to say, e^t times 1.

We see, in other words, that the slope of the function e^t is equal to the value of the function e^t for all t. The function e^t is the only function whose slope always equals its value. This property is useful. Since the slope of e^t is e^t, the slope of the slope of e^t is also e^t, and the slope of the slope of the slope is e^t.

When we work with e^{Rt} instead of e^t, going back to our original units of time, a similar argument leads to a slope of Re^{Rt}:

> The slope of e^{Rt} is Re^{Rt}.

We can understand the Taylor series for e^t in terms of slopes and slopes of slopes. First, we approximate e^t by its value at zero, $e^0 = 1$. Then, we improve our approximation by adding the rise produced by a slope of e^0 applied to a run of length t. Then, we add an extra rise, which is needed because the slope itself is increasing, at a rate given by the slope of the slope. The average of these increases between 0 and t equals half the overall increase all the way to t, so we have $(1/2)t$ more slope on average. This extra slope applied to our run of length t gives an extra rise of $(1/2)t^2$. We can go on in this fashion, with the slope of the slope of the slope, and so forth, but the expressions become more complicated, because we have to average over averages, picking up factors like 1/3 times 1/2. As we go on, we build the whole Taylor series for e^t. With the whole series, we can plug in $t = 1$ and obtain the numerical value of e to as many decimal places as we like:

$$e = e^1 = 1 + 1 + (1/2) + (1/2)(1/3) + (1/2)(1/3)(1/4) \ldots$$
$$= 2 + 0.500 + 0.167 + 0.042 + 0.008 + 0.001 \ldots = 2.718 \ldots$$

All smooth functions have Taylor series. For example, the Taylor series for $\log(1 + y)$ is $y - (1/2)y^2 + (1/3)y^3 \ldots$. This formula is easy to check. If $x = \log(1 + y)$ then $1 + y = e^x$. We can substitute the series for x into our Taylor series for e^x, and we find that we get back $1 + y$.

When y is small, $\log(1 + y)$ is close to y. We relied on this approximation in Section 1.2 to interpret R as a measure of proportional growth. We can write $R = (1/t) \log(K(t)/K(0))$ in the form $R = (1/t) \log(1 + y)$ with $y = (K(t) - K(0))/K(0)$. Approximating $\log(1 + y)$ by y tells us that $R \approx ((K(t) - K(0))/t)/K(0)$. As t goes to zero, we have the slope of $K(t)$ at zero divided by the value of $K(t)$ at zero. This argument holds valid not only for population size but for any smooth function.

> The slope of the logarithm of a function equals the slope of the function divided by the value of the function.

* 1.6 Logistic Growth

In exponentially growing populations, the growth rate R, the slope of the logarithm of population size, is constant. For most of human history, however, the value of R for the world's population has not been constant but increasing. In the last half-century it has been decreasing. Historical changes in growth rates do not fit any one pretty formula, but several mathematical expressions for populations with increasing or decreasing growth rates have become well known.

The facts from calculus reviewed in Section 1.5 allow us to calculate R when we are given a formula for population size over time. Later, methods in Chapter 2 will let us calculate population size from formulas for R. All these formulas include parameters, here called c, f, and g, which specify a particular case from a family of similar cases. Two families of cases which can represent accelerating population growth are treated in the exercises: $K(t) = \exp((f/g)(e^{gt} - 1))$ and $K(t) = (f/(f - t))^{1/g}$. In this section we work through a famous model in which population growth responds to available resources, the case of Logistic Growth:

$$K(t) = \frac{e^{gt}}{(e^{gt}/c) + f}$$

To calculate R from $K(t)$, we first take logarithms, yielding $\log K(t) = gt - \log(e^{gt}/c + f)$. The slope of the log of a function is the slope of the function divided by the value of the function, so

$$R = g - \frac{ge^{gt}/c}{e^{gt}/c + f} = g\,(1 - K(t)/c)$$

When the constant f is positive, K starts out smaller than c at time zero, R is positive, and K increases. If K starts out much smaller than c, the population starts out with nearly exponential growth. But as K grows toward c, the growth rate heads toward zero. Population size levels out at c. We think of c as something like the carrying capacity of the environment and $1 - K(t)/c$ as something like resources available to sustain growth. In the logistic model, population size approaches an equilibrium level equal to c. A negative value of f means that the starting population is above the sustainable level c. Then growth is negative, and the population trends downward to its equilibrium.

The logistic formulas give one example of population curves that could arise from demographic feedback along lines proposed by Rev. Thomas

Malthus in his 1798 work *An Essay on the Principle of Population* and later editions, a founding work of demographic theory. In a stylized version, we can picture larger population size and a larger supply of labor leading to lower wages. We can also picture lower wages leading to higher death rates and in some settings to lower birth rates. In this way, high population sizes can lead to negative growth rates, forcing population size down. Low population sizes can lead to positive growth rates, forcing population size up. There is feedback from population size back to population growth, pushing population size toward an equilibrium value, undoing temporary gains in wage rates but restoring temporary losses.

Debates about these ideas have gone on for two centuries and continue. Malthusian population regulation is an example of "homeostasis", from Greek words for "same" and "state". Other versions of homeostasis may also be found among animal populations. A thoughtful account is found in Lee (1987). Although processes of population regulation may seem natural enough, Malthus' ideas have a somber side. They hold that exponential population growth cannot go unchecked indefinitely and if "preventive checks" like family limitation do not bring population into a sustainable balance with resources, then the "positive check" of exacerbated mortality will intervene.

1.7 Doubling Times

Tremendous acceleration in average growth rates occurred between the dawn of civilization and the mid-twentieth century. The meaning of such values of R is not, however, easy to visualize. In order to make growth rates more intuitive, demographers often convert them to doubling times. The doubling time T_{double} is the time it would take a population to double at a given growth rate if the exponential model were exactly true. We start with the model $K(t) = \exp(Rt)K(0)$ and seek T_{double} such that

$$K(T_{\text{double}}) = 2K(0) = \exp(RT_{\text{double}})K(0)$$

$$2 = \exp(RT_{\text{double}})$$

$$\log(2) = RT_{\text{double}}$$

$$T_{\text{double}} = \log(2)/R \approx 0.6931/R$$

Table 1.4 World populations and doubling times over history

Date	Population	Growth Rate	Doubling Time
8000 B.C.	5 million	0.000489	1417 years
1 A.D.	250 million	−0.000373	−1858 years
600	200 million	0.000558	1272 years
1000	250 million	0.001465	473 years
1750	750 million	0.004426	157 years
1815	1,000 million	0.006957	100 years
1950	2,558 million	0.018753	37 years
1975	4,088 million	0.015937	43 years
2000	6,089 million		

Source: Estimates drawn from Cohen (1995, pages 30 and 400–401) and IDB (2012).

Table 1.4 shows some guesses at total world populations for various epochs in the past. The growth rate and doubling time for each period are shown on the row for the *starting date* of the period. Thus, the average growth rate from the origins of agriculture and settled life around 8000 B.C. up to 1 A.D., estimated at $R = 0.000489$, is shown in the row labeled "8000 B.C.". There was no year "0", since the number zero had not come into use when the calendar was established. The first period in the table is 8,000 years in length, and this growth rate equals $(1/8{,}000) \log(250/5)$. The same formula can be applied to verify other growth rates and doubling times in the table.

If the growth rate R is a negative number, as at the start of the Dark Ages, the doubling time comes out to be a negative number too. How do we interpret it? A negative time reckoned from now is a time in the past; the population would have been twice as big at some time in the past. We can also think of a negative doubling time as telling us a "half-life". If the doubling time is −100 years, then it takes 100 years for the population to decrease to half its size. Half-lives are familiar for populations of atoms in radioactive rocks, but they are not so common for humans.

How many doublings would have to occur if a population began with one primordial couple, an Adam and Eve, and grew to the 7 billion of 2012? That is to say, can we find a number j such that $7{,}000{,}000{,}000 = 2\,(2^j)$? Taking logarithms, we need $22.669176 = (j + 1) \log(2)$, or about $j \approx 32$

doublings. However, the human population may have passed through many spells of decrease as well as increase through human prehistory and may have started from a small group rather than a single couple. So 32 is only a rough net number. It is a thought-provoking one for the majority of present-day humans who have seen one doubling and more within their lifetimes.

Turning this calculation around, consider that each person has two bio-logical parents, and, in the absence of incest, four biological grandparents, eight great-grandparents, and 2^j positions in the ancestral tree at the jth generation. If all these positions were filled by distinct people, then each one of us would have to have nearly 7 billion ancestors a mere 32 generations back, around the year 1000. Of course, this cannot be. The explanation of the paradox is that people inevitably marry their distant cousins, so that most positions far up in an ancestral tree are not filled by distinct people. A discussion can be found in Wachter (1980). Rohde et al. (2004) go further to estimate dates when the most recent common ancestor of all currently living humans may have lived.

The properties of exponential growth fascinated thinkers of the eighteenth century, especially the feature that late increases come so much more rapidly than early increases. The growth cumulates very suddenly at the end. A Malthusian worldview, which sees the future stalked by the con-sequences of continuing rates of growth, has an explanation of why doubters might doubt: cumulative growth is nearly invisible until it is upon us.

HIGHLIGHTS OF CHAPTER 1

- The Balancing Equation
- Closed populations.
- Exponential Growth.
- The Population Growth Rate.
- Doubling Times.

KEY FORMULAS

$K(t + n) = K(t) + B(t) - D(t)$

$R = (1/T) \log(K(T)/K(0))$

$K(t) = K(0)e^{Rt}$

FURTHER READING

A Concise History of World Population by Massimo Livi-Bacci (2012) shows demographic methods at work for understanding trends and turning points in history. Original sources for much of what we study can be found in the new edition of Smith and Keyfitz (2013). The *Macmillan Encyclopedia of Population* edited by Demeny and McNicoll (2003) has readable overviews. The textbook by Preston et al. (2001) is worth consulting. For a deep and thoughtful treatment, the work by Hervé Le Bras (2008), entitled *The Nature of Demography*, translated from the French by Godfrey Rogers, is the best that can be found.

EXERCISES FOR CHAPTER 1

1. Between 1960 and 1975 the population of Indonesia grew from about 100.6 million to 137.5 million. Between 1990 and 2000 it grew from 187.7 million to 225.0 million. Find the growth rates between 1960 and 1975 and between 1990 and 2000. Have the growth rates increased or declined?

2. If the average growth rate for the Indonesian population between 2000 and 2020 turns out to be 18 per thousand per year, what will the population in 2020 be?

3. The population of Nigeria in 1960 was about 39.2 million. The average growth rate R during the 1960s was 23.99 per thousand per year. During the 1970s it was 28.41; during the 1980s, 29.41; during the 1990s, 35.169. It is predicted to be around 30 per thousand per year from 2000 to 2020. Draw a rough freehand graph of the logarithm of Nigerian population over time based on these data, label the axes, and predict the population in 2020.

4. How much longer would it take the population of Indonesia to double, as compared with Nigeria, under the rates predicted for 2000 to 2020?

5. Official U.S. Census counts are shown in Table 1.5. What were the yearly growth rates and population doubling times between the following years: (a) 1790 to 1900? (b) 1900 to 1950? (c) 1950 to 2000? (d) 1790 to 2000?

Table 1.5 U.S. Census counts in millions

1790	3.929	1850	23.192	1910	91.972	1970	203.212
1800	5.308	1860	31.443	1920	105.711	1980	226.546
1810	7.240	1870	39.818	1930	122.775	1990	248.710
1820	9.638	1880	50.156	1940	131.669	2000	281.421
1830	12.866	1890	62.948	1950	150.697	2010	308.745
1840	17.069	1900	75.995	1960	178.464		

6. If world population grew from 6.851 billion at mid-year 2010 to 7.017 billion at mid-year 2012, what was the growth rate R? If world population continued to grow at or near this rate, how long would it take for the population to triple? How long for population to grow by 1 billion more beyond the 2012 level?

7. Suppose the world's population began to decline at the rate of $R = 0.007$ per year. How many years would it take for population size to return from its 2012 level to its 1950 level?

8. If $R = 0.035$ and $t = 20$ years, what is e^{Rt}? What is the natural log of the square root of $\exp(Rt)$? What is the doubling time for a population growing at a rate of 35 per thousand per year?

9. At mid-year 2012 Brazil, Pakistan, and Nigeria had similar total populations, 194, 188, and 170 million, respectively. Growth rates were 0.011, 0.021, and 0.024 per year. Suppose growth continues at these rates for at least 8 years. Use the exponential model to project populations for these three countries in 2020. Would their rankings change?

10. What is the natural logarithm of 1 billion? From data in Table 1.2, working on a logarithmic scale, estimate the date at which China's population passed 1 billion.

11. Dates at which world population first exceeded each number of billions from 1 to 7 are estimated to be (1) 1800, (2) 1925, (3) 1960, (4) 1974, (5) 1987, (6) 1999, and (7) 2011. Find the growth rates between each of these dates.

12. Suppose we care about 20% accuracy in predictions of proportional increases in population for countries like Egypt with growth rates around 21 per thousand. How soon would multiplicative effects be sure to become important?

* 13. From the U.S. Census counts in Table 1.5, find the growth rate between 1900 and 2000 to six decimal places. Use this growth rate along with the population in 1900 to predict populations throughout the century from an exponential model with constant growth. Draw a plot showing the actual census counts as points and the predicted census counts as a curve. Differences between observed and predicted values reflect the effects of changing growth rates over time. Are these differences more or less important than the multiplicative effects visible in the steepening of the predicted curve?

* 14. World population growth rates are estimated at 0.017305 in 1986, 0.015794 in 1990, 0.014283 in 1994, 0.012871 in 1998, 0.011556 in 2002, and 0.011152 in 2010. Draw a graph of these values and use linear regression to find the slope and intercept of a straight line fitting the data. Use your straight line as a prediction and calculate the fitted values and the difference between fitted values and observations for 1990, 1994, 1998, and 2002. Is the line a good fit?

* 15. What is the range of values of the growth rate R for which $1 + Rt$ is within 5% of e^{Rt} when $t = 10$?

* 16. Find a formula for the approximate value of $K \log(1 + 1/K)$ for large K. Use your formula to find another way of calculating the number e.

* 17 Consider two possible formulas for populations with changing growth rates: (a) $K(t) = \exp((f/g)(e^{gt} - 1))$ and (b) $K(t) = (f/(f - t))^{1/g}$. In each case, find a formula for the growth rate R as a function of $K(t)$. Describe how the growth rate behaves as time increases.

* 18. Like the human population, the size of the universe is expanding. Size $K(t)$ is measured as the distance to some particular distant galaxy at time t divided by the present distance. The growth rate is called the Hubble constant. It is constant over space but changes over time according to the formula $R = g \sqrt{f + c/K(t)^3}$ with $g = 73 * 10^{-12}$ per year, $f = 0.74$, and $c = 0.26$. Construct a staircase plot for the size of the universe over the next billion years, using four steps of 250 million years each. You may take the growth rate determined by the size at the start of each interval to apply to the whole interval. Predict the factor by which the universe will expand in the next billion years. At a growth rate of 0.011, will the world population of humans expand more in 10 years than the universe will expand in a billion years?

2

Periods and Cohorts

2.1 Lexis Diagrams

We have managed to develop our model for exponential population growth
with no reference to the most important word in demography, the word *age*.
In effect, the exponential model treats all people as if they were alike. As
we shall see, it can be expanded into a model formulated in the language
of probability theory in which all members of a population have identical
constant risks of dying or of producing offspring without reference to sex or
age. But of course in any real population, even one for which the exponential
model gives a good approximation of population growth, the people in the
population are in fact aging.

Time enters demography in two distinct ways: through chronological time, measured by dates on the calendar, the same for everyone, and
through personal time, measured by age for each person, unique for each
person or, more exactly, to each set of people who share the same birthdate.
The Lexis diagram is a simple visual display which helps us keep track of
the relationships between chronological time t and age x. It is named for
Wilhelm Lexis, a demographer of the late 1800s. The horizontal axis represents chronological time, that is, calendar time. The vertical axis represents
age. Each person has a lifeline on a Lexis diagram, starting at the point with
coordinates $(t_b, 0)$, where t_b is the person's birthdate and 0 is the person's
age at birth. The line goes up to the right, with a slope equal to 1 (that is, at
an angle of 45 degrees) because *people age one year in one year.* Each lifeline

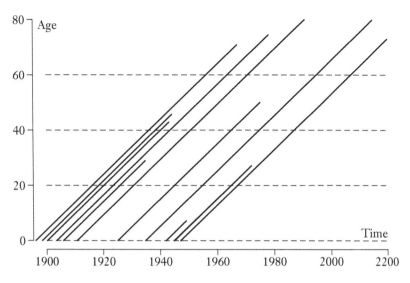

Figure 2.1   A Lexis diagram

continues up and to the right until the time and age of the person's death.
A Lexis diagram with 11 lifelines is shown in Figure 2.1.

To find how many people are alive at some instant of time, we draw a vertical line upward from the time point and count how many lifelines cross
that vertical line. That is the size of the population. Seven lifelines on Figure 2.1 would cross a line drawn at 1960. To find how many people survive
to some age, we draw a horizontal line across at the height corresponding
to that age and count how many lifelines cross that horizontal line. Five
people on Figure 2.1 survive to be 60 years old. If immigrants enter the
population, their lifelines start at the age and time of immigration, rather
than at their births. If we have a large population, some people share the
same birthdate and their lifelines partly overlap. We can imagine painting
our lifelines onto a board with heavy paint. The surface built up by the paint
is thick at any point of time and age where there are many people alive at
that time who are that age. It is thin where there are few people in the population at that time who are that age. The height of the painted surface
represents the density of people as a function of time and age. Such a three-
dimensional representation is called a Lexis surface, a generalization of a
Lexis diagram. The surface rises above a plane on which the axes for time
and age can be drawn, the so-called Lexis plane.

Let us focus on a group of people sharing the same birthdate. Later in time, all of those who survive will be found at the same older age. They age together. Their lifelines run diagonally up the Lexis diagram together. We call such a group of people a "cohort". "Cohort" is one of the most important words in demography.

We can define cohorts narrowly or broadly. We might form a cohort only out of people who share the same hour of birth. Such a cohort would have about 15,000 members around the world or about 500 members in the United States. Or we might form a cohort out of members with the same day of birth. Often, we take a broader perspective and form a cohort out of people with the same year of birth or with births within the same five-year timespan, called a quinquennium from the Latin words for "five" and "year". The essential point about a cohort is that time and age go up together.

A **cohort** is a group of individuals followed simultaneously through time and age.

Cohort experience is found on a diagonal stripe on a Lexis diagram. Years lived by cohort members are found on the lifelines inside a parallelogram stretching up from the axis at 45 degrees. In contrast, years lived by population members within a period of time are found in a vertical block on the Lexis diagram. Years lived within a given age group are found in a horizontal band on the Lexis diagram. Figure 2.2 illustrates the three ways of viewing demographic experience, in terms of cohort, period, and age.

We have been discussing the basic idea of a cohort, a group of people born together in time. Birth is the time of entry into the human population. We can extend the concept of cohort to embrace other sorts of entry. For example, demographers in Berkeley, California, talk about the cohort of students who enter graduate school together. Students entering in 2013 are the "thirty-fifth cohort". Likewise, we talk about marriage cohorts. Couples with weddings in 1982 form the Marriage Cohort of 1982. Duration of marriage takes the place of age. Age itself, after all, is the same as duration of life.

The word cohort was originally a military term, referring to a group of about 600 Roman infantrymen who marched along together. Ten cohorts

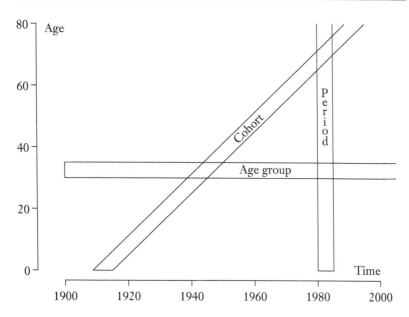

Figure 2.2 Cohort, period, and age

made a legion. In *Paradise Lost*, John Milton writes about a cohort of angels, "the cohort bright of watchful cherubim". We picture a birth cohort forming ranks along a stretch of the horizontal axis of the Lexis diagram and marching out along the diagonal through life together.

A cohort is special because it shares experiences. It arrives at the same point of history at the same age. The cohort born at the start of the twentieth century were all teenagers during World War I and fought as mature men in World War II. The cohort born immediately after World War II, at the start of the Baby Boom, experienced President Kennedy's assassination in high school and saw two of its members occupy the White House between 1992 and 2008. The book *Generations* by Strauss and Howe (1991) is an account of American history from 1584 into the future in terms of cohorts and their distinctive approaches to political and social problems over time.

2.2 Period Person-Years Lived

Demographers are constantly moving back and forth between thinking in terms of periods and thinking in terms of cohorts. The key tool for seeing relationships between formulas involving periods and formulas involving cohorts is the concept of *person-years lived*. We begin, in this section, by developing the concept of person-years lived in terms of periods. This concept helps us give a fuller description of our exponential model for population growth, which is essentially a model for the size of the period population. In later sections, we express the same concept of person-years lived in terms of cohorts. Our two ways of counting person-years, by period and by cohort, lead to an identity between period-based and cohort-based kinds of demographic measures, the Stationary Population Identity, derived at the end of this chapter.

We are led to the concept of person-years lived when we seek to refine the basic insight that brought us to the equation for exponential growth. We began in Chapter 1 with the insight that more people mean more births and deaths. We proceeded to divide births and deaths during an interval by population at the start of the interval to remove the most direct effects of population size. Now we ask, why take population at the start rather than at the end or in the middle? People who are present during part of the period can also have babies or become corpses. It is not just more people that mean more births and deaths, but more people present for more of the time.

Consider first an interval of time one decade long—say, the period from 2000 to 2010. Each full year that a person is present, he or she contributes one "person-year" to the total of "Period Person-Years Lived", or "PPYL", for the population in the period. We make two new definitions:

The Crude Birth Rate, or *CBR* (also written as *b*), is the number of births to members of the population in the period divided by the total period person-years lived.

The Crude Death Rate, or *CDR* (also written as *d*), is the number of deaths to members of the population in the period divided by the total period person-years lived.

We count up person-years in fractions of years as well as whole years. Each day a person is present in the population, he or she contributes 1 person-day, or $1/365$ person-year, to the period person-years lived. Each hour a person is present, he or she contributes 1 person-hour, or $1/8{,}766$ person-years, to the period person-years lived.

Whenever we know the whole sequence of population sizes throughout a period, say, the population sizes on each day over the period of a year, we can add up the person-years day by day. We take the number of people present on the first day times 1/365 of a person-year for each of them, plus the number of people present on the second day for each of them times 1/365 person-years, and add up all the contributions. For an even more precise calculation, we could use hours or minutes or seconds. As we take smaller and smaller subintervals, we have more and more of them to add up. When our subintervals are small enough, our sum is virtually equal to the area under the curve of population as a function of time during the period. This outcome is a fact of calculus, which we discuss further in the advanced (starred) sections in this chapter.

Whenever the sequence of population sizes throughout a period are unknown, we use an approximation for *PPYL*, the period person-years lived. The most popular practice is to take the population in the *middle* of the period and multiply by the length of the period. For example, to estimate period person-years lived in the United States in the period from 2005 to 2015, we take the mid-period count of 308.745 million from the 2010 Census and multiply by 10 years to obtain 3,087 million person-years in the period. Many countries like Great Britain estimate their populations in the middle of each year for just this purpose. If we do not know the mid-year population, then we can take the average of the starting and ending populations and multiply by the length of the period.

2.3 The Crude Rate Model

The concept of period person-years lived allows us to give a fuller statement of the assumptions behind our model of exponential growth. We imagine a closed population in which each person, each instant, is subject to a constant independent risk first of dying and second of contributing a baby to the population. Then b and d are the expected numbers of births per person per year and of deaths per person per year. The expected size of the population displays exponential growth.

Even for childbirth and dying, the model makes assumptions which are extreme simplifications. We know that risks of childbirth and dying are not the same from person to person and day to day. Women are more likely to give birth than men. Adults are more likely to give birth than children. Old people and infants are more likely to be about to die than students or professors. Summer days see more births than autumn days. But think of populations with a run-of-the-mill mix of people and seasons that blend into each other. For a crude model, we lump all the people and all their days together and attribute risk to all without distinction.

This Crude Rate Model allows perfect trade-off between people and days. People and days contribute on the same footing. Recall the proverb, "You can fool some of the people all of the time, and all of the people some of the time." When counting person-years, all of the people some of the time is just as good as some of the people all of the time. This model is appropriate if we do not know who the people are or what the days are. It assumes, first, a closed population, second, homogeneous risks among people, and, third, no measurement of change over time inside the period

We have been using the word "risk". Models that refer to risks or chances are really part of probability theory, where this model is called a "Birth and Death Process" model. When this model is an adequate description of a closed population within the limits of accuracy that we care about for some purpose, then the Growth Rate R equals the difference $b - d$. This fact is proved using calculus in Section 2.5. Of course, most actual populations are not closed and risks are not homogeneous over time, so in most cases R does not exactly equal $b - d$. Some demographers define a "Crude Growth Rate", or CGR, equal to the CBR minus the CDR plus a Crude Net Migration Rate, labeled MIG in Table 2.1.

Table 2.1 shows crude rates for the 10 most populous countries in the world at mid-year 2012. The IMR is the "Infant Mortality Rate" introduced in Section 2.4, and e_0 is the "expectation of life at birth" introduced in Section 2.6. Some of these statistics are subject to wide uncertainty.

The rates in Table 2.1 show substantial diversity from country to country, largely correlated with levels of economic development. But almost all countries today are much more like each other than like their counterparts of 200 or so years ago. Over the last century and a half, most societies have either passed through or moved well along the path of a "Demographic Transition" from "high-pressure" demographic regimes with high birth rates, high death rates, and low growth, to "low-pressure" regimes with low birth rates, low death rates, and low growth. In the mid-twentieth century, Kingsley Davis, Frank Notestein, and others developed this concept of Demographic Transition, viewing rapid population growth as a tempo-

Table 2.1   The world's 10 most populous countries (rates per thousand, population in millions for mid-year 2012)

Rank	Country	Pop.	CBR	CDR	MIG	R	IMR	e_0
1	China	1,350	12	7	−0	5	17	73
2	India	1,260	22	7	−0	16	47	65
3	USA	314	13	8	+3	9	6	78
4	Indonesia	245	19	6	−1	12	29	71
5	Brazil	194	16	6	−0	11	20	73
6	Pakistan	188	28	8	−2	21	64	63
7	Nigeria	170	40	14	0	24	77	47
8	Bangladesh	153	23	6	−3	14	43	65
9	Russia	143	12	15	+2	−1	8	68
10	Japan	128	9	9	0	0	3	83
*	world	7,017	20	8	0	12	46	69

Source: Author's estimates based on comparisons of *PRB*(2012) and *IDB* (2012).

rary phenomenon occurring between an initial drop in death rates and a subsequent drop in birth rates. It remains a question whether transitions still underway will proceed rapidly enough to allow a smooth path toward sustainable development. The measures in this chapter and later chapters are widely used to monitor accelerations and slowdowns in demographic transitions around the globe.

2.4 The Infant Mortality Rate

The Crude Birth Rate and the Crude Death Rate are period measures. We can calculate them using nothing besides what we can find in the rectangle for the period on the Lexis diagram. Most measures of mortality other than the *CDR* are based on cohort data and founded on cohort concepts, and we shall be studying them in Chapter 3. The Infant Mortality Rate, however, is another pure period measure. It is defined as follows:

$$IMR = \frac{\text{the number of deaths under age 1 in the period}}{\text{the number of live births in the period}}$$

The *IMR* is best understood by referring to a Lexis diagram like Figure 2.3. This figure shows the sources of contributions to the numerator and denominator of the *IMR*. The central square has a base of 1 year on the

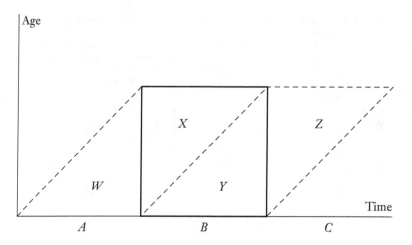

Figure 2.3   IMR contributions on a Lexis diagram

time axis (the 1-year period for this period rate). It has a height of 1 year
on the age axis for infants up to the age of 1 year. The square is made up
of two triangles labeled X and Y. Any lifeline which ends within the square
contributes a death to the numerator of the *IMR* for the period covered
by the square. Any lifeline that starts on the base of the square, labeled B,
contributes a birth to the denominator of the *IMR*.

From a certain point of view, the *IMR* is an odd hybrid measure. The
deaths in the numerator are not all happening to the babies whose births are
found in the denominator. Babies born outside the period in the preceding
year labeled A on the diagram may die as infants during the period in
the triangle X. They are counted in the numerator but omitted from the
denominator. Babies born during the period labeled B may die in the
triangle labeled Z after the end of the period. They are omitted from the
numerator but counted in the denominator. It is mathematically possible to
have an *IMR* greater than 1, if births labeled A far outnumber births labeled
B. Usually the mismatched terms balance each other out and the *IMR* is
close to the probability of dying before age 1 studied in Chapters 3 and 7.

The geometrical shapes in Figure 2.3 offer a preview of the distinction
between period age-specific rates and cohort age-specific rates that runs
through later chapters. Period deaths and period person-years lived come
from deaths and lifelines in the square bounded by solid lines comprising
triangles X and Y. Dividing these deaths by these person-years gives a

period age-specific mortality rate (in this case for the age group from 0 to 1) which will be written with a capital M. Cohort deaths and cohort person-years lived, on the other hand, come from deaths and lifelines in the parallelogram bounded by dashed lines comprising triangles Y and Z. Dividing these deaths by these person-years gives a cohort age-specific mortality rate, written with a small m. Were we looking at an older age group, say, from 20 to 21, we could also have a period age-specific fertility rate written with a capital F from childbirths and lifelines in a square and a cohort age-specific fertility rate written with a small f from childbirths and lifelines in a parallelogram.

Despite its theoretical oddity, the *IMR* is a handy measure. It uses only current information from vital registration. Unlike the lifetable measures presented in Chapter 3, it can be computed for countries that do not have a reliable census or other source for a count of the population at risk by age.

Infant Mortality Rates per thousand around the world range from about 1 for Iceland and 6 for the United States up to 110 for Senegal and 130 for Afghanistan. A century ago, however, rates as high as 350 were not uncommon. To some extent, the *IMR* depends on ages of mothers. Infants borne by teenagers and by older mothers are at higher risk, a point often forgotten by the popular press when it draws comparisons among countries and subgroups of the population.

* 2.5 Person-Years and Areas

We have seen in Section 2.2 that the period number of person-years lived in a population equals the area under the curve of population size over time. The *PPYL* in the period between time 0 and time T is the area under the curve $K(t)$ between 0 and T. In calculus, areas are written as integrals:

$$PPYL = \int_0^T K(t)\, dt$$

The symbol "dt" stands for an arbitrarily tiny piece of the whole time interval. We multiply the number of people alive in each piece by the length of the piece and add up over all the pieces. We take smaller and smaller pieces, hours, minutes, seconds, and in the limit we have a precise answer for the area.

We can find an exact formula for *PPYL* when the population is growing exactly exponentially, that is, when the growth rate is constant. We use a property of the exponential function called "self-similarity". If we take an exponential curve $f(t) = e^{Rt}$ and shift it T units to the left, we get a curve $g(t) = f(t + T)$ which is just the product of $f(t)$ times a constant e^{RT}, similar in the sense that it has the same shape but different size. Adding up areas starting from infinitely far back in the past, the area under the curve f up to time T is the same as the area under the curve g up to time zero, which, thanks to self-similarity, equals e^{RT} times the area (call it $\mathcal{A}$) under f up to time zero. Subtracting, we find the area under f between 0 and T to be $(e^{RT} - 1)\mathcal{A}$. What is $\mathcal{A}$? When T is very small, $\int_0^T f(t)\, dt$ is close to the area of the rectangle with base n and height $e^0 = 1$—namely, T—and our Taylor series tells us that $(e^{RT} - 1)\mathcal{A} \approx (1 + RT - 1)\mathcal{A}$, so $\mathcal{A}$ has to be $1/R$.

$$\text{Exponential Area} \quad \int_0^T e^{Rt}\, dt = \frac{e^{RT} - 1}{R}$$

When we multiply by $K(0)$ we obtain the full formula for the Period Person-Years Lived between 0 and T when the growth rate is constant: $PPYL = K(0)(e^{RT} - 1)/R = (K(T) - K(0))/R$.

As a first application, let us calculate how many person-years would have been lived altogether by members of the human race if the growth rate had always been equal to the present growth rate of around 0.012 per year. In billions, the answer is $(7 - 0)/0.012 \approx 583$ billion person-years. We come back to this answer in the next section, when we consider how many people have ever lived on earth.

As a second application, consider the *CBR* and *CDR* under the assumption that population size is growing exactly exponentially over the course of a year. Population increases by

$$K(1) - K(0) = K(0)(e^R - 1) = B - D$$

The difference between the *CBR* and the *CDR*, using our exact expression for the *PPYL* in the denominator, is

$$CBR - CDR = \frac{B - D}{K(0)(e^R - 1)(1/R)} = 1/(1/R) = R$$

Here is a sensible conclusion. The Growth Rate equals the difference between the Crude Birth Rate and the Crude Death Rate in a closed population subject to truly exponential growth.

As a third application, take the interval from 0 to T and substitute our Taylor expansion for the exponential in the formula for $PPYL$:

$$PPYL = K(0)(e^{RT} - 1)(1/R)$$
$$\approx K(0)(1 + RT + R^2T^2/2 + \ldots - 1)(1/R)$$
$$= K(0)(1 + RT/2 + \ldots)T \approx K(T/2)T$$

We see that the approximation for $PPYL$ in terms of the mid-period population $K(T/2)$ agrees with the exact expression up to the first nonconstant term (up to "first order") when the exponential model is true. It is a useful exercise to carry the expansions one step further, including the term R^3T^3. These expansions tell us the differences between the area formula, the mid-period approximation, and the average approximation $(T/2)(K(0) + K(T))$ as estimates of Period Person-Years Lived.

2.6 Cohort Person-Years Lived

Up to this point we have been counting person-years lived by period and calling them Period Person-Years Lived, or $PPYL$. We have been taking all the person-years from the first day, adding all the person-years from the second day, and so forth, counting up by subsets of time.

But we could have proceeded differently. We could have taken a cohort, counted the person-years lived by the first member of the cohort, added the person-years lived by the second member of the cohort, and so forth, for the whole cohort. This gives us a total Cohort Person-Years Lived, or $CPYL$. The person-years are the same things, but we are counting them up in two different ways. Referring back to Figure 2.3, for $PPYL$ we count person-years in a rectangle of the Lexis diagram (in that figure a square). For $CPYL$, we count person-years along a diagonal stretch which forms a parallelogram on the Lexis diagram.

If we add up all the cohort person-years lived and divide by the total number of members of the cohort (counted at birth, when the cohort is formed), we obtain a number e_0, the "expectation of life at birth." This is the average number of person-years lived in their whole lifetimes by members of the cohort, a quantity which will be discussed at length in Chapter 3.

To calculate e_0 we can measure the lengths of all the lifelines of cohort members with a ruler and take the average. Notice, however, that if 1 year corresponds to 1 inch on the axes, 1 year corresponds to 1.41 inches (the square root of 2 inches) on the diagonal, because of Pythagoras' theorem. In a right triangle, the square of the diagonal is equal to the sum of the squares of the other two sides, and 1 plus 1 equals 2.

The quantity e_0 is a cohort measure of survival (or of avoidance of mortality). The *CDR*, on the other hand, is a period measure of mortality. We calculate it from the lifelines in the rectangle on the Lexis diagram. The numerator for the rate is the number of lifelines which end in the box. (Often we mark the ends of lifelines with circles so we can see them.) Not every lifeline, of course, has a death on it in a particular period; for the numerator, we only count the circles. For the denominator, we are effectively adding up the length of all the lifelines in the box by counting how many cross each vertical line in a dense grid of vertical lines.

People wonder how many human beings have lived on our planet. Our methods allow us to make some relevant calculations. If we draw a curve of total population versus time over a long period, and if 1 year is 1 unit on the horizontal (time) axis, then the area under the curve is the total period person-years lived. If we know the average lifespan over the whole period, then the total person-years lived divided by the average lifespan gives us the number of people who lived those person-years.

In Section 2.5, using calculus, it was shown that when $K(t)$ is an exponential curve, the area under $K(t)$ between 0 and T is given by the quotient $(K(T) - K(0))/R$. Using the guesses at historical population sizes in Table 1.4, under the assumption of smooth exponential growth, the number of person-years between the origins of farming around 8000 B.C. and the birth of Christ in billions would be

$$(0.250 - 0.005)/0.000489 \approx 501 \text{ billion person-years}$$

If average lifespans over this period were around 25 years, then a total of about 20 billion people would have lived over this period of early human civilization.

For fully accurate results, we need to remember that people still alive at the end of the period still have some of their lifespans to live, and people already alive at the beginning of the period have already lived some of their lifespans. To obtain the total person-years for all the cohorts born between two dates, which contribute to the average lifespan of the cohorts, we have to add in a contribution for remaining life at the end and subtract away a contribution for expended life at the beginning.

This effect of extra life is small for small growth rates like the one in our previous calculation. But it can be large. For example, in Section 2.5 we saw that under the unrealistic assumption that the population had always been growing at its present rate of about 0.012 per year we would have about 583 billion person-years lived from the indefinite past up to the present. With a 2012 value for world-wide average lifespan of about 69 years, the formula we have been using would mislead us, suggesting $583/69 = 8.5$ billion people, of whom 80% or so would be alive today. The fallacy is that the 7 billion people alive today have something like 30 years apiece still to live on average, contributing another 210 billion person-years which would have to be added into the calculation.

Under the exponential model, the slower the growth rate, the more people have lived in the past and the smaller the proportion who are still living in the present. This outcome is reasonable. The slower the growth rate looking forward in time, the slower the population shrinks as we look back in time, and the more people we expect in the distant past.

When we ask how many humans have ever lived, some substantial uncertainty in the answer comes from prehistory. First, there are different choices for what counts as "humans" and what point in evolution should be taken as our starting point. Second, estimates of prehistoric population sizes and lifespans are speculative. Third, the exponential model is probably a poor guide to human prehistory. It may well be better to picture one or several periods of early rapid growth followed by long stretches of time in which populations remained roughly in balance with resources and predators or in which populations cycled through successive periods of shrinkage and expansion.

Genetic studies with the part of our genetic inheritance known as mitochondrial DNA suggest that all humans now living are descended in the female line from one woman who lived in Africa in something like 180,000 B.C. among a small group of other humans from whom we also descend through male and female lines. For a lower bound on total humans in prehistory, we reckon that the early group must have been at least 2, the average lifespan was less than 25, and the exponential model understates total person-years. We arrive at a lower bound of 2.3 billion people before the dawn of agriculture. As we have seen, the number of people living after that transition is even greater. The popular view that half or more of all people who have ever lived are living today is obviously wrong.

2.7 The Stationary Population Identity

Usually, period person-years lived and cohort person-years lived are different, because, though we are counting the same kind of thing, we are counting it for different groups of people or stretches of time. In special circumstances, however, we can count nearly the same batch of person-years in two ways, once by period and once by cohort, and get nearly the same answer. The special circumstances are these: First, the rates are unchanging. Second, the numbers are unchanging. This second condition means that total population is the same from year to year, and so are the number of births and the number of deaths. In this case the population is called "stationary".

We take care to distinguish the word "stationary", as demographers use it, from the word "stable." Populations which keep the same size are called stationary. The word "stable" is used for populations that are produced in the long term by unchanging demographic rates, whether their size is growing, constant, or declining. Stable populations are studied in Chapter 10. Here, we focus on stationary populations.

When the population is stationary, $K(t)$ equals the same number K, whatever the year t. The number of births per year B is also constant, equal to the number of deaths per year and also equal to the product of the Crude Birth Rate b times K people times 1 year for each year, amounting to $B = Kb$ births per year. In a period stretching from time 0 to time T, the total period count of person-years lived equals KT person-years.

Now consider the cohorts of people *born* in the same interval from time 0 to time T. Their lifelines, all at 45 degrees, are pictured on Figure 2.4. Most of the person-years on these cohort lifelines occur in the period and are the same as person-years we have already counted. However, the cohort count excludes years lived in the triangle OPQ in the Lexis diagram, which

Figure 2.4 Lexis diagram for a stationary population

are lived by people born before time 0, and the cohort count includes extra years lived in the triangle TUV by cohort members still living after the end of the period at time T. Now the triangle OPQ has the same shape and size as the triangle TUV, making the missing person-years cancel the extra person-years, since demographic rates and population sizes are unchanging over time. Therefore, the count of period person-years lived KT equals the count of cohort person-years lived.

We obtain the count of cohort person-years by multiplying $B = Kb$ cohort members born each year times e_0 years lived on average in each lifetime, times T cohorts in all, or $K\,b\,e_0\,T$, equal to the period count KT. Cancelling K and T, we obtain the "Stationary Population Identity":

$$1 = b\,e_0 \quad \text{when } R = 0$$

This identity is handy for quick estimates. For France in the 1600s, with a nearly stationary population, $e_0 = 30$, so the Crude Birth Rate must have been around $1/30$, or 0.033, per year. Since b is a rate, it has units of $1/\text{time}$, while e_0 has units of time. Their product is the dimensionless constant 1. The Stationary Population Identity is deep as well as useful. It connects a period fertility measure b to a cohort mortality measure e_0 in a stationary population. It reappears in various guises in many chapters of this book.

HIGHLIGHTS OF CHAPTER 2

- The Lexis diagram
- Cohorts
- Person-Years Lived

- The Infant Mortality Rate
- How many people have every lived.
- The Stationary Population Identity

KEY FORMULAS

$PPYL \approx K(T/2)\,T$

$IMR = \dfrac{\text{infant deaths in period}}{\text{live births in period}}$

$R = 0 \quad \text{implies } b\,e_0 = 1$

FURTHER READING

The book by Joel Cohen (1995) *How Many People Can the Earth Support?* has a captivating overview of population sizes and changing growth rates over time. Pages 11 to 13 of Keyfitz and Caswell (2005) discuss how many people have ever lived.

EXERCISES FOR CHAPTER 2

1. Of the world's 10 most populous countries, which has the highest rate of immigration today? Which has the lowest Infant Mortality Rate? What fraction of the world's population is comprised by these 10 most populous countries?

2. Mexico is the country with the eleventh largest population in the world. Its Crude Birth Rate during 2012 is reported to have been 20.44 per thousand, and 2,373,020 are reported to have been born. What mid-year population size would be consistent with these numbers?

3. Poland has a nearly stationary population, with $e_0 = 76$. There were about 380,000 births in 2012. What was the approximate size of the population?

4. Study the data in Table 2.1, and determine whether be_0 is typically greater than, equal to, or less than 1 in a growing population.

5. From an almanac or other source, find dates of birth and death for the presidents of the United States from Theodore Roosevelt to Barack

Obama. Draw a freehand Lexis diagram with the lifelines of these presidents. Label the axes clearly.

(a) Draw and label a line representing the age 30 and a line representing the year 1945.

(b) Draw and label the area containing person-years lived by people between the ages of 20 and 30 in the years between 1964 and 1968.

(c) Draw and label the area representing the whole lifetime experience of the cohort aged 10 to 30 in 1917.

6. Work out an estimate of how many humans have ever lived based on the estimate for the time before the dawn of agriculture given in the text and the estimates of population sizes given in Table 1.4 under the assumption of constant rates of growth between the years cited in the table. For average lifespans, use 30 years before 1750, 40 years for 1750 to 1950, 50 years for 1950 to 1975, and 60 years for 1975 to 2000.

* 7. Explain briefly what step in the derivation of the stationary population identity $be_0 = 1$ fails if the population is growing rather than stationary.

* 8. Apply Taylor expansions to three expressions for the Period Person-Years Lived over an interval from 0 to T:

(a) the mid-period approximation $K(T/2)T$

(b) the average approximation $(K(0) + K(T))(T/2)$

(c) the exponential area $K(0)(e^{RT} - 1)/R$

Find formulas for the differences among these three expressions up to a term in T^3. Which is largest and which is smallest, or does the ordering depend on R and T?

* 9. Suppose the Growth Rate for a population $K(t)$ is given by $R(t) = g(1 - K(t)/c)$. Find a formula for the Growth Rate of $Z(t) = (c - K(t))/K(t)$ and use it to find a formula for $K(t)$ in terms of g, c, and $f = Z(0)/c$.

10. The number of redwood trees in a certain triangular valley along the Jedediah Smith River is believed to have changed very little over the last thousand centuries. The expectation of life of trees that survive to the age of 10 is a further lifespan of 500 years. Trees about age 10 can be recognized because they are about as tall as a human adult. Suppose there are 2,000 trees in the valley as tall or taller than human adults. How many 10-year-old trees should you expect to find in the forest?

3

Cohort Mortality

3.1 Cohort Survival by Analogy

We begin our study of mortality by focussing on cohorts. We look at the lifelines and the deaths that occur in the diagonal stripe on the Lexis diagram that represents a particular cohort's experience, and we introduce measures of survival and probabilities of dying as a function of age for the cohort. We could, instead, look at the rectangle on a Lexis diagram that represents some period and consider the lifelines that cross the rectangle and the deaths that fall inside it. That is more complicated, because in that case the people at risk of dying at different ages are different people. When we trace the experience of a cohort over time, the people at risk of dying at different ages are the same people. That makes cohort measures conceptually simpler than period measures and gives us an incentive to begin by studying cohort measures.

In Chapter 7 we go on to study period mortality and adapt our cohort-based calculations to period data. The advantage of cohort measures is their conceptual simplicity. The disadvantage is their being out of date. To have complete measures of cohort mortality for all ages, we have to wait until all members of the cohort have died, and by then rates for young ages hark back to the distant past. The most recent cohorts with complete mortality data are those born around 1900. Measures of period mortality are more complicated, but they use more recent data.

Table 3.1   An analogy between populations and cohorts

Population Growth	Cohort Mortality
Time t	Age x
Population size $K(t)$	Cohort survivors ℓ_x
Multiplier $A = 1 - D/K$	Survival probability $1 - q$
Growth Rate R	Hazard rate h (with minus sign)
Area under $K(t)$, PPYL	Area under ℓ_x, CPYL, L
Crude rate d	Age-specific rates m

The basic measures of cohort mortality are elementary. All we have to do is to take our model for exponential population growth and apply it to a closed population consisting of the members of a single cohort. We change the symbols in the equations but keep the equations themselves.

If our population consists of a single cohort, then after the cohort is born, no one else enters the population. Babies born to cohort members belong to the babies' own, later cohorts, not to their parents' cohort. So, for this cohort "population", the only changes in population size come from deaths to members of the population. The measures we have studied in Chapter 1 reappear with new names. We have a tight analogy between population growth and cohort mortality illustrated in Table 3.1.

In a cohort, age x takes the place of time. The number of surviving members of the cohort at age x, ℓ_x, takes the place of population size at time t, $K(t)$. The initial cohort size ℓ_0, taking the place of $K(0)$, is called the "radix". Cohort deaths, with little d, take the place of population deaths with capital D. The multiplier A for calculating $K(t+1)$ as the product $AK(t)$ is given by $1 + (B - D)/K$, as we know from Chapter 1. For a cohort, after age zero, births are out of the picture and A is $1 - D/K$.

We write the cohort counterpart of $1 - D/K$ as $1 - d/\ell$ or $1 - q$. It is a probability of survival. The letter q in this expression stands for the probability of dying. The probability of surviving is 1 minus the probability of dying. As a cohort ages across an interval from x to $x + n$, each member either dies or survives. There is no other alternative, so the probabilities have to add to 1.

The counterpart of the growth rate is called the "hazard rate". Like the growth rate, the hazard rate is defined using logarithms, as we shall shortly see. Just as the area under the $K(t)$ curve gives Period Person-Years Lived, so the area under the ℓ_x curve gives Cohort Person-Years Lived. Its symbol will be a capital L. Crude rates as functions of time, with period person-years in their denominators, correspond to "age-specific" rates for cohorts, with cohort person-years in their denominators. Each measure for population growth has a partner among the measures for cohort mortality.

The important step in Chapter 1 is to let us see growth as a process of multiplication. The same is true of cohort mortality. But we have to be careful. It is not the mortality rates that multiply. Nor is it the probabilities of dying. It is the probabilities of *surviving*.

We write the age x as a subscript on the cohort survivors ℓ_x, whereas we write the time t inside parentheses by the population size $K(t)$. The notation is different but the idea is the same. The multiplicative rule for population growth

$$K(t+n) = A\,K(t)$$

carries over to a multiplicative rule for cohort survivorship:

$$\ell_{x+n} = (1 - {}_nq_x)\ell_x$$

The letter q in this formula has an extra subscript n, written *in front of* the letter. This left-side subscript specifies the length of the interval. Thus ${}_nq_x$ is the probability of dying within an interval of length n that starts at age x and ends at age $x+n$. Similarly, ${}_nd_x$ are cohort deaths between ages x and $x+n$ and ${}_nL_x$ are cohort person-years lived in this interval. This traditional notation dates from long before typewriters and computers.

The ℓ_x cohort members alive at age x split into two groups, the ${}_nd_x$ members who die before age $x+n$ and the $\ell_x - {}_nd_x = \ell_{x+n}$ members who survive to age $x+n$.

${}_nq_x$ is the **probability of dying** between ages x and $x+n$ among cohort members alive at age x, equal to ${}_nd_x/\ell_x$.

$1 - {}_nq_x$ is the **probability of surviving** from age x to age $x+n$ among cohort members alive at age x, equal to ℓ_{x+n}/ℓ_x.

A cohort born in 1984 reached age 18 in 2002, and about 1,767,644 were alive at their birthdays. Only about 724 of them died before age 19. We see that their probability of dying is

$$_1q_{18} = 724/1{,}767{,}644 = 0.000410$$

and their probability of surviving is

$$1 - {_1q_{18}} = 1{,}766{,}920/1{,}767{,}644 = 0.999590$$

Happily, probabilities of dying are low in developed countries at such early adult ages.

Another way of expressing the pace of death within cohorts is by means of hazard rates, used widely in advanced work. The hazard rate is the counterpart of the population growth rate. Just as we measure population growth with slopes of logarithms of population size, so we can measure cohort losses with slopes of logarithms of numbers of survivors. We insert a minus sign to make the hazard rate into a positive number, since cohorts grow smaller, not larger, as they age:

> The **hazard rate** for a cohort is minus the slope of the logarithm of the number of cohort survivors as a function of age,

For example, the cohort of boys born in the United States in 1980 started out with 1,853,616 members. As many as 1,836,853 of them survived to their first birthday. We calculate the hazard rate from the logarithms of ℓ_0 and ℓ_1:

$$h = -(1/1)\left(\log(1{,}836{,}853) - \log(1{,}853{,}616)\right)$$
$$= -(14.423564 - 14.432649) = 0.009085$$

If we write the hazard rate in the interval starting at age x as h_x (omitting any subscript for n), our formulas for cohort survivorship resemble our formulas for exponential population growth:

$$\ell_{x+n} = \ell_x\, e^{-nh_x}$$

3.2 Probabilities of Dying

A hazard rate is a rate like R, whereas $_nq_x$ is a probability. The word "probability" suggests a random process. Here, we introduce randomness into our picture by always referring in principle to a randomly selected member of our cohort. At a deeper level, the occurrence of death appears partly random and partly determined by causes, themselves partly random and partly determined by prior causes. For understanding the mathematics, it may be helpful to imagine the devil playing with a deck of cards. The ace of spades means death. The deck is shuffled. If the devil draws the ace of spades, you die. If the devil draws any other card, you survive. But, it being the devil, the deck may be stacked with more than one ace of spades.

It takes some experience to become accustomed to demography's traditional subscript notation. As mentioned in Section 3.1, in the expression $_nq_x$ the left subscript gives the width of the age interval and the right subscript gives the starting age. Thus $_{10}q_{20}$ is the probability of dying between 20 and 30, not between 10 and 20. One must also be careful not to confuse $_nq_x$ with n multiplied by q_x, which would look superficially like n multiplied by ℓ_x. It is wise in the latter case to use parentheses and write $(n)(\ell_x)$. Finally, note that $_{10}q_{20}$ goes from 20.00000 to 29.99999. We call this interval "the interval from 20 to 30" (including exact age 20, excluding exact age 30), but some other authors call it "the interval from 20 to 29".

Demographers frequently find themselves with data for one set of age intervals when they need answers for different intervals. They may have data for 1-year-wide intervals and need answers for 5-year-wide intervals. They may have data for 15-year intervals and need answers for 5-year intervals. They may have tables for ages 25 and 30 and need to know how many women survive to a mean age of childbearing of, say, 27.89 years. Problems that involve working out $_nq_x$ values for different x and n are called "$_nq_x$-conversions". They provide valuable practice in the basic skills of demography.

From our analogy with population growth comes the key point that we go from ℓ_x to ℓ_{x+n} by *multiplication*. We go from ℓ_{65} to ℓ_{85} by multiplying by $1 - _{20}q_{65}$. We go on from ℓ_{85} to ℓ_{100} by a further multiplication by $1 - _{15}q_{85}$. So we go all the way from ℓ_{65} to ℓ_{100} by multiplying by the product $(1 - _{20}q_{65})(1 - _{15}q_{85})$.

> ## Survival Probabilities Multiply

The important thing to remember is that we do not multiply the $_nq_x$ values. We multiply the $1 - _nq_x$ values. To survive 10 years you must survive the first year *and* survive the second year *and* survive the third year, and so on. These "ands" mean multiplication. To die, you can die in the first year *or* in the second year *or* in the third year, and so on, but you only do it once, and there is no multiplication. So, while we are ultimately interested in q, we work with $1 - q$.

When we do not have direct data for short intervals of interest, like 1-year-wide intervals, we need an assumption. The basic assumption we shall always make is this one:

> We assume the probability of dying is constant within each interval where we have no further information.

Thus, if we do not know $_1q_{20}$ or $_1q_{21}$ but we do know $_2q_{20}$, we assume that the probability of dying is constant between ages 20 and 22, that is, that $_1q_{20} = _1q_{21}$, so that they both equal some value q. Then $(1 - q)^2$ has to equal $1 - _2q_{20}$. More generally, for y between x and $x + n - 1$,

$$(1 - _1q_y)^n = 1 - _nq_x$$

$$1 - _1q_y = (1 - _nq_x)^{1/n}$$

$$_1q_y = 1 - (1 - _nq_x)^{1/n}$$

For example, for the cohort of U.S. women born in 1980, $_2q_{20} = 0.000837$. We calculate $_1q_{20}$ to be $1 - (1 - 0.000837)^{1/2}$, or 0.000419. For the cohort of women born in 1780 in Sweden, a country replete with early data reported, for example, in Keyfitz and Flieger (1968), $_5q_{20} = 0.032545$. Then

$$_1q_{20} = 1 - (1 - 0.032545)^{1/5} = 0.006595.$$

For another example, suppose we know that $_5q_{80} = 0.274248$, and we want to find the probability of dying each year which would, if constant, account for the observed 5-year mortality and survivorship. We calculate

$$1 - (1 - {}_5q_{80})^{1/5} = 1 - (1 - 0.274248)^{1/5} = 0.062098$$

Sometimes more elaborate conversion problems arise. For example, we might have sources which told us three values:

$$\ell_{65} = 0.915449; \qquad \ell_{75} = 0.799403; \qquad {}_{35}q_{65} = 0.930201$$

We might want the probability of surviving from 70 to 100 for comparison with some other source. (The numbers here come from a forecast of survival for the U.S. cohort of women born in 1980.) Our unknown $1 - {}_{30}q_{70}$ equals $1 - {}_{35}q_{65}$ divided by $1 - {}_5q_{65}$. The numerator is $1 - 0.930201$. We calculate the denominator as $(1 - {}_{10}q_{65})^{5/10}$ since we have no other information between 65 and 75. That denominator is the square root of ℓ_{75}/ℓ_{65}, or 0.934471. Our survival probability from 70 to 100 thus comes out to be 0.074694.

The best way to solve complicated conversion problems is to begin by drawing a diagonal line on a Lexis diagram. Then, mark off each age for which there is information about survivorship at that age. Next, mark off ages which are the endpoints of intervals over which there is information about mortality within the interval. Between each marked age, assume a constant probability of dying, and apply the conversion formulas.

3.3 Columns of the Cohort Life Table

3.3.1 King Edward's Children

Since the 1600s it has been customary to arrange ℓ_x and ${}_nq_x$ as columns in a table along with a special set of other measures of mortality. Such a table is called a "lifetable". The rows correspond to age groups. The columns correspond to different measures. From a mathematical point of view, all the main columns of the lifetable contain the same information, in the sense that with some standard assumptions any one column can be computed from any other. But the columns present information from different perspectives for use in different applications. Some columns focus on survivors, some on the dying, some on average life remaining. The choice of the columns and their

Table 3.2   Children of King Edward III of England

1330–1376	Edward, The Black Prince
1332–1382	Isabel
1335–1348	Joan
1336–?	William of Hatfield (died young)
1338–1368	Lionel of Antwerp, Duke of Clarence
1340–1398	John of Gaunt, Duke of Lancaster
1341–1402	Edmund Langley, Duke of York
1342–1342	Blanche
1344–1362	Mary
1346–1361	Margaret
1355–1397	Thomas of Woodstock, Duke of Gloucester

names and symbols are fixed by tradition. Each column is a function of age, so the columns of the lifetable are sometimes called "lifetable functions".

We introduce the cohort lifetable with an example drawn from the 1300s. King Edward III of England was born in 1312 and reigned from 1337 to 1377. He had eleven children, and birth and death dates are known for all but one. Many appear as characters in Shakespeare's history plays. They may be familiar from *Richard II*, *Richard III*, *Henry IV, Parts I and II*, and other stories of the Wars of the Roses. A Lexis diagram for them is shown in Figure 3.1, derived from data in Table 3.2. We treat these children born between 1330 and 1355 as a cohort and calculate the cohort lifetable.

For our example we restrict ourselves to the 10 children for whom dates of birth and death are known. This lifetable understates mortality since we omit a child (William of Hatfield) who died young. For a better lifetable, calculated in one of the exercises, we fill in the missing date with a plausible value—a process called "imputation"—yielding a lifetable for all 11 children rather than 10.

Lifetables begin with a column labeled x. The entry in this column is the *starting* age for the age group. In the next column, sometimes omitted, we write the width n of the age interval, the difference between the value of x for this row and the value for the next age group found in the next row. Generally, lifetables are constructed with 1-year or 5-year intervals. A table with 5-year-wide intervals except for a 1-year-wide and a 4-year-wide interval at the start is the most common form. It is called an "abridged lifetable" in older works. Our example, instead, uses two 10-year-wide

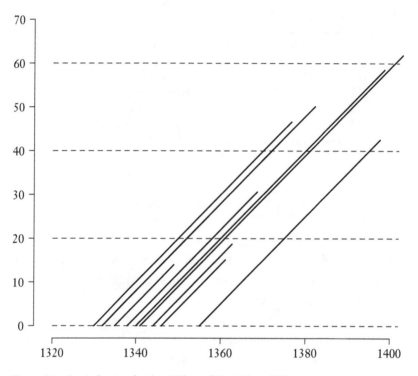

Figure 3.1   Lexis diagram for the children of King Edward III

intervals and two 20-year-wide intervals, providing practice with intervals of different widths. With a cohort of only 10 members, these intervals are quite narrow enough.

The last listed age is 60. This last row of the lifetable applies to all ages from 60 on up. It is called the "open-ended age interval" since it has no maximum age. This row requires special treatment. We write ∞, the mathematical symbol for infinity, for the length of this interval. Of course, no one survives forever. We write ∞ because we are not setting any upper limit of our own.

The survivorship column ℓ_x leads off the data-driven entries of the cohort lifetable. The first-row entry, ℓ_0, is the radix, the initial size of the cohort at birth. In our example the radix equals 10, the number of children whose lives and deaths we are following in the table. By leaving out William of Hatfield, we conveniently obtain a round number radix which is also an actual starting cohort size. The choice of radix is up to us. A lifetable can be built up from any radix, an actual size or a convenient size, as we discuss in Section 3.3.3.

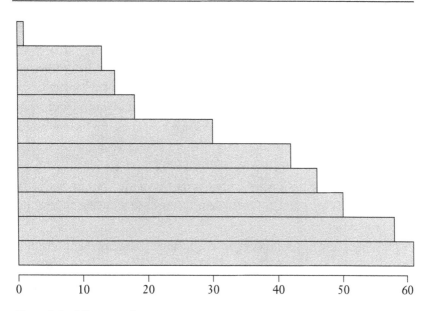

Figure 3.2   Lifespans and ℓ_x

We can read the ℓ_x values off the Lexis diagram. The value of ℓ_{10} is the number of princes and princesses surviving at least till age 10, that is to say, the number of lifelines which cross a horizontal line for age 10. All but Blanche survive, so $\ell_{10} = 9$. Only six lifelines cross the mark at age 20, so $\ell_{20} = 6$. Five cross 40, whence $\ell_{40} = 5$, and one crosses 60, whence $\ell_{60} = 1$.

There is an appealing way to draw a graph of ℓ_x as a function of x. Figure 3.2 has a shaded horizontal bar for each child. The lengths of the bars are the lengths of life of the children, ordered with the shortest at the top and the longest at the bottom. We mark off ages along the horizontal axis. The top of the shaded area is made up of steps. The height of the steps over any age x is the value of ℓ_x. The bars there belong to the cohort members still alive. This kind of plot for a large population has lots and lots of very thin bars. We often draw a smooth curve through the mid-points of the right-hand sides of the bars so that ℓ_x, instead of taking steps down, becomes a continuous function. But each horizontal line still belongs to the bar for some person. Demographers often draw the bars with different colors for the portions of each person's life spent in and out of some activity like rearing children or being married or being free from disability.

The lower edge of any person's bar lies some percentage of the way between the bottom and the top of the steps. This percentage represents the percentage of the whole cohort that the person leaves behind in the world when he or she departs. It is his or her personal value of ℓ_x at the instant after death, converted to a percentage. Joan, whose bar lies second from the top, leaves 80% of her siblings (excluding William) behind. The Black Prince, seventh from the top, leaves 30% behind. Such percentages are studied further in Section 3.4 and Chapter 8. They can be interpreted as a kind of reverse measure of luck. People who leave a low percentage of their cohort behind them may be considered lucky to live to great age. However, length of life is not the same as quality of life. Mozart died at 35, Alexander the Great at 32. The ancient Greeks had a saying: "Those the gods love die young."

The column which follows ℓ_x in the lifetable contains the probability of dying in the interval given that one is alive at the start. This is the $_nq_x$ measure that we have already studied. Its formula is

$$_nq_x = 1 - (\ell_{x+n}/\ell_x)$$

For the first age group we have $1 - 9/10$, which is 0.100. For the second age group, $1 - 6/9$ or 0.333, then 0.167, then 0.800, and then what? There is no ℓ_{x+n} value for this last row. However, if you are alive at 60, we know the probability that you will die at some age above 60. The probability is 1. Death is certain. We can fill in the last entry automatically. It is always 1.

We go on to insert a column which gives deaths between ages x and $x + n$. The formula is $_nd_x = \ell_x - \ell_{x+n}$. This column counts the lifelines that end in each age interval on the Lexis diagram. We now have a lifetable with the columns shown in Table 3.3.

Table 3.3   Five columns of King Edward's family lifetable

x	n	ℓ_x	$_nq_x$	$_nd_x$
0	10	10	0.100	1
10	10	9	0.333	3
20	20	6	0.167	1
40	20	5	0.800	4
60	∞	1	1.000	1

Cohort Mortality   59

3.3.2 From $_nL_x$ to e_x

The remaining columns of the lifetable all relate to cohort person-years lived, the "CPYL" of Chapter 2. In order to calculate person-years, we need an extra minor column called $_na_x$. This column tells us how many years within an interval people live on average if they die in the interval. Usually, this quantity is about half the width of the interval, $n/2$, except for infants and toddlers, for whom we shall have special formulas in Chapter 7.

In our example we happen to have years of birth and death, and we can work out averages. For example, Joan lives from 1335 to 1348 and so dies somewhere between 2 to 4 years beyond her tenth birthday. Mary lives between 7 to 9 years and Margaret between 4 and 6 years beyond their tenth birthdays. The average is $(1/2)(2 + 4 + 7 + 9 + 4 + 6)/3 = 5.33$, our value for $_{10}a_{10}$. Similarly, we find $_{10}a_0 = 0.50$ and $_{20}a_{20} = 10$ and $_{20}a_{40} = 9$ and $_\infty a_{60} = 1$, the middle ones quite close to $n/2$. These calculations are not very important, since we usually just fill in $n/2$.

When we have our values for $_na_x$, we are ready for cohort person-years lived. This lifetable column is called $_nL_x$ or "big L". Think of "L" standing for life. Big L is one of the four most important columns together with ℓ_x ("little ℓ"), $_nq_x$, and the e_x column coming soon. The formula is

$$_nL_x = (n)(\ell_{x+n}) + (_na_x)(_nd_x)$$

and it gives the number of Cohort Person-Years Lived between ages x and $x + n$

The value of $_nL_x$ is made up of two contributions. Those who survive the whole interval, ℓ_{x+n} in number, each contribute a full n years to $_nL_x$. Those who die during the interval, $_nd_x$ in number, contribute on average $_na_x$ years. That is where we use $_na_x$. Our formula adds these two contributions together. We usually have $_na_x = n/2$, and then our formula simplifies to

$$_nL_x = (n/2)(\ell_x + \ell_{x+n})$$

If we have a smooth curve of ℓ_x values, those familiar with calculus can also calculate big L as the area under the little ℓ curve between x and $x + n$. In our example, $_{10}L_0 = 10 * 9 + 1 * 0.5 = 90.5$ and $_{10}L_{10} = 10 * 6 + 3 * 5.33 = 76$, and so on.

The big-L column helps us fill in all the rest. We divide cohort deaths $_nd_x$ by Cohort Person-Years Lived $_nL_x$ for the lifetable death rate $_nm_x$, which is less prominent in cohort lifetables than in the period lifetables of Chapter 7. The column $_nm_x$ is the age-specific counterpart of the Crude Death Rate. It is a rate, measured per unit of time. The lifetable death rate measured over a very short interval starting at x is very close to the hazard rate. For the first row of our example, we have $_{10}m_0 = 1/90.5 = 0.011050$

If we add up all the person-years to be lived beyond age x, we obtain T_x, the person-years of life remaining for cohort members who reach age x. The formula is $T_x = {_nL_x} + {_nL_{x+n}} + {_nL_{x+2n}} + \cdots$. Our T_x is easiest to compute by first filling in the whole $_nL_x$ column and then cumulating sums from the bottom up. In our example, T_{60} is 1 and T_{40} is $1 + 56 = 57$, and so forth.

The main use of T_x is for computing the expectation of further life beyond age x, e_x. The T_x person-years will be lived by the ℓ_x members of the cohort who reach age x, so e_x is given by the formula $e_x = T_x/\ell_x$. The expectation of life at age zero, that is, at birth, is often called the "life expectancy".

It is good to remember that e_x is the expectation of future life beyond age x. It is not an average age at death. To obtain the average age at death for cohort members who all survive to age x, we add x and e_x. Not all lifetables include $x + e_x$, but it is helpful for checking whether ages are plausible. The expectation of future life e_x does not always go down. It often goes up after the first few years of life, because babies who survive infancy are no longer subject to the high risks of infancy. The column $x + e_x$, however, must always go up. If it does not, a mistake has been made. The remaining columns of the lifetable for our example are shown in Table 3.4.

The expectation of life at birth is often taken as an index of overall mortality. But it gives a poor idea of lifespan, since it is heavily affected by infant mortality, which may be heavy. A better index of lifespan is $10 + e_{10}$.

Table 3.4   Right-hand columns of a lifetable

x	$_na_x$	$_nL_x$	$_nm_x$	T_x	e_x	$x + e_x$
0	0.50	90.5	0.011	334	33.4	33.4
10	5.33	76.0	0.039	243	27.0	37.0
20	10.00	110.0	0.009	167	27.8	47.8
40	9.00	56.0	0.071	57	11.4	51.4
60	1.00	1.0	1.000	1	1.0	61.0

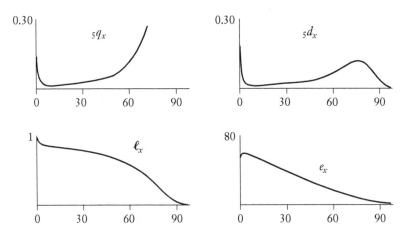

Figure 3.3   Typical shapes of lifetable functions

The different lifetable functions express the same basic information from different points of view. In practical work demographers often have to start with entries for some column and work out entries for another or to start with bits and pieces of data from a few columns and solve for some missing piece of information. The exercises contain several puzzles of this kind.

Each lifetable function has a characteristic shape illustrated in Figure 3.3. The probability of dying in the upper left of Figure 3.3 drops after infancy and rises steadily in old age. Lifetable deaths at upper right show a spike at birth and a bulge in old age which fades away as fewer and fewer cohort members are left alive to die even in the face of ever-increasing death rates. Survivorship at lower left dips after birth, drops slowly into middle age, and accelerates downward in old age. The expectation of future life ticks upward after birth and steadily decreases afterward. Table 3.5 reviews the names and formulas for the cohort lifetable columns calculated from the survivorship column ℓ_x. See also the collection called "Useful Formulas" in Appendix B.

3.3.3 The Radix

We return to the radix ℓ_0, which plays the role of the cohort's initial size. This initial size has a name of its own, the "radix", which is the Latin word meaning "root". The phrase "plays the role" reminds us that the radix need not be the whole size of an actual cohort. One Census Bureau estimate of

Table 3.5   Cohort lifetable formulas

Formula	Name
$_nq_x = 1 - (\ell_{x+n}/\ell_x)$	Probability of dying
$_nd_x = \ell_x - \ell_{x+n}$	Cohort deaths
$_nL_x = (n)(\ell_{x+n}) + (_na_x)(_nd_x)$	Person-years lived
$_nm_x = {}_nd_x/{}_nL_x$	Lifetable death rate
$T_x = \sum_x^\infty {}_nL_a$	Remaining person-years
$e_x = T_x/\ell_x$	Expectation of life

the initial size of the cohort of U.S. males born between 1945 and 1950 is 9,025,382. This is not a convenient number. An initial size of 1,000 or 100,000 or 1 would be easier. Demographers feel free to choose a radix to suit their tastes. They think of drawing a random sample of some size like 1,000 from among the newborn babies and think of the lifetable as following this "sample cohort" through life. With a random sample, survival of the sample mirrors survival for the whole cohort. If the sample cohort starts with 1,000 members and has 300 left alive at age 80, the real cohort would have $(300/1000) * 9,025,382 = 2,707,615$ members alive at age 80. With a radix of 1, we can interpret ℓ_x as the expected *proportion* of the cohort surviving to age x.

This freedom to choose the radix fosters flexibility and neatness. Conceptually, however, it is worthwhile to be picturing an actual group of people, a whole cohort or a sample, starting with ℓ_0 members and living out their lives, surviving, aging, and dying.

It helps to keep in mind what depends on the choice of the radix ℓ_0 and what does not. Multiplying the initial size by, say, 1,000 alters some quantities and leaves others the same, as can be seen by calculating all columns with a new radix. Which quantities do change? Here is a list: *YES:* $\ell_x, {}_nL_x, {}_nd_x$; *NO:* $_nq_x, {}_nm_x, e_x$.

One calculation employing the radix is the construction of a combined-sex lifetable from separate single-sex lifetables. Because men and women die at different rates, we usually construct separate lifetables for them. Sometimes, however, we want a lifetable for everyone. Let f_{fab} stand for the fraction female at birth in the cohort, a quantity discussed in detail in Chapter 4, and assume that the single-sex lifetables have the same radix ℓ_0. We set

$$\ell_x^c = \left(f_{\text{fab}}\right) \ell_x^{\text{female}} + \left(1 - f_{\text{fab}}\right) \ell_x^{\text{male}}$$

Our new ℓ_x^c ("c" stands for "combined sex") has the same radix as the single-sex tables, as we see from plugging in $x = 0$. The cohort begins with $(f_{\text{fab}})\ell_0$ baby girls and $(1 - f_{\text{fab}})\ell_0$ baby boys, and the survivors in the cohort consist of all the women who survive plus all the men who survive. This survivor-based approach for combining lifetables will be used for period as well as for cohort lifetables. We do not average $_nq_x$ values or $_nm_x$ values, but instead always work with the survivorships ℓ_x.

* 3.4 Hazards and Survivors

Hazard rates, although they are not one of the traditional columns of the lifetable, play a prominent role in advanced studies. The hazard, being a rate, has units of 1/time. The faster the members of the cohort are dying, the higher is the hazard rate. It can take any value equal to or greater than zero. We often write the hazard rate as a function h_x depending on age x and speak of the "hazard function" or "hazard curve" or simply of the "hazard". It is also often called the "force of mortality". Some authors prefer the Greek letter μ, pronounced "mu" or "myoo", for the hazard. Calculations with hazards are treated in more detail in Chapter 8. Here, we introduce basic ideas.

Being equal to minus the slope of the logarithm of the survivorship function ℓ_x, the hazard function plays a role very like the role of the Growth Rate R. It enters into an exponential formula for survival from x to $x + n$:

$$\ell_{x+n} = \ell_x \, e^{-hn}$$

The formula connecting the hazard function to the probability of dying $_nq_x$ has two minus signs, one inside and one outside the exponential function:

$$_nq_x = 1 - e^{-hn}$$

In these formulas h is taken to be constant between x and $x + n$. When h varies continuously, areas come into the picture. The area under the hazard curve has a name of its own, the "cumulative hazard", often written with a capital "H" as H_x. The cumulative hazard is minus the logarithm of ℓ_x/ℓ_0. Using calculus to express areas as integrals and writing a for ages within an interval and x for age at the end of the interval, we have

$$\ell_x = \ell_0 \, e^{-\int_0^x h_a da} = \ell_0 \, e^{-H_x}$$

When we multiply the hazard at an age a by survivorship to age a, the product $h_a \, \ell_a$ tells us the density of deaths at a, in the sense that the area under the curve $h_a \, \ell_a$ between x and $x + n$ is $_n d_x$. The total area under the curve is the radix ℓ_0, since everyone born into the cohort eventually dies. When we multiply the cumulative hazard at an age a by survivorship to age a, the product $H_a \, \ell_a$ tells us about hazards undergone up to age a by the living. In a lifetable with unit radix, the total area under this curve turns out to be a measure of how wide a spread is found among ages at deaths for cohort members. James Vaupel has given the name "disparity" to this total. See Zhang and Vaupel (2009).

The disparity measure can be written either as $\int \ell_a \log(1/\ell_a) da$ or as $\int H_a \exp(-H_a) da$, and it usually turns out to equal the integral $\int e_a \, (h_a \ell_a) da$, that is, further life expectancy lost by those $h_a \ell_a$ cohort members dying at age a. The ratio of disparity to life expectancy is often called "lifetable entropy" (see Keyfitz and Caswell [2005, p. 81]) although, as statisticians and physical scientists use the word entropy, the entropy of the normalized survivorship distribution is really $\int (\ell_a/e_0) \log(e_0/\ell_a) da$. Disparity is closely related to the statistical standard deviation of ages of death in a cohort; the standard deviation of ages of death beyond age 10 is an alternative measure analyzed by Edwards and Tuljapurkar (2005). In developed countries both measures have decreased a great deal over the last century or so.

In our lifetable for King Edward's children, we saw how each member of a cohort can be assigned a number on a percentage scale equal to the percentage of the cohort that the member leaves behind at death. We now consider a lifetable of contemporary relevance, the predicted cohort lifetable for U.S. women born in the early 1990s taken from forecasts by the actuaries of the U.S. Social Security system. This predicted ℓ_x curve with a radix of 1 is shown in Figure 3.4. All but 0.014 of these women survived to their twentieth birthdays. Think of the particular woman who dies leaving exactly 75% of her cohort behind. We find the woman's age at death by drawing the upper horizontal dashed line across the graph until it hits the ℓ_x curve. Then we drop a line down to the axis to the answer, 77.14 years. Under these predictions, early deaths are not so very early. The lower horizontal line in Figure 3.4 picks out the woman who leaves only 25% of the cohort behind, dying at 93.69 years. The woman leaving 50% behind dies at 87.08 years.

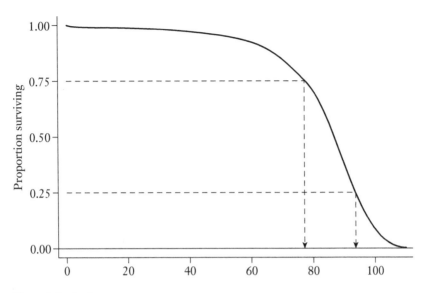

Figure 3.4   An ℓ_x curve

Our method of matching individuals with their ages at death in Figure 3.4 has important applications. If we start with an ℓ_x curve, we can construct an artificial population whose survivorship follows this curve by generating a sample of uniform random numbers between zero and one, treating them as proportions left behind and applying our method to generate ages at death for them, in effect inverting the ℓ_x curve. In practice, this approach is usually carried through on a logarithmic scale with cumulative hazards instead of survivorships, and it is explored further in Section 8.4.

The predictions about longevity in Figure 3.4 help give an idea of how long a lifetime young American women of today may want to plan for. Men have their turn in Chapter 8. The predictions assume that current trends continue. That may prove overly optimistic. Obesity, antibiotic resistance, terrorism, resource depletion, and many other threats may keep us wary, although there are also reasons for hope.

* 3.5 Gompertz Hazards

Mortality is ordinarily a story about the very young and the fairly old. Evolution driven by natural selection arranges, as best it can, to keep death rates low for creatures of reproductive age. Hazard functions typically are shaped somewhat like a tired letter "J", high in infancy, low in early adulthood, and rising into old age. Demographers have put effort into special models for infant mortality and for old-age mortality. Here, we introduce the most popular of them all, the Gompertz model for old-age mortality, followed by a brief account of a few models for infant mortality. These are our first examples of model lifetables, studied extensively in Chapter 7.

For older ages, mathematical curves for describing cohort mortality have come back into fashion. Since the 1970s, models that use conveniently simple curves for the whole age range have come into disrepute, because we know that overall patterns of mortality are not simple. Different causes of death predominate at different ages, and there is no reason that their combination should be some familiar curve given by a simple formula. When we restrict attention to later life, however, the situation is different. At advanced ages, the idea of a definite cause of death is less well-defined. Often, older people have many contributing infirmities at the time of death, and the choice of one cause over others is arbitrary. Belief in a simple curve as a summary of the overall outcome may be more plausible.

The Gompertz model, first published by Benjamin Gompertz in 1825, is a model for the hazard function at adult ages. It says that this hazard function takes the form of an exponential curve:

$$h_x = \alpha \; e^{\beta x}$$

Such an exponential hazard is shown in Figure 3.5, starting at age 40 when the model begins to be sensible. The formula for h_x is equivalent to the provision that the graph of the logarithm of the hazard function as a function of age be a straight line:

$$\log(h_x) = \log(\alpha) + \beta x$$

We follow the approach introduced in Section 1.4 of Chapter 1, specifying the ingredients of the model, digesting its meaning by working forward from some choices of parameter values to predictions, and then working backward from empirical data to parameter estimates.

As we have said, the quantity being modeled is the hazard function, a "leading column" which is not always one of the columns of a lifetable but which determines all the rest. The formula has the same form as our model

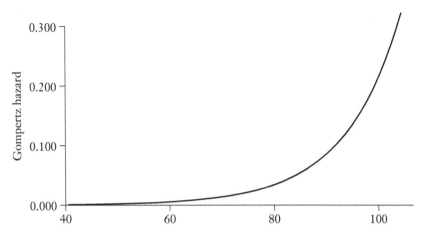

Figure 3.5   A Gompertz hazard function

for exponential growth, but with different symbols and different meanings. The Gompertz model has two parameters. The parameter α determines the initial level of the hazard, and the parameter β, which specifies the slope on a logarithmic scale, determines the rapidity of increase of mortality with age, what is often called "senescent" mortality.

Working forward from parameter values to predictions is easy. We plug the parameter values into the formula. For example, suppose we are given values $\alpha = 0.000133$ and $\beta = 0.080$. What is the predicted hazard for age 85? We calculate

$$h_{85} = (0.000133)e^{(85)(0.080)} = 0.119$$

These parameter values pertain to the cohort of Swedish women born in 1910. Sweden has some of the earliest and best mortality data in the world. Our α and β parameters are derived from the Human Mortality Database (HMD), listed in Appendix A. Age 85 is the point at which women enter the category of the "oldest-old". At age 100 they become centenarians. If the Gompertz model continued to hold at extreme ages, how high would the hazard rate rise by age 100? We calculate

$$h_{100} = (0.000133)e^{(100)(0.080)} = 0.396$$

In reality, exponential increases in hazard rates begin to slacken for centenarians and supercentenarians.

Continuing to work forward, we can also take our parameters and predict values of other columns in the lifetable like survivorship. We could tabulate lots of h_a values and add them up to find H_x and ℓ_x values from them, but it is faster to recall the formula from Chapter 2 for the area under an exponential curve. With α in place of $K(0)$ and β in place of R, our formula from Section 2.5 implies

$$\int_x^y \alpha \, e^{\beta z} \, dz = \frac{\alpha}{\beta} \left(e^{\beta y} - e^{\beta x} \right) = \frac{h_y - h_x}{\beta} = H_y - H_x$$

For our Swedish women, the probability of survival from 85 to 100 is predicted to be

$$\ell_{100}/\ell_{85} = \exp(-(H_y - H_x))$$

$$= \exp(-(0.396467 - 0.119414)/(0.080)) = 0.031331$$

Only about 1 in 30 of these 85-year-olds live on to be centenarians.

We have used our formula for ratios of survivorships at adult ages. We could write out a formula for ℓ_x itself, with exponentials inside exponentials, $\ell_x = \ell_0 \exp(-(\alpha/\beta)(\exp(\beta x) - 1))$. But this formula would give the wrong answers, because the Gompertz model is wrong for ages under about 40. It only gives correct answers when age "zero" in the formula actually stands for some other adult age.

Still continuing to work forward, we can predict cohort deaths by multiplying the hazard rate at x by the survivors to x at risk of dying, yielding the product $h_x \, \ell_x$. The curve of cohort deaths slopes upward at younger ages, reaches a peak or "mode", and then drops as fewer members are still alive at risk of dying. The age of the peak is called the "modal age at death". A bit of calculus shows that the modal age at death under a Gompertz model turns out to be

$$x_{\text{mode}} = (1/\beta) \log(\beta/\alpha)$$

For our Swedish cohort, the modal age at death is close to 80 years.

The formula for the modal age at death is gratifying, because there is no simple exact formula for life expectancy under a Gompertz model. For low-mortality populations, however, there is a handy approximation for the average age at death of those dying beyond age 40 when a Gompertz model applies:

$$e_{40} + 40 \approx x_{\text{mode}} - 0.577215/\beta$$

The constant 0.577215 is called Euler's constant, named after Leonhard Euler, who took the first steps toward the creation of stable population theory studied in Chapter 10. In the Gompertz formulas, α is the hazard rate that would apply at age zero if we pretended that hazards at older adult ages could be extrapolated all the way back to birth with exponential formulas. We can also express α as a function of x_{mode} and β and rewrite the Gompertz hazard function as $h_x = \beta \, \exp(\beta(x - x_{\text{mode}}))$.

Having studied how to work forward from parameters to predictions, we now turn to the question of how to work backward from observations to parameter values. As in Chapter 1, we begin by taking a transformation, in this case a logarithm, and turn our problem into the problem of finding the slope and intercept of a straight line:

$$\log(h_x) = \log(\alpha) + \beta x = (\text{intercept}) + (\text{slope})(x)$$

Figure 3.6 is a plot with observed values of $\log(h_x)$ on the vertical axis and ages x on the horizontal axis. When we fit a straight line to the points on the plot, the slope is an estimate of β and the exponential function applied to the intercept is an estimate of α. The observed hazards here are actually taken from the actuaries' forecasts for the cohort of U.S. women born in the early 1990s studied in Section 3.4. The graph is quite straight above age 40,

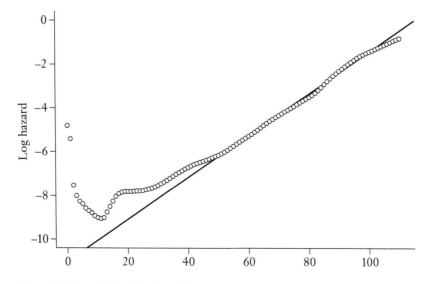

Figure 3.6 Logarithm of the hazard function

Table 3.6 Fitting Gompertz parameters

	X	Y	$X * X$	$X * Y$
	50	−6.153	2,500	−308
	65	−4.798	4,225	−312
	80	−3.510	6,400	−281
	95	−1.797	9,025	−171
Sum	290	−16.258	22,150	−1,072
Mean	72.5	−4.0645	5,537.5	−268

agreeing with the model. Truly empirical hazard functions are often found to be just as straight, not only for humans, but for other species from flies, worms, and birds to horses and chimpanzees. This cross-species regularity has, as yet, no full theoretical explanation.

We find the slope and intercept for a straight-line fit to $\log(h_x)$ by the recipe for linear regression from Section 1.4, plugging the means of columns from Table 3.6 into the formulas given there and in Appendix B:

$$\text{slope} = \frac{(-268) - (72.5) * (-4.0645)}{(5537.5) - (72.5) * (72.5)} = \frac{26.67625}{281.25} = 0.094849$$

$$\text{intercept} = (-4.0645) - (0.094849)(72.5) = -10.941040$$

Our estimate of α is the exponential of the intercept, $17.716 * 10^{-6}$. The modal age at death is 90.52 years. The fitted line is superimposed on Figure 3.6. We note that our forecasts for U.S. women growing up in the new century imply a β value only a little larger than the one for Swedish women from the last century, but the level parameter α decreases a great deal.

Advanced work requires a more sophisticated method for estimating α and β from ages at death. If we are given ages at death $X_1, X_2, \ldots$ from a sample from a population, then α and β can be chosen to maximize $\sum \log(h(X_i)\ell_{X_i})$, when h and ℓ have the Gompertz form.

Infant and child mortality are more difficult to model than old-age mortality, and there is nothing comparable in empirical power to the Gompertz. A Makeham model is derived from the Gompertz by adding to the exponential hazards a constant independent of age, whose value constitutes a third parameter. The constant improves fit for early adult ages and can be interpreted as an "exogenous" force of mortality. *Exo* is a Greek root for "outside", as contrasted with *endo* for "inside". In principle, exogenous hazards come from threats outside the body, endogenous hazards from failings inside the body, although the distinction is often a fuzzy one.

For childhood mortality, there is a Siler model which adds a decreasing exponential hazard term with two more parameters to the Makeham model, for five parameters in all. For mortality within the first year of life, there is an older model invented by Jean Bourgeois-Pichat in 1951. Today the model is out of date, because medicine succeeds in saving many premature babies, altering the age-pattern of infant deaths, but the model has served historians well. Like the Makeham model, it distinguishes between exogenous and endogenous mortality with two parameters, which we call a and b, setting

$$_nq_0 = a + b \left(\log(1 + 365\,n)\right)^3$$

Here, the interval n is measured in fractions of 1 year, so $365\,n$ registers days after birth. We work backward from observations to parameter estimates by transforming n to $X = (\log(1 + 365\,n))^3$ and forming Y from observations of survival to age n for some fractional ages between the first month and the first year of life. As before, we find a and b using linear regression. The parameter a estimates the level of endogenous mortality, which can be assumed until recently not to change too much from case to case, and the parameter b estimates the force of exogenous mortality, particularly driven by infections, a parameter which varies widely and spreads deaths out through the first year of life. An example is included in the exercises. In a famous application, E. A. Wrigley proposed that changes in estimated values of a in pre-industrial English parishes reflected changes, not in true endogenous mortality, but in faulty registration of infant deaths, and he used Bourgeois-Pichat's model to correct for under-registration.

3.6 Annuities and Insurance

The earliest applications of lifetable methods in the 1600s and 1700s were to annuities. The idea is to assure yourself a steady income (for instance, after retirement) by buying now from an annuity company for a single payment of money P, the purchase price, a policy under which the company agrees to pay you an annual benefit B for as long as you live. (No relation to B for births.) Annuities and insurance are social institutions that typically become familiar only after school or college when starting a job or a family. With an annuity, you pay now and collect benefits as long as you live. If you die soon, the company wins. If you live long, the company loses. The company sets the purchase price to break even or come out ahead. We deal here with "actuarially fair rates", where the profit is zero. In practice, a margin for profit is added on.

The purpose of buying an annuity is to share risk. If you are going to die soon, you might want to spend a lot of money while you are alive to enjoy it. But if you turned out to live for a long time, you might run out of money. The risk of running out of money is removed by buying an annuity. The purchase price ought to depend on the age of the buyer. When the British parliament first tried to raise money by selling annuities at a price independent of age, Dutch financiers bought annuities for their teenage daughters and parliament lost money.

To derive formulas connecting P and B, we imagine all ℓ_x members of a cohort buying annuities at the same age x. Some members live long. Others live less long. Over the first n years after purchase, cohort members live a total of $_nL_x$ person-years, each one receiving a benefit B each year, for $B\,_nL_x$ in benefits overall. Over all future ages, total benefits amount to

$$B\,_nL_x + B\,_nL_{x+n} + B\,_nL_{x+2n} + B\,_nL_{x+3n} \cdots = B\,T_x$$

The total purchase amount is $P\ell_x$. Equating purchase to benefits implies $P = Be_x$.

It looks as if an annuity with a benefit of \$10,000 a year purchased at age 20 could cost half a million dollars. But annuities do not cost such huge sums. Why not? The answer is that the company can invest money and earn interest while it is waiting to pay future benefits. Time elapses between purchase and receipt of benefits.

To take interest into account, it is useful to imagine the company opening a separate bank account for each future n-year period. It invests the money for early benefits in short-term investments and money for the distant future in long-term investments. We calculate the price of an annuity by figuring out how much money the company must put into each account at the start in order to have enough money to pay out the benefits from that account when the time comes.

Write i for the interest rate. For the first account, the company has to deposit enough money to pay out benefits B_nL_x on average half-way through the first period, leaving on average about $n/2$ years for money to grow through compound interest. At compound interest, 1 dollar grows to $(1+i)^{n/2}$ dollars in $n/2$ years. So the company needs to deposit about $B_nL_x/(1+i)^{n/2}$ in the first account. For the next account, money can earn interest for an average of $n+n/2$ years, so $B_nL_{x+n}/(1+i)^{n+n/2}$ is needed. In a period starting when the cohort reaches age y, the deposit is $B_nL_y/(1+i)^{y-x+n/2}$. In all, the company needs to deposit

$$\frac{B_nL_x}{(1+i)^{n/2}} + \frac{B_nL_{x+n}}{(1+i)^{n+n/2}} + \frac{B_nL_{x+2n}}{(1+i)^{2n+n/2}} + \cdots$$

For the price P per person, we divide by the number of buyers ℓ_x.

Lifetables with an open-ended interval starting at a top age $x$max introduce a subtlety. What average time should apply for earning interest? Our rule is to replace $n/2$ with $e_{x\text{max}}$, since people alive at the start of the interval will live about $e_{x\text{max}}$ further years.

As an example, suppose King Edward III had bought annuities with a benefit of £100 a year (a vast sum in English pounds in the 1300s) for all five of his surviving children when they were age 10. His expeditions into Scotland left many Scottish widows. Suppose the present-day company called the Scottish Widows had had a fourteenth-century precursor which could earn 10% interest per year. For the total price in pounds of the princely annuities, we find

$$\frac{100 * 56}{1.10^{10}} + \frac{100 * 1.0}{1.10^{21}} = 2{,}159 + 13 = 2{,}172$$

Insurance policies resemble annuities, but the company promises to pay an amount once when you die, not year by year when you are living. With fully funded insurance, the purchase price P is paid at the start, and all formulas are the same as for annuities, except that deaths to cohort members $_nd_x$ take the place of person-years lived. Such policies were once common, but today more often companies sell term insurance, where the benefit is paid only to cohort members who die in the next year, $_1d_x$ of them. There are many variations on annuities and insurance, most of them easy once the basic ideas are clear. Annuities may be purchased at age x and start paying benefits only at some later age z, implying that the sum over terms $_nL_y$ only starts at $y = z$. Buyers may have a mix of ages; each age can be treated separately and results added together. All these calculations require skills with lifetables, providing employment for demographers.

3.7 Mortality of the 1300s and 2000s

The lifetable for Edward III's children is quite a good picture of mortality in England in the later 1300s, despite all the reasons that this small sample of unusual people should be different from the rest. The two anomalies are the low level of infant deaths, underregistered here, as elsewhere, for we have omitted William of Hatfield, and the abbreviated life course after age 60, which would usually be longer. Note the heavy early female mortality, again a frequent feature of medieval life and death. In this family, deaths of mothers in childbearing are not the principal source of early adult women's mortality. They would have been a grievous cause of mortality for many families.

It is instructive to think about the changes between these days and our own. With regard to early life, infant and child mortality has dropped dramatically over the last hundred years, and the death of a baby has become an unusual event. Today, families who lose a child may feel singled out for tragedy, whereas once it was a part of life for the majority of families and most children experienced a brother's or a sister's death.

The other great change is the survival today of large numbers of people into their eighties and beyond. Engrained in our culture is the view of lifespan found in Psalm 90, verse 10:

> The days of our years are three-score years and ten;
> And if by reason of strength they be fourscore years,
> Yet is their strength labour and sorrow.

From Biblical times down to the era that present-day grandparents still remember, active healthy life beyond age 80—four score—was rare. A few people did live to great age. Life expectancies, affected as they are by infant mortaliy, are no guide to maximum ages attained by humans. In our lifetable for a family of the 1300s, the value for e_0 is 33, but Edmund Langley lives past 60. The pharoah Ramases II of Egypt, the adversary of Moses, is recorded as having lived beyond 90. His mummy survives as confirming evidence. But such cases were extremely rare. Today, almost all of us have family members or neighbors who live active lives into their late 80s and 90s, and alert people celebrating their hundredth birthdays are to be found in many communities. The result is a change in attitudes about what it means to be old and what kind of life can be lived at extreme old age.

The members of the cohort in our example provide a striking illustration of these changing attitudes. John of Gaunt, the Duke of Lancaster, dies at age 58. For us, 58 no longer even seems like old age. But Shakespeare presents John of Gaunt as an ancient man. He is introduced with the words "Old John of Gaunt, time-honoured Lancaster" as he totters onto the stage to give his famous dying speech, "This royal throne of kinds, this sceptred isle, . . . This fortress built by Nature for herself against infection and the hand of war . . . This blessed plot, this earth, this realm, this England."

HIGHLIGHTS OF CHAPTER 3

- $_nq_x$ conversions
- The cohort lifetable
- Hazard functions
- Gompertz models
- Annuities

KEY FORMULAS

$h_x = (-1/n) \log(\ell_{x+n}/\ell_x)$

$1 - {}_1q_x = (1 - {}_nq_x)^{1/n}$

$\ell_{x+n} = \ell_x(1 - {}_nq_x)$

$_nL_x \approx (n/2)(\ell_x + \ell_{x+n})$

$e_x = T_x/\ell_x$

Gompertz $h_x = \alpha \, e^{\beta x}$

FURTHER READING

For more details on lifetables, see Namboodiri and Suchindran (1987). The Human Mortality Database (HMD) developed by John Wilmoth along with Vladimir Shkolnikov is a pre-eminent source for data on death rates. Chapter 1 of Le Bras (2008) is a thoughtful overview.

EXERCISES FOR CHAPTER 3

1. Mortality for contemporary cohorts varies considerably across the globe.
   (a) For Kenyan children born in 2005, $_1q_0 = 0.053112$ and $_4q_1 = 0.026376$. What is $_5q_0$?
   (b) For Chilean girls born in 2000, $_1q_0 = 0.008941$, $_4q_1 = 0.001832$ and survivorship to age 10 is $\ell_{10} = 0.984178$. What is $_5q_5$?
   (c) For Taiwanese young women born in 1978, $_5q_{25} = 0.024740$. What is the value of $_1q_{27}$?

2. For the cohort of Russian men who were born in 1930, reaching age 35 in 1965, $_5q_{35} = 0.027857$ and $_5q_{40} = 0.041386$. For the later cohort born in 1960, $_5q_{35} = 0.04049$ and $_5q_{40} = 0.064856$. Estimate $_2q_{39}$ for each of the two cohorts. It is unusual to see mortality worsen in a developed country, as it has in Russia since the breakup of the Soviet Union.

3. The cohort of French women born in 1890 were 28 years old when, at the end of World War I, the influenza pandemic of 1918 struck. With a radix $\ell_0 = 100,000$, cohort deaths were $_{27}d_0 = 29,006$, $_1d_{27} = 512$, $_1d_{28} = 1,052$, $_1d_{29} = 439$, and $_1d_{30} = 405$. Find $_1q_x$ for $x = 27, 28$, and 29. If the cohort's actual initial size was 409,907, how many excess deaths did the cohort suffer in 1918, compared to the average of 1917 and 1919?

4. Projected probabilities of survival for U.S. women and men for a cohort born in the early 1990s are shown in Table 3.7, taken from the same forecasts as Figure 3.4 with a radix of 1. Projected cohort life expectancies are $e_0 = 78.91$ for men and $e_0 = 83.31$ for women. Suppose you belonged to this cohort. What is your probability of surviving from your present age to age 75? To age 90? To 100? Assume constant values

of $_1q_x$ between 0 and 17 and between 17 and 25 (but not above 25). If you are older than 25 set your age back to 25. What is your present expectation of further life e_x and the corresponding lifespan $x + e_x$?

5. For the children of King Edward III, whose birth and death dates are given in Table 3.2, how much would the expectation of life at birth change if William of Hatfield were added with a death age of 1 month?

6. Can it ever happen that $_nq_x$ is smaller than $(_{2n}q_{x+2n})/2$?

7. Can it ever happen that $_nL_x$ is smaller than $(_{2n}L_{x+2n})/2$?

8. Taking up a career as a teacher at the age of 25, a young American man belonging to the cohort born in 1990 (see Table 3.7) buys an annuity which promises to pay him a benefit of $100,000 per year starting at age 75 up to the age he dies. The open-ended interval has $e_{x\max} = e_{100} = 2.1$ years. Assuming an interest rate of 5% per year with actuarially fair rates, how much should his annuity cost?

9. A population maintains itself in a stationary state with the addition of 1,000 births and 200 immigrants aged exactly 20 each year. Write down a formula for the size of this population. One or more lifetable quantities may occur in your formula.

* 10. Table 3.8 shows hazard rates for the cohort of British women born in 1910 whose oldest members are now centenarians. Fit a Gompertz model to these hazards, estimating the α and β parameters. How well does the Gompertz prediction for h_{90} fit the recorded value of 0.167692?

Table 3.7 Survivorship forecasts for a U.S. cohort

x	17	25	75	90	100
Male ℓ_x	0.98436	0.97571	0.70231	0.26753	0.03327
Female ℓ_x	0.98809	0.98488	0.78552	0.39044	0.07363

Table 3.8 Hazard rates for British women born in 1910

x	50	60	70	80
h_x	0.004631	0.010672	0.025325	0.063001

* 11. By experimenting with various cases, find out whether it is always, sometimes, or never true that the hazard rate per year in a 1-year age interval is greater than the probability of dying in that 1-year interval.

* 12. From data from the English village of Colyton for 1750 to 1799 from Wrigley (1977), one learns that the probability of infants dying within 31 days of birth appears to be 0.046. The cumulative probability of dying within 61 days of birth is 0.054. Within 91 days of birth it is 0.062 and within 181 days of birth it is 0.071. Estimate the endogenous mortality rate by the method of Jean Bourgeois-Pichat.

13. For Kuwaiti women in 1980, estimates show $_5q_{65} = 0.154$, $_5q_{70} = 0.183$, $_5q_{75} = 0.305$, and $_5q_{80} = 0.409$. For men, the estimates are $_5q_{65} = 0.188$, $_5q_{70} = 0.304$, $_5q_{75} = 0.402$, and $_5q_{80} = 0.458$. Consider a cohort of 53% women and 47% men at age 65. Compute values of $_5m_x$ for a combined-sex lifetable from age 65 to 85. Plot $\log(_5m_x)$ versus x. How near do the points come to a straight line?

* 14. Combine the expressions for the hazard h_x and survivors ℓ_x under a Gompertz model into an expression for the density of cohort deaths at age x. Consider the logarithm of this density. Find an expression for its slope and solve for the age at which this slope vanishes. In this way, verify the formula for the modal age at death under the Gompertz model and find an expression for the value of the hazard rate at the modal age at death.

4

Cohort Fertility

4.1 Generational Renewal

In our studies so far we have dwelt mainly on the beginning and ending of lifelines on a Lexis diagram, on the start of life when one is born into a cohort and on the end of life when one takes one's exit by dying. Indeed, on our Lexis diagrams we have been marking nothing at all along the lifeline, as if nothing happened in between. It is reminiscent of a modern poem in which the poet thinks of her father and the inscription on his tombstone: a date of birth, a date of death, and nothing in between but a dash.

In between, among other things, comes childbearing. We focus here on a cohort of women—we consider men briefly later—and we focus at the beginning on their daughters. Figure 4.1 is a Lexis diagram for a sample of 10 women drawn from the 5,994,000 women born into the 5-year birth cohort born between 1930 and 1935 in the United States. One of these women died 4 months after birth. You can see the tiny lifeline on the middle left. Another woman died at the age of 30. You can see the lifeline end. The remaining eight women survived through to the end of the ages of childbearing. Two of them had two daughters each, four of them had a single daughter, and two of them had no daughters. Each of these births is a droplet along the mother's lifeline. On this diagram, a dotted line shows the droplet dropping to the axis, to the point where each daughter begins her own lifeline on the Lexis diagram. Visually, the lifelines of the cohort

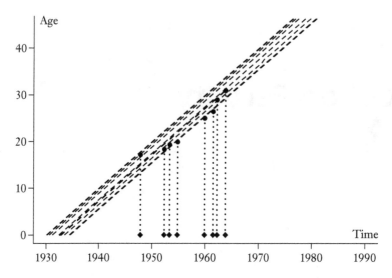

Figure 4.1 Cohort fertility on a Lexis diagram

of mothers resemble the left edge of a rainbow, and the cohort's daughters are like a gentle rain falling on the earth beneath.

In our picture we are seeing a process of generational renewal. If we call the cohort of women the first generation, then their daughters are the second generation. The cohort's daughters' daughters are the third generation. The ratio of the total number of daughters borne by cohort members to the initial number of women in the cohort is a generational replacement ratio, the ratio of the size of the second generation to the first. We call this ratio the "Net Reproduction Ratio" or, less precisely but more commonly, the "Net Reproduction Rate", or "*NRR*".

Published data more commonly record numbers of babies rather than numbers of daughters, so we need to convert from babies of both sexes to daughters when we calculate an *NRR*. The conversion factor, as previously mentioned, is the "fraction female at birth", or f_{fab}. Take as an example the cohort of U.S. women born in 1934. These were the mothers who generated the peak of the Baby Boom. The 1,054,933 women in the 1934 cohort had a total of 3,231,638 babies, of whom 1,576,094 were daughters, for a ratio of 0.4877. The *NRR* is given by

$$NRR = \frac{(3,231,638) * (0.4877)}{1,054,933} = 1.494$$

Table 4.1   Generation sizes and the *NRR*

Cohort	Babies	f_{fab}	Cohort Size	*NRR*
1910	2,665,122	0.4871	1,353,682	0.959
1922	3,579,318	0.4866	1,408,021	1.237
1934	3,231,638	0.4877	1,054,933	1.494
1947	3,788,342	0.4871	1,884,884	0.979

In a closed population, if cohort after cohort each has a Net Reproduction Ratio greater than 1, then we expect each generation to be larger than the next, and so we expect a growing population. If cohorts have *NRR* values equal to 1 over the course of many generations, then we expect a stationary population, and if cohorts all have *NRR* values less than 1, then we expect a contracting population.

When totals for cohorts and their babies are available, the calculation of the *NRR* is elementary. Table 4.1 shows some birth cohorts of U.S. women, with the number of babies borne by the cohort, the fraction female at birth, and the number of women in the cohort. (Several approximations have been employed.) We multiply the second and third columns and divide by the fourth to obtain the *NRR*. We see the *NRR* rising up to the 1934 cohort of Baby Boom mothers and falling back below 1 as the Baby Boom gave way to a "Baby Lull".

Frequently, the fraction female at birth is not published. In such cases a default value is needed. This fraction is generally a little less than one-half. Current studies suggest that nearly equal numbers of boys and girls are conceived and slightly more male fetuses normally survive to birth. The default value we adopt is $f_{fab} = 0.4886$. When the true value is known, we always use it, but when it is unknown, we use 0.4886.

The advantage of using a special number like 0.4886 for our default rather than a common number like 0.5000 is ease of recognition. The number 0.4886 occurs nowhere in formulas except as f_{fab}, whereas 0.5000 may occur in formulas for many other reasons. The choice 0.4886 was the fraction in America at the time this book began. Demographers often quote sex ratios on a percentage basis in place of fractions female. The sex ratio at birth implied by our default fraction is $100 * (0.5114)/(0.4886) = 104.67$.

A word about names is in order. The name "Net Reproduction Rate" is more common than "Net Reproduction Ratio", but to call the *NRR* a "rate" is a misnomer. A rate in demography is a value per unit of time, per year, per month, per decade. The *NRR* is a pure ratio. It is not expressed in units of time. Eugene Grebenik, long editor of the journal *Population Studies*, insisted on this point, and we follow his practice. Other names in use are the "Generational Replacement Ratio" and, occasionally, the "Net Reproductive Ratio".

The *NRR* is an input–output ratio. The potential future mothers starting life in a cohort are the "input". Their baby daughters in the next generation are the "output". The essential feature of an input–output ratio is that input must be measured in the same units as output. We compare apples to apples or oranges to oranges, not apples to oranges. Since we are measuring input as a count of females, we need to measure output as a count of females. We have women as input, so we need daughters as output, not sons plus daughters. Furthermore, we have newborn women as input. We count the size of the cohort at birth, not at some later age. Therefore, we need to count newborn daughters as output, not daughters at some later age. We compare like to like. As an alternative, we could take women at the start of childbearing as input. But then we would need to take daughters surviving to the start of childbearing as output. Mortality comes into the *NRR*, but only once, through the mortality of potential mothers.

Some members of a cohort die before beginning or completing childbearing. Their deaths reduce the eventual total number of daughters and so affect the *NRR*. The *NRR* is a measure of reproduction net of the effects of mortality, that is, remaining after mortality has been taken into account. Mortality diminishes a cohort's production of offspring just as taxes diminish a person's spendable income. The Net Reproduction Ratio is like a person's net income after taxes. There is also a Gross Reproduction Ratio. It is like gross, pre-tax income and excludes losses due to mortality.

The word "net" derives from a Latin root meaning "shining". The Net Reproduction Ratio is the shining measure of demography, one of the most important quantities demographers study. We spell it out in the following definition:

> The **Net Reproduction Ratio** is the number of daughters per newborn prospective mother who may or may not survive to and through childbearing.

4.2 Age-Specific Fertility

The presentation of the *NRR* in the previous section as a ratio of generation sizes brings out the concept clearly. In practice, however, the common method for calculating the *NRR* makes use of age-specific fertility rates.

An age-specific fertility rate is like a Crude Birth Rate insofar as it has babies in the numerator and person-years in the denominator. But it is unlike a Crude Birth Rate insofar as the babies are only the babies born to women in a particular age range and the person-years are only person-years lived by the women within that age range. Note that there are two restrictions on the person-years. They have to be lived within the particular range of ages, and they have to be lived by women, not (as with the Crude Birth Rate) by men and women.

We take an age interval from x to $x + n$. For a cohort, we write $_nf_x$ for the ratio formed by taking babies of both sexes born to women in the cohort while the women are between ages x and $x + n$ and dividing by the cohort person-years lived by women in the cohort between those ages. (As we shall see in Chapter 6, for a period age-specific fertility rate we shall use a capital "F" and write $_nF_x$ for the ratio of babies born to women aged x to $x + n$ in the period to period-person-years lived by women between those ages.) The abbreviation "ASFR" stands for age-specific fertility rate.

> The **cohort age-specific fertility rate** (ASFR) $_nf_x$ is the number of children borne by women in the cohort between ages x and $x + n$ per person-year lived by women in the cohort between ages x and $x + n$.

Age-specific fertility rates are rates, not probabilities. They have units of 1/time. Babies are persons, so the babies in the numerator cancel the persons part of the person-years in the denominator, leaving 1/years. Doubling the width of the age interval would increase both the numerator and the denominator and would not drastically change the rate. An age-specific fertility rate $_n f_x$ is the counterpart for fertility of the age-specific mortality rate $_n m_x$ in the lifetable, which has the same denominator but a numerator with deaths in place of births.

It is usual to concentrate on age-specific fertility rates for women, since women's age is a more obvious determinant of fertility. We can if we wish count births by age of father and divide by person-years-lived by men in the age interval. Such male *ASFR*'s are rarely used, since ages of fatherhood are less narrowly restricted biologically and socially and since data on fathers' ages are rarely tabulated.

We must bear in mind that "female" *ASFR*'s pertain to female parents but to both male and female babies. Sons and daughters enter into the numerator, person-years for mothers into the denominator. If the numerator is further restricted to daughters, the resulting rate should be labeled as a "daughters-only" *ASFR*, for instance by $_n f_x^{\text{daughters}}$, or by multiplying $_n f_x$ by the fraction female at birth. Mathematical demographers often work with daughters-only rates, and sometimes this restriction is mentioned in the text but omitted from the notation.

4.3 ASFRs and the NRR

A Net Reproduction Ratio is most often calculated from a table of age-specific fertility rates. We shall see in Chapter 6 that this calculation is the easiest one to generalize from cohort-based to period-based rates.

Since $_n f_x$ has babies divided by person-years, to recover a count of babies we need to multiply back by person-years. These person-years are the person-years lived by the female members of the cohort, and we borrow them from the $_n L_x$ column of the female cohort lifetable. After we form the products $_n f_x \, _n L_x$, we need to add them up over all ages of childbearing. We also need to convert from babies to daughters, and divide by the initial cohort size. These steps give the following age-based formula for the *NRR*:

$$NRR = \sum {}_n f_x \, {}_n L_x \, f_{fab}/\ell_0$$

Table 4.2 A cohort *NRR* from U.S.
age-specific rates

x	$_5f_x$	$_5L_x$	Babies
0	0	4770	0
5	0	4726	0
10	0	4712	0
15	0.0811	4698	381
20	0.2384	4681	1116
25	0.1969	4662	918
30	0.1033	4637	479
35	0.0313	4604	144
40	0.0046	4561	21
45	0.0009	4503	4
			3,063

The notation $\sum$ means "add up over all the age intervals with different starting ages x". The symbol $\sum$ is the capital Greek letter sigma and stands for "sum".

Calculation of the *NRR* from age-specific rates is illustrated in Table 4.2 with data for a sample of 1,000 U.S. women randomly selected from the cohort born in 1934 treated in previous sections. We multiply the age-specific fertility rates in the $_nf_x$ column by the lifetable person-years lived in the $_nL_x$ column (with a radix of 1,000) to obtain the column for babies. The sum of the column for babies is 3,063. We multiply the sum by the fraction $f_{\text{fab}} = 0.4877$ for this cohort from Table 4.1 and divide by the radix, arriving at an *NRR* of $3,063 * 0.4877/1000$, or 1.494, agreeing with the calculation from generational sizes in Section 4.3.

Two other summary measures employed throughout demography can be calculated from age-specific fertility rates. They are the Total Fertility Rate, or *TFR*, and the Gross Reproduction Ratio, or *GRR*. Both are usually calculated from period rather than cohort data, and they will be discussed again in Chapter 6. However, the concepts of the *TFR* and *GRR* are cohort concepts, just like the concept of the *NRR*. Both the *TFR* and the *GRR* are measures of fertility rather than generational renewal. Both of them exclude the effects of mortality. They tell us how many babies or daughters a cohort would produce in the absence of mortality. In the absence of mortality, each member of a cohort would live n person-years in the interval from x to $x + n$. We replace $_nL_x/\ell_0$ by n in our formulas. When we keep babies of both sexes, we obtain the *TFR*. When we restrict to daughters by multiplying by the fraction female at birth, we obtain the *GRR*:

$$TFR = \sum (_nf_x)(n); \qquad GRR = \sum (_nf_x)(n)(f_{fab})$$

When all the age intervals in a data table have the same width n, we can add up the $_nf_x$ column and multiply by n at the end to obtain the *TFR*. Then we multiply by f_{fab} to obtain the *GRR*. The *TFR* implied by Table 4.2 is close to 3.3. The *TFR* is not exactly the same as the expected total of children for women who do live through ages at childbearing. Women who survive to 50 might not be a typical subset of all women. They might, for instance, have had lower fertility in their twenties than women with poorer prospects for survival. We use the fertility for all women in their twenties, those who will not survive to older ages along with those who will, and similarly for every age group, when we compute a *TFR*.

4.4 Cohort Parity

The age-specific rates we have been studying track childbearing across the lifecourse. As women in a cohort reach the end of their years of childbearing, we can also assess completed cohort fertility. Sometimes data come in the form of a distribution of children ever born. Such data make possible a third way of calculating the *NRR*.

The number of live births that a woman has had is known as her parity. This word has the same spelling as the more familiar word "parity" meaning "equality" which occurs in phrases like "parity of pay". But the word "parity" in demography is derived from a different root, the same root as for "parent", for "parturition" (which means childbirth), or for "post partum" (which means "after childbirth"). A woman is "nulliparous" when she has never borne children.

We write $w(j)$ for the count, or "tally", of women in a cohort who have parity j. Unless otherwise noted, parities are measured after all members of the cohort have completed childbearing. Thus, $w(0)$ cohort members have borne no children, while $w(1)$ have borne one child, $w(2)$ have borne

Table 4.3   Completed parity for U.S. women born in 1934

j	0	1	2	3	4	5	6	7	8	9	10
$w(j)$	76	97	233	241	166	90	47	30	12	5	3

two children, and so forth. The sum of all the $w(j)$ is the initial cohort size. The index j labels children ever born, not children surviving.

If we are given a tally of women by parity for a cohort, we can find the NRR by the following formula:

$$NRR = \frac{(0 * w(0) + 1 * w(1) + 2 * w(2) + 3 * w(3) \ldots)(f_{\text{fab}})}{w(0) + w(1) + w(2) + w(3) \ldots}$$

Each woman at parity 1 contributes one child, each woman at parity 2 contributes two children, and so on. We multiply by f_{fab} to convert from children to daughters and divide by initial cohort size. Table 4.3 shows completed parity for a sample of 1,000 women from the U.S. cohort born in 1934.

To estimate the NRR, we multiply the first row by the second row and add the products: $0 * 76 + 1 * 97 + 2 * 233 \ldots + 10 * 3 = 3{,}063$. We multiply by 0.4877 and divide by 1,000, yielding $NRR = 1.494$, agreeing with our previous calculations.

The leading use for measures based on parity is the study of fertility limitation across history and around the world. A conceptual framework is described in Section 4.5. Here, by way of preparation, we introduce some key measures for this purpose, Parity Progression Ratios. The Parity Progression Ratio at parity j, written $PPR(j)$, is the fraction of women in a cohort who, having reached parity j, go on to have another baby, reaching at least parity $j + 1$ and perhaps going further, ending at some parity greater than j. If $w(j)$ women are ending up at parity j, then $w(j) + w(j + 1) + w(j + 2) \ldots$ women reached at least parity j, ending up at parity j or more, and $w(j + 1) + w(j + 2) + \ldots$ of these women went on at least to parity $j + 1$. The fraction progressing from j to $j + 1$ is the ratio $PPR(j)$ given by

$$PPR(j) = \frac{w(j + 1) + w(j + 2) + \ldots}{w(j) + w(j + 1) + w(j + 2) \ldots} = \sum_{j+1}^{\infty} w(i) / \sum_{j}^{\infty} w(i)$$

Table 4.4   Dutch women age 50 by parity, 2009

j:	0	1	2	3	4	5
$w(j)$:	22,275	15,151	49,972	22,897	6,378	1,690
$j+$:	119,570	97,295	82,144	32,172	9,275	2,897
$PPR(j)$:	0.814	0.844	0.392	0.288	0.312	0.417

Source: Human Fertility Database (HFD) (May 2013).

In sigma notation, the starting index is written below the sigma symbol and the ending index above it. Of course, these sums do not go all the way to infinity but only to the highest parity observed, above which $w(i) = 0$. In the sample of U.S. women in Table 4.3, all 1,000 reach at least parity 0, and $1,000 - 76 = 924$ reach at least parity 1, so $PPR(0) = 0.924$. Observe that PPR's are always labeled by the starting parity. The ratio labeled 0 goes from 0 to 1. Since $924 - 97 = 827$ reach parity 2, $PPR(1) = 827/924 = 0.895$. Similarly, $PPR(2) = (827 - 233)/827 = 0.718$.

The tally of women at each parity in Table 4.3 has been obtained by following girls born in 1934 as they grow, die or survive, and go on to bear all their children. These are tallies that take cohort mortality into account, allowing us, as we have seen, to compute a cohort NRR. Often, data come in a different form, from women who have survived to an age like 50 and then report numbers of children ever born. Mean completed parity for these surviving women would be an estimate of the cohort TFR. Multiplying by f_{fab} would give an estimate of the cohort GRR instead of the NRR.

Table 4.4 shows a tally by parity for 50-year-old Dutch women (that is, women in the Netherlands) in 2009, survivors of the 1-year birth cohort centered on mid-year 1959 reported in the Human Fertility Database (HFD). Only parities up to 5 are found in the table, but we also know that there were 1,207 women at parities 6 and above, so we can add up backward starting from the right to find the row for $j+$ from the row for $w(j)$. Dividing the entry for $j + 1+$ by the entry for $j+$ yields $PPR(j)$. For example, $1,207 + 1,690 = 2,897$ is the entry for 5+, and $1,207/2,897 = 0.417$ is $PPR(5)$.

Notice how PPR values drop off abruptly after $PPR(1)$. There is no mystery here. Many couples want no more than two children and use contraception to avoid going on to higher parities. Notice also that PPR

values trend upward again at higher parities. In most populations there is a subset of women and their spouses who want large families or want "as many children as the Lord sends". Parities above 5 or 6 or more have a heavy representation of such women, who bring up the progression ratios. European countries, including the Netherlands, have become known for so-called lowest-low fertility far below replacement levels, even more pronounced for cohorts born later than the cohort in Table 4.4. Whether fertility in these societies will rebound is a subject for lively debate.

A sharp contrast to the Netherlands is offered by Parity Progression Ratios for the central African country of Malawi based on interviews with 770 women aged 45 to 50 in a Demographic and Health Survey (DHS) for 2004. Here, $PPR(0) = 0.978$, $PPR(1) = 0.976$, $PPR(2) = 0.940$, and $PPR(j)$ is still above 0.600 through parity $j = 9$. From parity 11 onward the ratios do drop to around 0.300, which is no surprise, since women only reach high parities at ages close to the end of their reproductive spans. Just as we can start with tallies w and calculate PPR's, so we can start with PPR's along with total cohort size and calculate the w's. Here, of 770 total women in our sample, $770 * PPR(0) = 753$ reach at least parity 1, so $770 - 753 = 17$ must be found at parity 0. Some $753 * PPR(1) = 735$ reach at least parity 2, so $753 - 735 = 18$ must be found at parity 1. This example is treated further in the exercises. Sustained high PPR's constitute evidence that family limitation practices are not widespread, in a sense which we now make more precise.

4.5 Natural Fertility

The decline of fertility in most Western and many Eastern societies and the persistence of high fertility and rapid population growth in sectors of the Third World are the demographic facts which more than all others shape the contemporary world. Demographers have devoted sustained attention to devising measures to track fertility decline and, particularly, conscious fertility limitation. We now describe an approach which has informed the last half-century of demographic thought.

The modern study of fertility limitation began with Louis Henry, who worked at the Institut National d'Études Démographiques (INED) in Paris in the years following the Second World War. His ideas were taken up and extended by the Cambridge Group for the History of Population and Social Structure in England under the leadership of Peter Laslett, E. Anthony Wrigley, and Roger Schofield, and then at the Office for Population Research at Princeton University under Ansley Coale. Louis Henry saw that to understand the onset of fertility limitation in a society, it was paramount to be able to describe the pattern of fertility before these practices came into use. He was interested in conscious, intentional fertility limitation, what we now call "family planning", and he was particularly interested in being able to analyze data which would distinguish between the absence and the presence of practices by which couples attempt to stop childbearing after desired family-size targets have been achieved. Data on couples' intentions do not, of course, exist to any extent for previous centuries, and even today the gap between reported intentions and observed behavior is often great. Henry therefore asked what tell-tale signs would appear in the kind of fertility data that do exist from earlier centuries that would indicate family limitation of a modern, conscious kind.

Louis Henry focussed on parity. As we have said, parity is a person's number of children. When further childbearing is made to depend on the number of previous children, it is called "parity-specific control". Parity-specific control presumes both that couples want to limit their family sizes and that they have the means to do so. A leading sign of parity-specific control is the kind of drop in Parity Progression Ratios at some parity featured in Section 4.4. Another sign can be recognized when fertility rates specific to combined categories of age and parity can be estimated and we can see whether rates for women of the same age differ according to their parities. This form of evidence is featured later in this section.

In an article in the *Eugenics Quarterly* in 1961, Louis Henry proposed using the term "natural fertility" in a technical demographic sense to mean "fertility in the absence of parity-specific control". In some ways, this choice of words was unfortunate. It suggests that human populations were in some sort of "state of nature" before they began to practice modern versions of family limitation. It also suggests that parity-specific control is the only important form of fertility control, which is not true. Nonetheless, Henry's definition of "natural fertility" has one great virtue. It is an operational

Table 4.5   Fertility rates specific for age and parity

Parity	0	1	2	3	4	5	6+
Nigeria	0.272	0.225	0.257	0.244	0.279	0.284	0.233
Netherlands	0.146	0.221	0.079	0.075	0.090	NA	NA

definition. Whether there is parity-specific control can be inferred from Parity Progression Ratios and from fertility rates specific to parity and age. By calculating ratios and rates, we can measure whether fertility is "natural fertility" in Henry's sense.

The concept of a demographic rate specific for some cross classification of categories like age, parity, marital status, or ethnicity is straightforward. Each combination of, say, age and parity specifies a group of women and an interval—for example, women at parity 3 between ages 30 and 35. The numerator for their rate includes all their births at parity 3 before age 35. Births at parity 3 move women out of the category and on to parity 4. The denominator for their rate includes all person-years lived at parity 3 while they are still between ages 30 and 35.

The important point is to match the set of events in the numerator to the set of years of exposure on the denominator. For a marital fertility rate, the numerator only includes births to married women, and the denominator only includes years lived in the married state. If a woman is divorced and later remarries, the person-years unmarried do not contribute to the denominator. For a parity-specific rate, after a woman has a birth counted in the numerator, she is then at the next parity, and her person-years after the birth do not count in the denominator for the original parity group.

Since 2000, most countries have experienced some departures from natural fertility, but surveys from earlier decades are often consistent with an absence of parity-specific control. The 1990 DHS sample of Nigerian women provides an illustration. In Table 4.5, the row labeled "Nigeria" shows estimates of age- and parity-specific fertility rates for women 30 to 35 in 1990, a cohort born between 1955 and 1960. Each rate is a quotient of births divided by person-years. For example, women between 30 and 35 in the survey reported 60 first births since the age of 30 and 220.4 years spent over the age of 30 at parity 0 (before their first births), yielding the rate of

$60/220.4 = 0.272$ entered in the table. At parity 1, some 101 second births from 448.2 person-years yields the rate of $101/448.2 = 0.225$.

For Nigeria, the rates in Table 4.5 are all quite close to each other, regardless of parity. "Regardless of parity" is the point. We are seeing evidence of natural fertility. Of course, there is some variation from column to column. These are estimates based on a sample, subject to chance variations which statisticians call sampling error. But for these Nigerian women of the same age the variations with parity are small. That becomes clear when we compare them to the row labeled "Netherlands", which comes from Human Fertility Database statistics for women aged 30 in 2009, the whole of a cohort born in 1979. In that row, fertility rates drop by nearly a factor of 3 as we look from parity 1 to parities 2 and up. So few women are found at parities 5 and up that estimates are not available (NA). The contrast between Nigeria and the Netherlands is a contrast between the absence of parity-specific control and the presence of parity-specific control.

Parity Progression Ratios and fertility rates specific to parity as well as age supply evidence about deviations, if any, from natural fertility, but they do not themselves summarize the strength of fertility limitation on some simple scale. Measures based on parity that do so are available in the Cohort Parity Analysis of David et al. (1988). More frequently, demographers resort to measures which exploit age-based data to infer patterns of parity. These measures are typically computed from period rather than cohort rates, and they are presented in Sections 6.7 and 6.8.

Like the approaches in this section, many of the innovative measures now applied to contemporary populations were pioneered by historical demographers. Methods were especially devised to take advantage of pre-industrial data drawn from local records of baptisms, marriages, and burials kept in parish churches in England, France, and other countries within the European orbit. A technique called "family reconstitution" was developed at INED, refined by the Cambridge Group, and widely applied. The technique involves comparing names that appear in the registers, matching baptisms to the marriages of parents, matching husbands and wives back to their own baptisms, and matching burials back to marriages and baptisms, building small family genealogies one by one. From the reconstituted families of a parish, estimates of age-specific mortality and age- and parity-specific fertility can be constructed. Due to movements in and out of parishes and imperfections in the records, data are incomplete. Statistical methods were developed for confirming the presence of a family in a parish with records subsequently excluded from the computation of rates, in order to avoid statistical distortions. Most of the early research on natural fertility was based on family reconstitution. The authoritative work is Wrigley et al. (1997).

Biologists observe that differences in age-specific fertility rates from species to species are often much greater than differences among members of the same species. Flies have fertility rates thousands of times as high as falcons. In this sense, a species has its own characteristic level of fertility. This perspective tempts one into thinking that levels of fertility for humans subject to natural fertility might be pretty much the same from person to person and society to society, and differences would only appear when fertility patterns diverged from natural fertility.

Louis Henry discovered that this expectation is wrong. If one takes natural fertility to mean the absence of parity-specific control, then there turn out to be huge variations in the overall level of fertility in human societies from time to time and place to place. This is partly because biological and environmental factors affect fertility levels (without introducing parity-specific patterns), partly because biological and environmental factors interact with cultural practices that differ, and partly because not all forms of family limitation are parity specific.

In thinking about variations in natural fertility, it is worthwhile to introduce some technical distinctions in vocabulary. Fecundity is the biological capacity for childbearing. Fecundability is the probability of conceiving for a woman subject to a continuous exposure to the risk of pregnancy. Fertility is the outcome level of childbearing, which depends not only on fecundity but on the decisions and behaviors of couples within their social, cultural, and environmental context. These are the distinctions in English. The French call fertility *fécondité* and fecundity *fertilité*, creating confusion for the unwary. There are technical terms for infertility. Primary sterility is the lack of capacity ever to have children, either for individuals or for couples. Secondary sterility is a loss of capacity to have children, after some children have been born. Post-partum amenorrhoea is temporary infecundity for women following childbirth. Lactational amenorrhoea is temporary infecundity accompanying breastfeeding, which generally abates when breast milk is supplemented with other food.

These definitions call attention to some of the reasons that levels of fertility vary widely among societies which still have natural fertility in Louis Henry's sense. A chief reason is lactation. Different cultures have different norms about nursing and weaning and supplementation which interact with the human endocrine system to produce different lengths of lactational amenorrhoea. A second reason is abstinence. Customs differ with regard to "post-partum abstinence", when couples refrain from sexual intercourse following childbirth. Such cultural practices have strong effects on birth intervals and may have beneficial effects on the survival of infants and the health of the mother. Periods of abstinence do not generally depend on parity and so do not count as parity-specific control. But their effects on child spacing may be well understood and intentional and may reasonably be classified as a form of family limitation different from parity-specific control.

Another reason for levels of fertility to vary in natural fertility populations is nutrition. Nutrition affects fecundity, but only mainly at the extremes. In famines, women stop ovulating. During the Dutch hunger-winter of 1944, Nazis starved the population of Holland and most childbearing was suppressed. The medical condition of anorexia nervosa leads to amenorrhoea among teeneage girls. What is at stake is the net balance of nutritional intake compared to the demands placed on the body. Women athletes are often amenorrhoeic. Net nutritional status has strong effects on human heights and on capacity for physical labor. Impressive though unequal improvements in nutrition over the last three centuries have been a major driver of economic development and indirectly of population growth, as described in Floud et al. (1990) and Floud et al. (2011).

However, direct effects on growth rates through linkage between nutrition and fecundity are thought to be modest except at extremes of malnutrition. Studies by Jane Menken in the 1990s documented high fertility among poorly fed women in Bangladesh. A mother's nutritional status and the hormonal signals it stimulates can affect the viability of a fetus after conception, but late in pregnancy it appears that the human body is programmed to support the fetus at the expense of the mother, even under famine conditions.

Understanding of nutrition and hormones and their links to demographic outcomes, discussed, for example, by Ellison (2001), is of great theoretical importance. One can imagine evolutionary processes of natural selection favoring physiological responses that reduce fecundity when food is scarce and increase it when food is plentiful. This would be an example of a "homeostatic" mechanism, in the sense introduced in the discussion of Thomas Malthus in Chapter 1. As before, homeostatic means maintaining the same state. A thermostat keeps a house at the same temperature. As the house cools, it turns on the heat and warms it up. As the house warms, it turns off the heat, till the house cools down again. Homeostatic mechanisms in demography are mechanisms which regulate population growth in relation to resources. When resources are plentiful, growth rates are to rise. When resources are scarce, growth rates are to drop. Most species in nature appear to be subject to homeostatic controls of one sort or another. Homeostatic mechanisms may operate through mortality or fertility, and effects on fertility may operate through biological fecundity or through social practices. In historical times the principal homeostatic mechanisms for human populations appear to come largely from economic arrangements and cultural and social institutions, but there remains much to be learned.

Economic, social, and cultural factors do not themselves prevent births. Demographers distinguish between background causes and the pathways through which they impinge on the biological processes of having children. The pathways are called proximate determinants. Proxima is the Latin word for "nearest". Proximate determinants are the nearest causal factors to the actual outcomes that can be measured from ordinary demographic sources like surveys without special medical examinations. Examples of proximate determinants are contraception, induced abortion, post-partum infecundity, and states like marriage which affect sexual activity. A popular method for separating out the numerical contributions of the proximate determinants by Bongaarts and Potter (1983) is often taught in courses on fertility. Other methods for assessing fertility limitation are typically computed from period data. We return to them in Chapter 6.

HIGHLIGHTS OF CHAPTER 4

- The Net Reproduction Ratio
- Age-specific fertility rates
- Parity and Parity Progression Ratios
- Natural fertility
- Nutrition and fertility

KEY FORMULAS

$$NRR = \frac{(\text{births to women in cohort})(f_{\text{fab}})}{\text{women in cohort}}$$

$$NRR = \sum ({}_n f_x)({}_n L_x)(f_{\text{fab}})/\ell_0$$

$$NRR = \frac{(0 * w(0) + 1 * w(1) + 2 * w(2) + 3 * w(3) \ldots)(f_{\text{fab}})}{w(0) + w(1) + w(2) + w(3) \ldots}$$

$$TFR = \sum ({}_n f_x)(n)$$

$$GRR = \sum ({}_n f_x)(n)(f_{\text{fab}})$$

$$PPR(j) = \sum_{j+1}^{\infty} w(i) / \sum_{j}^{\infty} w(i)$$

FURTHER READING

The World We Have Lost by Laslett (1971) (first edition, 1965) continues to shape the study of fertility and historical social structure. For new directions, see the work by Johnson-Hanks, Bachrach, Morgan, and Kohler Johnson-Hanks et al. (2011).

EXERCISES FOR CHAPTER 4

1. Find the *TFR* and *GRR* from the U.S. age-specific cohort rates in Table 4.2. How close is the *GRR* to the *NRR*?

2. Table 4.6 shows estimates of cohort age-specific fertility rates and person-years lived for the cohort of Swedish women born in 1800. The radix is 1,000. Find the cohort *NRR*, *TFR*, and *GRR*. How close is the *GRR* to the *NRR*?

3. Some 34 baby girls were born in a single week in July at Stanford Hospital. Fifty years later, a survey is sent out asking them, among other questions, how many daughters they have borne. It turns out that one of them died as an infant. All 33 of the others respond. The following are the numbers of daughters they report: 1, 0, 1, 1, 2, 1, 1, 0, 1, 3, 1, 2, 2, 1, 4, 1, 0, 1, 1, 0, 2, 0, 1, 2, 0, 0, 1, 1, 1, 0, 3, 2, 3. Calculate the Net Reproduction Ratio for this July cohort.

Table 4.6   Data for the 1800 cohort of Swedish women

x	$_5f_x$	$_5L_x$	x	$_5f_x$	$_5L_x$
15	0.0122	3,134	35	0.2131	2,663
20	0.1038	3,036	40	0.1136	2,509
25	0.2211	2,930	45	0.0182	2,351
30	0.2408	2,808			

Source: Keyfitz and Flieger (1968).

Table 4.7   Women by completed parity, Malawi, 2004

Parity j:	0	1	2	3	4	5	6	7
Women $w(j)$:	17	18	44	45	48	62	107	95

Parity j:	8	9	10	11	12	13	14	15
Women $w(j)$:	96	92	69	47	22	5	2	1

Source: Demographic and Health Survey (DHS), Malawi, 2004.

4. Table 4.7 shows women by parity at ages 45 to 50 in the whole sample from the 2004 DHS in Malawi discussed in Section 4.4. Calculate counts of women at and above each parity along with the values of $PPR(j)$ for all j.

5. From Table 4.7, calculate estimates of the cohort *TFR* and *GRR* for this cohort from Malawi. What is the mean completed parity for women at and above parity 8? By how much would we underestimate the *TFR* if all women at and above parity 8 were assigned to parity 8?

6. Imagine that we could ask each of the children of the women in Table 4.7 to report the number of their siblings ever born. (In fact, it would be hard to do so, since some children would have died.) There are $j\,w(j)$ children from a family of size j, and each one has $j - 1$ siblings ever born. Work out the mean number of siblings for children ever born in Malawi implied by the data in the table.

5

Population Projection

5.1 Transition Matrices

Transition matrices are tables used for population projection. Official presentations of projections are often filled with disclaimers cautioning the reader that projections are not predictions. They do not tell us what the world *will* be like but only what the world *would* be like if a particular set of stated assumptions about future vital rates turned out to be true. The assumptions may or may not bear any relation to what actually happens.

Such disclaimers are disingenuous. Projection is not just a game with computers and pieces of paper. We do projections for a purpose, and that purpose is to foresee, as best we can, the future of the population. The choice of credible assumptions about vital rates is as much a part of the art and science of projection as are the formulas we use to implement the calculations. Here, we concentrate on the formulas. A synopsis of assumptions and their rationale may be found in Bongaarts and Bulatao (2000).

The record of demographers at guessing future vital rates has not been good. The community as a whole failed to predict the Baby Boom of the 1950s and 1960s, and it failed to predict the Baby Lull of the 1970s and 1980s. It largely failed to predict the continuing trend toward lower mortality at older ages in industrialized countries. These failures show that we do not yet understand the mechanisms that drive demographic change. We crave deeper theories with better predictive power.

Although demographers have an unenviable record of prediction, they can pride themselves on doing better, by and large, than economists, seismologists, or those who bet on horses. The choice of assumptions about future fertility, mortality, marriage, divorce, and immigration may be fraught with pitfalls, but the methods for using those assumptions to calculate future population sizes and age distributions are well developed and satisfactory. In this chapter we study these methods of calculation. We feature tools based on matrices and vectors, with projection over discrete steps of time with populations split up into discrete age groups. Section 5.7 adds a brief discussion of the deeper mathematics of projection that takes time and age to be continuous variables.

Sophisticated projections can treat a population classified by many characteristics including race, ethnicity, education, marital status, income, and locality as well as sex and age. In fact, so much detail is not common, although progress is being made, under a European team led by the demographer Wolfgang Lutz, for incorporating education into worldwide projections. Despite the potential for complexity, the basic ideas are well illustrated by simple projections which focus on a single sex and on all races and ethnicities together and which subdivide the population only by age. We devote ourselves to this simple case.

The main tools for projecting the size and age distribution of a population forward through time are tables called "Leslie matrices". It was P.H. Leslie who published a description of their use in 1945. The same approach was aired a few years earlier by H. Bernardelli and by E.G. Lewis, but their work did not become widely known until Leslie published his. The approach is closely related to the subject of Markov chains in probability theory, mentioned again in Section 5.7, but what is being projected with Leslie matrices are expected numbers of individuals rather than probabilities. Leslie matrices are a special case of transition matrices. When demographers project a distribution of marital status, parity, education, or other variables into the future, they use general transition matrices. When they project age structure, they use the special transition matrices that Leslie defined.

We begin by defining a transition matrix.

A transition matrix is a table with rows and columns
showing the expected number of individuals
who
END up in the state with the label on the ROW
per individual
at the START in the state with the label on the COLUMN.

A Leslie matrix, as we have said, is a special case of a transition matrix in which the states correspond to age groups. With Leslie matrices, the processes of transition are surviving and giving birth. The Leslie matrix describes a one-step transition. We project the population forward one step at a time. The time between START and END, the projection step, should be equal to the width n of all the age groups.

The fact that the step size has to equal the age group width is crucial. For projection, we generally pick one sex, usually females, and we divide the female population into age groups of width n. This width may be 1 year, 5 years, 15 years, or some other convenient number. If we are using age groups that are 1 year wide, then we have to project forward 1 year at a time, and so to project 10 years into the future requires 10 projection steps. If we are using 5-year age groups, then we have to project forward 5 years at a time, and so to project 10 years into the future requires only two projection steps.

Here, we assume a closed population. This assumption is relaxed in Chapter 11, where migrants are included in projections. In this chapter, people enter the population only by being born to members already in the population, and people leave it only by dying. Our projection treats childbirth as a possible transition along with survival. That means that the people who end up in some state may not be the same people who start in any one of the states. Instead, they may be the babies of people who start in the various states. We are concerned with the expected numbers in the state for the row per person in the state for the column, without regard to how the people are channeled there.

5.2 Structural Zeros

The logic of the transition process is built into a transition matrix through the pattern of zeros that occur. Some age groups owe no part of their numbers at the end of the step to certain other age groups. Suppose we have $n = 5$. We have 5-year-wide age groups and we are projecting forward 5 years in one step. No teenagers owe their numbers to 40-year-olds 5 years before. Thus the value of the Leslie matrix element in the row for 15 to 20-year-olds and the column for 40-year-olds has to be zero. This is a "structural zero". We know it is zero because of the logic of the processes of aging and childbirth. We do not have to consult data to see whether the expected number comes out to be zero. We can tell beforehand.

Most of the elements of a Leslie matrix are structural zeros, and we can fill them in immediately. Continue assuming 5-year-wide age groups, and consider the third row of a Leslie matrix, giving expected numbers of 10-to-15-year-olds. We expect no 10-to-15-year olds at the end of 5 years per person aged 0 to 5 at the start, because no 0-to-5-year-old can be over age 10 in only 5 years. So the entry in the first column in this row is a structural zero. The next entry need not be zero, however, because we do expect some 10-to-15-year-olds at the end of 5 years per person aged 5 to 10 at the start. Any such person who survives 5 years will make it into the state labeled by the row. In this example, the entry in the third row in the third column is another structural zero. No one 10 to 15 at the start can stay 10 to 15 five years later. The next entry is also zero. No one can get younger. In the third row, only the entry in the second column is not a structural zero.

The same logic tells us that, below the first row, all elements are structural zeros except the subdiagonal, the set of entries one below the main diagonal. No one can jump an age group, stay in the same age group, or get younger. They can only move (if they survive) into the next age group. We see how important it is for the projection step to be the same as the age-group width to avoid a higgeldy-piggeldy mixing of groups.

So far, we have skipped the first row. What about the first row, for people who end up aged 0 to 5 at the end of 5 years? No one can survive into this row. But these elements are not structural zeros, because there can be babies born during the projection step who are found in this age group at the end of the step. The number of babies depends on the number of potential parents (mothers, in a females-only projection) in the various age groups at the start. So the entries in the first row are not structural zeros.

Whether the upper-left element of a Leslie matrix equals zero or not depends on the age-group width. If n is 5, we do not expect there to be any babies in 5 years to people 0 to 5 at the start. But if n is 15, we do expect babies in the next 15 years to people aged 0 to 15 at the start. Whether the upper-left element is zero depends on n and on empirical knowledge about youngest ages of childbearing. Therefore, the upper-left element, despite often equalling zero, is not regarded as a structural zero. The following diagram shows the structural zeros and sources of nonzero entries in a segment of a Leslie matrix:

	0 to 5	5 to 10	10 to 15	15 to 20	20 to 25
0 to 5	kids	kids	kids	kids	kids
5 to 10	survivors	0	0	0	0
10 to 15	0	survivors	0	0	0
15 to 20	0	0	survivors	0	0
20 to 25	0	0	0	survivors	0

Another way of representing information about structural zeros is a diagram of permitted transitions. We mark states within circles and draw an arrow from one state to another one if there is a nonzero element for that column-row pair, that is, if any individuals can show up in the receiver state at the point of the arrow from individuals in the sender state at the shaft of the arrow.

Such arrow diagrams, like programmer flow charts, are helpful when transitions are not between age groups but between states like marital statuses with a logic all their own. Consider a model with four states, single (S) in the sense of never married, married (M), widowed (W), and divorced (D). Suppose the projection step is too short for us to expect anyone to get both married and divorced or divorced and remarried within a single step. In other words, multiple transitions within one step are not numerically significant. An arrow diagram for such a model is shown in Figure 5.1.

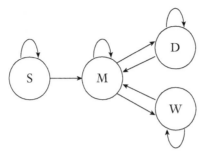

Figure 5.1 Permitted transitions among marital statuses

The structural zeros in the transition matrix corresponding to Figure 5.1 go into slots marked "0" in the following matrix:

	Single	Married	Widowed	Divorced
Single	x	0	0	0
Married	x	x	x	x
Widowed	0	x	x	0
Divorced	0	x	0	x

5.3 The Leslie Matrix Subdiagonal

We generally denote a matrix by a single capital letter like A. We pick out an element in a particular row and column with subscripts. The first subscript is for the row and the second subscript is for the column. Thus $A_{3\,2}$ is the element in the third row and second column, for survivors from the second age group to the third age group. By contrast, $A_{2\,3}$ is the element in the second row and third column. This is a structural zero, since no member of the third age group can grow younger and turn up in the second age group at the end of a projection step. This notation for elements of matrices is universal. For our particular matrices it may seem confusing, because the subscript for the destination age group comes first, and the subscript for the origin age group second, in the reverse of chronological order. The notation can be illustrated by writing

$$A_{\text{to, from}} \quad \text{or} \quad A_{\text{row, column}}$$

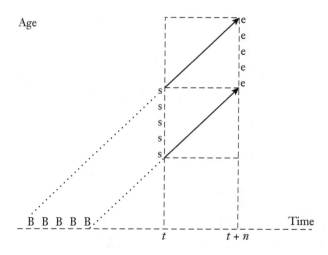

Figure 5.2 Contributions to the Leslie matrix subdiagonal

We now want to develop a formula for the elements along the subdiagonal of the Leslie matrix, which represent transitions of survival. We continue to use 5-year-wide age groups, and consider $A_{3\,2}$, the expected number of people aged 10 to 15 at the end, per person aged 5 to 10 at the start. The age group of 5-to-10-year-olds at the start, at time t ("today"), is composed of cohorts born between times $t-10$ and $t-5$. We follow the experience of five 1-year birth cohorts on the Lexis diagram in Figure 5.2.

On the diagram, the "B" symbols represent single-year cohorts at birth, the "s" symbols represent them at the start of the projection step, and the "e" symbols represent them at the end. The basic assumption which we make is that we may ignore changes in sizes of cohorts at birth inside each 5-year period, pretending that all changes in initial cohort sizes occur in jumps between periods. We also assume that the same lifetable applies to all the 1-year cohorts in this 5-year group of cohorts.

Let us trace the experience of some of the cohorts on the diagram. The earliest cohort, today's 10-year-olds, had some size ℓ_0 at birth. Now, at the start of the projection step, it has ℓ_{10} members left. The latest cohort contributing to the age group, today's 5-year-olds, had, by assumption, the same size ℓ_0 at birth and now has ℓ_5 members left. The whole 5-year age group is about five times as large as the average size of its youngest and oldest cohorts and now amounts to

$$(5/2)(\ell_5 + \ell_{10})$$

Five years from now, at the end of the projection step, as the cohorts reach the points marked "e", the oldest cohort will have ℓ_{15} members left and the youngest cohort will have ℓ_{10} members left. The whole age group will amount to

$$(5/2)(\ell_{10} + \ell_{15})$$

We recognize these sizes as our usual approximations for $_5L_5$ and $_5L_{10}$ from the person-years lived column of the lifetable. Had we split our age group into arbitrarily many small cohorts and added them all up, we would have obtained the corresponding $_nL_x$ values exactly.

Thus the subdiagonal element of the Leslie matrix is the ratio of the 10-to-15-year olds at the end to the 5-to-10-year-olds at the start, that is,

$$A_{3\,2} = \frac{_5L_{10}}{_5L_5}$$

In general, with the bottom age of the age group x expressed in terms of the column number j by $x = jn - n$, we have

$$A_{j+1,\,j} = \frac{_nL_{x+n}}{_nL_x}$$

Each subdiagonal element of a Leslie matrix is a ratio of big-L values. The age label on the *numerator* comes from the *row*. The age label on the *denominator* comes from the *column*. The Leslie matrix with formulas on the subdiagonal looks like this one:

	0 to 5 kids	5 to 10 kids	10 to 15 kids	15 to 20 kids	20 to 25 kids
0 to 5					
5 to 10	$\frac{_5L_5}{_5L_0}$	0	0	0	0
10 to 15	0	$\frac{_5L_{10}}{_5L_5}$	0	0	0
15 to 20	0	0	$\frac{_5L_{15}}{_5L_{10}}$	0	0
20 to 25	0	0	0	$\frac{_5L_{20}}{_5L_{15}}$	0

A point needs to be mentioned that will become clearer in later sections. The cohort whose lifetable supplies the numerator and denominator in the subdiagonal element $_nL_{x+n}/_nL_x$ is the cohort born between $t - x - n$ and $t - x$. That is a different cohort for each age group x. The big-L values for different columns of the Leslie matrix are big-L values from different cohort lifetables. They are in fact big-L values from the period lifetable which will be introduced in Chapter 7. The period lifetable stitches together survival experience for different cohorts as they move through the same time period, just as the Leslie matrix does. At this stage, the key concept is the way that ratios of big-L values supply subdiagonal matrix elements. The source of the big-L values is a detail deferred to Section 5.8 and Chapter 7.

* 5.4 The Leslie Matrix First Row

Outside the subdiagonal, the only elements in a Leslie matrix which are not structural zeros are found in the first row. These are the elements that take account of population renewal, as babies are born to parents and survive to be counted at the end of the projection step. The formulas for the first row are more complicated than those for the subdiagonal, and we develop them one step at a time.

The formulas we develop are for projecting the female population. Daughters rather than babies of both sexes are at stake in the first row. Whenever we do projections, we must have the same kinds of people coming out as going in. We cannot have babies of both sexes coming out without having parents of both sexes going in. Joint projections which keep track of males and females and interactions between them are possible in principle, but building a simple and appealing two-sex model is a problem that remains largely unsolved. One-sex projections could be done for males, inserting fertility rates for sons and fathers, but ages of motherhood are more regular than ages of fatherhood. Usually the female population is projected and counts of males are estimated from projected counts for females.

When projecting females, we must remember that we need fertility rates for *daughters only*. Since published fertility rates are usually for babies of both sexes, we need to multiply by the fraction female at birth, f_{fab}, or by our default fraction 0.4886.

We seek a formula for the expected number of daughters aged 0 to n at the end of the projection step per woman aged x to $x + n$ at the start. As before, we write $j(x)$ for the corresponding column with $x = j(x)(n) - n$.

Here is a sneak preview. Our formula turns out to be

$$A_{1,j(x)} = \frac{{}_nL_0}{2\,\ell_0}\left({}_nF_x + {}_nF_{x+n}\frac{{}_nL_{x+n}}{{}_nL_x}\right)f_{\text{fab}}$$

We build up our formula by introducing complications one at a time. The element $A_{1,j(x)}$ pertains to daughters entering the population over n years by being born to mothers aged x to $x + n$ at the start. How many daughters per potential mother should there be?

A first guess would be to multiply the daughters-only age-specific fertility rate $({}_nF_x)(f_{\text{fab}})$ for women x to $x + n$ by the years at risk in the interval, namely n, yielding a first crude version of our formula:

$$(n)({}_nF_x)(f_{\text{fab}})$$

The capital "F" in ${}_nF_x$ indicates a period age-specific fertility rate, yet to be discussed in Chapter 6, instead of a small "f" for ${}_nf_x$, the cohort age-specific fertility rate already discussed in Chapter 4. Strictly speaking, ${}_nF_x$ and ${}_nf_x$ are both approximations to the relevant rate, and either capital F or small f could be used in the formula, but capital F is the customary choice.

For a better, second version we recognize that not all baby daughters survive to the end of the projection interval. The first age group counts kids aged 0 to n at the end of the step, not newborns. So we need a formula for the proportion of babies born during the n years who survive to be counted. Babies born early in the period have to survive to be nearly n years old. Babies born late in the period have to survive only a little while. We need an average of survivorships. When we were finding a formula for subdiagonal elements, we also averaged survivorships, but now our newborn cohorts start at birth, along the bottom axis of the Lexis diagram. Whereas before we were comparing lifelines crossing two sides of a parallelogram, now we are comparing lifelines crossing two adjacent sides of a right triangle. The base of the triangle covers the interval from t to $t + n$ and the perpendicular side reaches up from age 0 to age n above time $t + n$.

As before, we ignore changes in initial cohort size within the interval. Out of any ℓ_0 girls born near the start of the interval, about ℓ_n survive to the end. Out of any ℓ_0 born close to the end, nearly all ℓ_0 survive to the end. On average, from $(n)(\ell_0)$ births we expect $(n)(\ell_n + \ell_0)/(2)$ survivors, which we recognize as our standard approximation for $_nL_0$. Multiplying the ratio of survivors to births by the factors in our first crude formula, we obtain an improved candidate:

$$\left(\frac{_nL_0}{(n)(\ell_0)}\right)(n)(_nF_x)(f_{\text{fab}})$$

The factors of n in numerator and denominator ultimately cancel out but are helpful for understanding along the way.

For a third version, we take into account the aging of potential mothers during the projection interval. Women aged x to $x + n$ at the start only spend on average about half of the next n years in their starting age group. They grow older and spend about half the interval in the next age group. So in place of n years at $_nF_x$, we have about $n/2$ years at $_nF_x$ and $n/2$ years at $_nF_{x+n}$. But $n/2$ and $n/2$ are not quite the right breakdown. Not all women survive into the next age group. A full accounting is complicated. But if we pretend that all deaths between the starting s's and the ending e's in Figure 5.2 take place at the dashed age-group boundary at age $x + n$, then the fraction of women surviving into the next age group is the ratio we have already computed for the subdiagonal entry—namely, $_nL_{x+n}$ divided by $_nL_x$. Reducing time spent in the older age group by this survival fraction, we arrive at our full formula:

$$A_{1,\,j(x)} = \frac{_nL_0}{2\ell_0}\left(_nF_x + _nF_{x+n}\frac{_nL_{x+n}}{_nL_x}\right)f_{\text{fab}}$$

There is one further subtlety which we mention in passing. We have derived our formula leaving open the choice of the interval width n. Usually, n is 1 year or 5 years or some other small number of years, and age-specific fertility for the youngest age group from 0 to n will be zero. We say that the youngest age group is part of the "preprocreative span". All higher mammals have substantial preprocreative spans. Newborns do not immediately start procreating, that is, producing infants. This is not true of non-human populations like populations of neutrons inside atomic bombs. It is a special characteristic of the kind of species to which we belong.

Occasionally, we want Leslie matrices with wider intervals, 10, 15, or 20 years wide, longer than the human preprocreative span. The fertility for the youngest age group will then not equal zero, and it is possible for children born during the projection step to grow up and bear their own children during a single projection step. Our formulas so far make no allowance for grandchildren. A full correction is complicated, but a rough-and-ready one may be introduced by inserting $(2)(_nF_0)$ in place of $_nF_0$ in the formula for the upper-left element of the Leslie matrix. When fertility before age n is zero, this change has no effect. When it is not zero, the correction improves accuracy.

More complicated formulas are possible, apportioning person-years of fertility more precisely between age groups, but the formula we have derived, which came into general use with Keyfitz and Flieger (1968), is sufficient for almost all applications. It can be rewritten in a revealing way by consolidating fractions:

$$\frac{(_nL_0)(f_{\text{fab}})}{2\ell_0} \frac{(_nF_x)(_nL_x) + (_nF_{x+n})(_nL_{x+n})}{_nL_x}$$

The denominator depends on the age group x. But if we multiply the element for age group x by $_nL_x$ we remove this dependence. Even better, multiply the element for age group x by $_nL_x/_nL_0$ and add together the terms for $x = 0$, $x = n$, $x = 2n$, and so on. The sum is

$$\frac{f_{\text{fab}}}{2\,\ell_0}\left(\sum(_nF_x)(_nL_x) + \sum(_nF_{x+n})(_nL_{x+n})\right)$$

Notice that the first term in the second sum is exactly the same as the second term in the first sum. The second term in the second sum is the same as the third term in the first sum, and so forth. The only difference is in the first term. The first term in the first sum is for the group from 0 to n. The first term in the second sum is for the group from n to $2n$. So the second sum has no term for the group from 0 to n. When n is small, that makes no difference, since fertility for that group is zero. When n is large, if we insert our special correction for grandchildren, we then have twice the term for the youngest age group shown in the last equation, and we can use the "extra" term to make up for the missing term in the second sum. The result is

$$\sum A_{1,\,j(x)}(_nL_x/_nL_0) = \sum(_nF_x)(_nL_x)(f_{\text{fab}})/\ell_0$$

We recognize the sum on the right as the Net Reproduction Ratio.

The factors by which we just multiplied the elements in the first row can themselves be calculated from the subdiagonal elements of the Leslie matrix. They are products of subdiagonal elements. Thus we have a simple formula for finding the *NRR* from the Leslie matrix elements. But all we have on the subdiagonal are ratios. We cannot find $_nL_0$ itself, and thus we cannot fully disentangle fertility from mortality or recover fertility rates themselves from Leslie matrix elements.

5.5 Projecting Fillies, Mares, Seniors

We now work through an example of a Leslie matrix and a population projection employing it. For the sake of convenience we would like to have no more than three rows and columns, but we would also like to retain familiar 5-year age groups. These requirements rule out humans but can be happily met with horses. The demography of horses in the wild is poorly documented. Our example refers instead to a population of horses in a stable, with rates of survival and fertility that are stylized but credible. We project a population of females. Young female horses are "fillies", here 0 to 5 years old. In general, mature females are mares. We reserve the name "mares" for 5-to-10-year-olds and call more senior mares over age 10 "seniors". Horses mature fairly quickly and may live to ages like 30, but in our stable they only give birth to offspring, "foals," between ages 5 and 15. We only project the population up to age 15. Leslie matrices often stop at the last age of reproduction, since sizes of older age groups can be computed directly from the relevant lifetable.

Age-specific fertility rates in our stable are reported at $_5F_5\ f_{\text{fab}} = 0.400$ and $_5F_{10}\ f_{\text{fab}} = 0.300$, with zero below age 5. Note that the reported rates have already been multiplied by the fraction female at birth and so pertain to female offspring only. The lifetable radix is 1, and $\ell_5 = 0.900$, $\ell_{10} = 0.600$, and $\ell_{15} = 0.000$.

We have three parts of the Leslie matrix to fill in, the structural zeros, the subdiagonal elements, and the first row. The first step in writing down the Leslie matrix is to fill in the structural zeros. In our 3 by 3 dimensional case, the matrix resembles a game of tic-tac-toe. Noughts go on the structural zeros. Crosses for nonzero elements go on the first row and subdiagonal.

The first row has three crosses in a row, so the crosses win:

$$\begin{pmatrix} X & X & X \\ X & 0 & 0 \\ 0 & X & 0 \end{pmatrix}$$

Our second step is to compute survivorship ratios for the subdiagonal:

$$A_{21} = \frac{(5/2)(0.9 + 0.6)}{(5/2)(1.0 + 0.9)} = 0.7895; \quad A_{32} = \frac{(5/2)(0.6 + 0.0)}{(5/2)(0.9 + 0.6)} = 0.4000$$

The next step is to compute the first row. The formula presented in the starred Section 5.4 for the element in the first row and jth column, with $x = jn - n$ is longwinded but easy to apply:

$$A_{1j} = \frac{nL_0}{2\,\ell_0} \left({}_nF_x + {}_nF_{x+n} \frac{{}_nL_{x+n}}{{}_nL_x} \right) (f_{\text{fab}})$$

Our radix is 1 and n is 5, so the first fraction on the right, the same for all j, is ${}_5L_0/2 = (5/2)(1.0 + 0.9)/2 = 4.75/2 = 2.375$

We begin with $j = 1$ and ask about the upper-left element of our Leslie matrix. Is it zero? The fertility rate for the first age group is indeed zero; we imagine that fillies in our stable, although capable of bearing offspring, are being taken riding or racing or having other amusements and are kept away from colts and stallions till they turn 5. But ${}_5F_0 = 0$ does not imply $A_{11} = 0$. Fillies 0 to 5 at the start of a step will pass the age of 5 during the next 5 years and bear foals at the rates for 5-to-10-year-olds. So A_{11} is not zero. Instead, we find

$$A_{11} = \frac{4.75}{2}(0 + 0.400\frac{3.75}{4.75}) = 0.7500$$

Similarly, for foals from mares aged 5 to 10 we have

$$A_{12} = \frac{4.75}{2}(0.400 + 0.300\frac{1.50}{3.75}) = 1.2350$$

For foals from seniors we have

$$A_{13} = \frac{4.75}{2}(0.300 + 0.000) = 0.7125$$

So our Leslie matrix comes out to be

$$\begin{pmatrix} 0.7500 & 1.2350 & 0.7125 \\ 0.7895 & 0 & 0 \\ 0 & 0.4000 & 0 \end{pmatrix}$$

Now we use our Leslie matrix for projection. Suppose at time $t = 0$ our stable has no fillies, four mares, and two seniors. How many fillies, mares, and seniors should we expect after 5 years?

First, how many fillies? The rule for our calculation comes directly out of the definition of a transition matrix. By definition, the upper-left element of our Leslie matrix, 0.7500, is the number of fillies to expect at the end of the 5-year step per filly at the start. But there are no fillies in our starting population, so the contribution here is zero. Again by definition, 1.2350 is the number of fillies at the end per mare at the start. We have four mares at the start, so we have a contribution of $1.2350 * 4 = 4.94$ fillies. The element 0.7125 is the number of fillies at the end per senior at the start. We have two seniors at the start for a contribution of $0.7125 * 2 = 1.425$ fillies. Altogether, we expect $0 + 4.940 + 1.425 = 6.365$ fillies at time $t = 5$.

Our answer is not coming out in whole numbers but in fractions. What is 0.365 of a horse? Our Leslie matrix elements are not specifying actual numbers but "expected numbers" which, in a statistical sense, are averages. We interpret 0.365 to mean that we have a little more than a one-third chance of having an extra horse and a little less than two-thirds chance of having no extra horse. Our projected count of 6.365 fillies tells us to expect six or seven fillies, more likely six than seven.

We restate our calculation:

(0.7500 fillies per starting filly) $*$ (0 starting fillies)

$+$ (1.2350 fillies per starting mare) $*$ (4 starting mares)

$+$ (0.7125 fillies per starting senior) $*$ (2 starting seniors)

We are working our way across the first row of our matrix as we work our way down through our starting population counts, element times count plus element times count plus element times count. If we write our population counts at time t as a vector $K(t)$, then we are applying the standard rule for matrix multiplication. Our expected fillies at time t equals the top element of a vector equal to the matrix product of the matrix A times the vector $K(0)$.

The general rule for matrix products says that $K(t) = A\,K(0)$ means $K_i(t) = \sum A_{i\,j} K_j(0)$, summing over columns j of the matrix and elements j of the vector on the right. The jth element of the vector $K(t)$ is $_nK_x(t)$. As before, $x = jn - n$.

Does matrix multiplication give us the right answer for expected older horses at $t = 5$? It does. Expected mares at $t = 5$ equal

$$(0.7895 \text{ mares per starting filly}) * (0 \text{ starting fillies}) + 0 + 0$$

With the second row of our matrix, we go across the columns as we go down the starting vector, multiplying and adding up. Similarly, expected seniors at $t = 5$ are

$$0 + (0.400 \text{ seniors per starting mare}) * (4 \text{ starting mares}) + 0$$

In summary:

$$\begin{pmatrix} 6.365 \\ 0.000 \\ 1.600 \end{pmatrix} = \begin{pmatrix} 0.7500 & 1.2350 & 0.7125 \\ 0.7895 & 0 & 0 \\ 0 & 0.4000 & 0 \end{pmatrix} \begin{pmatrix} 0 \\ 4 \\ 2 \end{pmatrix}$$

Matrix notation makes it easy to see what happens next:

$$K(10) = AK(5) = AAK(0)$$

Here $AA = A^2$ is not ordinary multiplication but matrix multiplication. In general

$$K(nk) = A^k\,K(0)$$

In our crude model of exponential growth, we had an equation that looked like this one, but it had ordinary numbers rather than vectors and took no account of age. Now we have an equation with matrices and vectors which take account of age. The equation has the same form as before but a new and richer interpretation. It is the generalization to closed age-structured populations of the Crude Rate Model with which our study of populations began. Further generalizations for populations that are not closed will come to the fore in Chapter 11 in the study of migration.

* **5.6 Multi-State Tables**

There are revealing connections between lifetables and transition matrices. A lifetable describes transitions between the two states "alive" and "dead" and time (measured from birth) is the same as age for a cohort, so we can write the lifetable formula for ℓ_x as a product of transition matrices:

$$\begin{pmatrix} \ell_{15} \\ \ell_0 - \ell_{15} \end{pmatrix} = \begin{pmatrix} 1 - {}_5q_{10} & 0 \\ {}_5q_{10} & 1 \end{pmatrix} \begin{pmatrix} 1 - {}_5q_5 & 0 \\ {}_5q_5 & 1 \end{pmatrix} \begin{pmatrix} 1 - {}_5q_0 & 0 \\ {}_5q_0 & 1 \end{pmatrix} \begin{pmatrix} \ell_0 \\ 0 \end{pmatrix}$$

$$\begin{pmatrix} K(15) \end{pmatrix} = \begin{pmatrix} A(10) \end{pmatrix} \begin{pmatrix} A(5) \end{pmatrix} \begin{pmatrix} A(0) \end{pmatrix} \begin{pmatrix} K(0) \end{pmatrix}$$

Suppose we follow a cohort through several or more states, not just life and death. For instance, we might distinguish four states for health, illness, disability, and death, or dozens of states for different kinds of illness and disability along with health and death. In such a setting, numbers in each state may go up as well as down, as individuals enter as well as exit the state. There are increments as well as decrements to the counts of individuals by state. These more general tables are called "increment-decrement lifetables" or "multi-state lifetables". Notation for them can be developed along the lines of Chapter 3, but many demographers prefer matrix notation, as we do here.

For a multi-state table, each interval of age or duration has its own transition matrix. In our tables, we include being dead as one of the states. Once in this state, an individual cannot exit it, so we call the state of being dead an "absorbing state". When the absorbing state is included, everyone who starts in some state ends in some state, and we can interpret the entries in each transition matrix as probabilities.

Transition matrices are easy to calculate when data are available from a survey that follows the same individuals across time, reporting the state in which each one is found at successive rounds of observation called survey waves. Such a survey is called "longitudinal" to distinguish it from a cross-sectional survey in which all respondents are observed only once. The Health and Retirement Study (HRS) of the U.S. National Institute on Aging (NIA) is a leading example of a longitudinal demographic survey. For estimating transitions during an interval between two waves, we collect all respondents in a particular cohort in state j at the start of the interval, track down their state at the end of the interval, and divide the number in state i at the end by the number in state j at the start, yielding the transition matrix entry A_{ij}. For example, states might register levels of disability assessed from the numbers of limitations on activities of daily living (ADLs) like walking or feeding oneself and limitations on instrumental activities of daily living (IADLs) like paying bills.

From the transition matrices, we can construct a generalized version of ℓ_x—namely, a matrix L such that $L_{i\,j}(x)$ is the probability of finding an individual in state i at age x given that the individual starts in state j at age zero. The counterpart of our radix is $L(0) = I$, where I is the identity matrix with 1s on the diagonal and 0s elsewhere. Although L is written with a capital letter, it is the counterpart of little ℓ, not of big-L in the lifetable. We go from $L(x)$ to $L(x + n)$ by projecting with the matrix $A(x)$:

$$L(x + n) = A(x)\, L(x) = A(x)\, A(x - n) \cdots A(n)\, A(0)\, I$$

The multi-state counterpart of life expectancy is a matrix whose entry in the ith row and jth column is the expectation of total time spent in state i for individuals starting in state j. It is obtained by writing down the counterpart of person-years lived, $(n/2)(L(x + n) + L(x))$ for each x and summing these matrices over x. We are not obliged to start at age zero. If we want the total time spent after age y by individuals starting in state j at age y, we can use a matrix inverse, written L^{-1}, and replace $L(x)$ by matrix products $L(x)\, L^{-1}(y)$ for $x = y, y + n, \ldots$. Leading applications include healthy life expectancy, when i labels a state of good health, and disability-free life expectancy, when i labels a state without limitations on ADLs and IADLs, calculations featured in detail in advanced accounts.

Estimation of the A matrices directly from longitudinal data parallels our construction of cohort lifetables working with ℓ_x and $_nq_x$. When we take up period lifetables in Chapter 7, our point of departure will be age-specific mortality rates rather than survivorships and probabilities, rates suited for estimation from cross-sectional data. Period mortality rates have occurrences of events (deaths) in the numerator and exposure to risk (period person-years lived) in the denominator. Multi-state transition matrices can also be estimated from occurrence-exposure data. A matrix U is formed whose off-diagonal element $U_{i\,j}$ is minus the total number of transitions from state j into state i in the course of the period divided by the total person-years lived in state j in the period. Diagonal elements of U are filled in to make the elements in each column sum to zero. The convention is for positive elements to represent losses. Gains to state i off the diagonal are the negatives of losses. The elements of U are somewhat like hazard rates, studied further in Chapter 8.

The transition matrix A for an age interval of width n is estimated from a U matrix by setting $A = \exp(-nU)$. The exponential function of a matrix is evaluated by plugging into the Taylor series from Chapter 1, where U^2 is the matrix product of U with itself, and so on,

$$A = \exp(-nU) = I - nU + (n^2/2)U^2 - (n^3/6)U^3 + \cdots$$

An approximation is $A \approx (I + (n/2)U)^{-1}(I - (n/2)U)$. Multi-state lifetables are a special case of Markov chains, objects studied in courses on statistics, but the notation is different, with rows and columns reversed. Among demographers, notations also differ. Our U may be denoted by the Greek letter small μ or capital M.

Each off-diagonal element U_{ij} of U has a numerator which includes all the transitions from j to i in the period, including repeated moves. An individual may move from j to i, then move back to j, then return to i. The individual contributes two moves to the numerator of U_{ij}. Including repeats, taking account of back-and-forth moves within an interval, makes U an indicator of "gross flows". The projection matrix A, on the other hand, registers "net flows". It registers where individuals are found at the end of the interval, regardless of the hither and thither in between. The distinction between gross flows and net flows comes up again in the study of migration in Chapter 11. With ordinary lifetables, gross flows are the same as net flows, since there is no backward flow on earth from being dead to being alive again. With multi-state tables, the distinction matters and differences between U and A may give valuable information.

* 5.7 Population Renewal

The projections with Leslie matrices and other transition matrices which we have been studying determine the present from the past and the future from the present step by step in discrete steps of time. But time itself, as we experience it, flows smoothly from the past through the present into the future. For practical forecasting, matrices fill the bill, but for underlying theory, we want to express relationships in continuous time. Projection in continuous time is called population renewal. The two ideas at stake are truisms of the human condition:

- The babies of today come from the mothers of today.
- The mothers of today come from the babies of yesterday.

The first idea is implicit in the first row of the Leslie matrix, and the second idea is implicit in the subdiagonal. We introduce notation to express them in terms of continuous age and time. Obvious as these ideas are, at first encounter they may seem amazing. A mother shows her little one a picture of a little one and asks, "Do you know who that is?" "Me?" "No, that's Mommy."

We set up our equations for a closed female population. The babies here are all daughters. We write $k(x, t)$ for the density of women age x at time t, the height of the Lexis surface described in Chapter 2, the limit of $_n K_x(t)/n$ as the interval width n goes to zero. We write $f^{(d)}(x, t)$ for daughters-only age-specific fertility at age x at time t, equal to f_{fab} times the limit as $n \to 0$ of cohort fertility $_n f_x(t - x)$ for the cohort born at $t - x$, which is the same as f_{fab} times the limit of period fertility $_n F_x(t)$ as $n \to 0$. We write $\ell_x(t - x)$ for cohort survivorship for the cohort born at $t - x$ with unit radix, and $B(t)$ for the density of births of girls at time t. For the daughters of today coming from the mothers of today, we have

$$B(t) = \int k(x, t) \, f^{(d)}(x, t) \, dx$$

For the mothers of today coming from the daughters of yesterday, we have

$$k(x, t) = B(t - x) \, \ell_x(t - x)$$

Putting the relationships together, we arrive at the Renewal Equation:

$$B(t) = \int B(t - x) \, \ell_x(t - x) \, f^{(d)}(x, t) \, dx$$

The Renewal Equation expresses births at time t as a weighted sum over births at earlier times. The weights are products of cohort survivorship and fertility. When we are given all the survivorship and fertility rates as well as the births up to time t, we might like to plug in the values on the right-hand side and find future births. But the quantity on the left-hand side is present births, births at time t, not future births. The Renewal Equation is not entirely a plug-in kind of equation. We can test whether a candidate solution for the whole trajectory of births is indeed a solution by plugging into the equation, but we need mathematical methods more advanced than those in this book for finding solutions from scratch.

The theoretical value of the Renewal Equation becomes especially apparent when age-specific rates of fertility and mortality are unchanging over time and we consider a population in which births are growing (or declining) exponentially at rate R, so that $B(t) = B(0)e^{Rt}$ and $B(t - x) = B(0)e^{Rt}e^{-Rx}$ equal to $B(t)e^{-Rx}$:

$$B(t) = B(0)e^{Rt} = \int B(0)e^{Rt}e^{-Rx}\ell_x f^{(d)}(x)dx$$

We divide out $B(0)e^{Rt}$ from both sides and obtain a preview of the Euler–Lotka equation at the heart of the theory of stable populations studied in Chapter 10:

$$1 = \int f^{(d)}(x)\ell_x\, e^{-Rx}\, dx$$

Unchanging age-specific rates of childbirth and survival in a closed population starting with almost any starting age structure do lead in the long run to exponential growth under quite general conditions, with a growth rate that does satisfy the Euler–Lotka equation. A precise version of this statement is a deep result called the Renewal Theorem, first proved for a significant class of cases by David Blackwell in 1948 and extended by William Feller and collaborators. David Blackwell was the first African American elected to the U.S. National Academy of Sciences. There is a whole branch of statistics called "Renewal Theory" which treats many kinds of populations which can age, survive, reproduce or be replaced, and in due course die, among them stars, lightbulbs, lions, automobiles, empires, and morning glory flowers.

* 5.8 Variable *r* and the Lexis Surface

The Renewal Equation puts a cohort perspective in the foreground. The factor $B(t - x)$ is the initial size of the cohort reaching age x at time t and $\ell_x(t - x)$ is the survivorship of this cohort to this age. A Leslie matrix, in contrast, applies to a period, the period of the projection step. It serves to project cohorts forward in time and age, but only with respect to changes that are happening to them within the period. In this sense the subject of Leslie matrices is a natural stepping-stone between our study of cohort measures in the last two chapters and our study of period measures in the next two.

A closer look at the period perspective built into Leslie matrices leads into an approach and notation called "Variable r" invented by Samuel Preston and Ansley Coale (1982) building on work of Neil Bennett and Shiro Horiuchi (1981). The "r" in Variable r is the growth rate of an age group, when an age group is regarded as a population on its own. It is variable because it varies from age to age. It is written with a small rather than a capital letter "r". The rate for ages a to $a + n$ is defined in the usual way, $r_a = (1/n) \log({}_n K_a(t + n)/{}_n K_a(t))$. Age-group growth rates measure changes along horizontal bands in the Lexis plane. Subdiagonal elements of the Leslie matrix, as we know, measure changes along diagonal stripes in the Lexis plane. The two can be put together to measure changes along verticals as well, as illustrated in Figure 5.3. Like Figure 5.2, this figure displays one projection step from time t to $t + n$. Yearly births B over the n years of the interval are denoted by $n B$ and for brevity later letters of the alphabet, small $c, d, e,$ and f label age group sizes at t, and capital $C, D, E,$ F, G label sizes at $t + n$. We track the ratio of sizes along the zigzag path shown in the figure:

$$G = \frac{nB}{1} \frac{C}{nB} \frac{c}{C} \frac{D}{c} \frac{d}{D} \frac{E}{d} \frac{e}{E} \frac{F}{e} \frac{f}{F} \frac{G}{f}$$

The fractions with capital and small copies of the same letter in numerator and denominator are ratios that can be expressed in terms of the age-group growth rates: ${}_n K_a(t)/{}_n K_a(t + n)$ equal to $\exp(-n\, r_a)$. The fractions mixing letters in numerator and denominator are Leslie matrix subdiagonal elements each of the form ${}_n L_{a+n}/{}_n L_a$. But bear in mind that the big-Ls

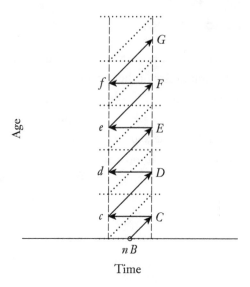

Figure 5.3   Zigzag paths with Variable r

in each of the separate fractions come from a separate cohort lifetable, the
lifetable for the cohort born between $t - a - n$ and $t - a$. When we multiply
the fractions together, we are piecing together the survival experience of
different cohorts as they each pass through the same period. As we shall
see in Chapter 7, a lifetable pieced together in this way from the period
experience of different cohorts is what we mean by a period lifetable. The
product of the fractions for ages a from 0 up to an age x is the *period lifetable*
ratio $_nL_x^P/_nL_0^P$ marked with a superscript "P" for "period". Setting the
lifetable radix to 1, we arrive at an expression for age-group sizes involving
the quantities r_a:

$$_nK_x(t+n) = n\,B\left(\frac{_nL_x^P}{n}\right)\exp\left(-n\sum_0^{x-n}r_a\right)$$

What is the point? The computation of r_a starts with age-group sizes; a
long formula is not needed to find them back again. The point is protection
against census coverage errors. Censuses often undercount or double-count
members of certain population subgroups. Coverage fractions, ratios of
reported counts to true counts, tend to vary systematically by age and may be
somewhat stable from census date to census date. In that situation, starting
from reported census counts at times t and $t + n$ and independent estimates

of the period lifetable and births, the formula based on r_a may allow a more accurate reconstruction of true counts by age.

The expressions involving Variable r imply some elegant formulas. The average of the age-group growth rates for groups with labels from 0 to $x - n$ is $\bar{r}_x = (1/x) \sum_0^{x-n} nr_a$. This average is not the same as the growth rate of the whole age group from 0 to n, but it leads to a compact formula for the density of population $k(x, t)$ on the Lexis surface defined in Section 5.7. We divide by n, let n go to zero, write $B(t)$ for the density of births at time t, and find

$$k(x, t) = B(t)\ell_x^P(t)\, e^{-x\,\bar{r}_x(t)}$$

Multiplying population by rates of fertility, summing over age, and dividing out $B(t)$, we also find

$$1 = \int f(x, t)\, \ell_x^P(t)\, e^{-x\,\bar{r}_x(t)}\, dx$$

Here is an equation in the presence of changing rates analogous to the Euler–Lotka equation. It reduces to the Euler–Lotka equation when ℓ_x and $f(x, t)$ are constant over time and all the age-group growth rates are the same, entailing a population with exponential growth.

Besides illustrating Variable r, Figure 5.3 leads us to a relationship prominent in mathematical demography. Consider any one zig and zag from the diagram—say, from D to E. We see that $E/d = (F/D)(D/d)$ or $(1/n)\log(E/d) = (1/n)\log(E/D) + (1/n)\log(D/d)$. When we let the interval width n go to zero, the left-hand side measured along the diagonal converges to minus the hazard rate $h(x, t)$, written here as a function of x and t. The first term on the right measures the rate of change of $\log(k(x, t))$ in the vertical direction with t held fixed, and the second term on the right is an age-group growth rate r_x, which measures the rate of change of $\log(k(x, t))$ in the horizontal direction with x held fixed. In calculus, these kinds of directional slopes holding some things fixed are called "partial derivatives", written with curly ∂s, and the resulting equation is a partial differential equation

$$\frac{\partial \log(k(x, t))}{\partial x} + \frac{\partial \log(k(x, t))}{\partial t} = -h(x, t)$$

This equation dates back to McKendrick (1926). It can be paired with the Renewal Equation, which determines $k(x, t)$ along the boundary $x = 0$, to fill in values of $k(x, t)$ across the whole of the Lexis Surface. Arthur and Vaupel (1984) use this equation to clarify and extend the logic of Variable r, and applications to mortality, more advanced than those in this book, are found in Bongaarts and Feeney (2002), Barbi et al. (2008), Canudas-Romo and Schoen (2005), and Wachter (2005).

HIGHLIGHTS OF CHAPTER 5

- Transition matrices.
- Leslie matrices, zeros, subdiagonal, and first row
- Multi-state lifetables
- Population Renewal
- Variable r

KEY FORMULAS

$$A_{j+1, j} = \frac{_nL_{x+n}}{_nL_x}$$

$$A_{1, j(x)} = \frac{_nL_0}{2\,\ell_0} \left(_nF_x + _nF_{x+n} \frac{_nL_{x+n}}{_nL_x} \right) f_{fab}$$

$$K(tn) = A^t K(0)$$

$$B(t) = \int B(t - x)\ell_x(t - x) f^{(d)}(x, t)\, dx$$

FURTHER READING

Projection matrices are widely used in population biology along with demography. Chapter 3 of Keyfitz and Caswell (2005) covers basic ideas and Chapter 17 has a crisp account of multi-state lifetables, which are explained in detail by Schoen (1988).

EXERCISES FOR CHAPTER 5

1. Let A be a Leslie matrix for projecting a population of horses through a 5-year interval, and let $K(0)$ an initial vector of age-group counts at time $t = 0$ given by

$$A = \begin{pmatrix} 0.8894 & 1.3650 & 0.2600 \\ 0.7058 & 0 & 0 \\ 0 & 0.4200 & 0 \end{pmatrix}; \qquad K(0) = \begin{pmatrix} 1 \\ 6 \\ 0 \end{pmatrix}$$

Find the population vector at $t = 5$ years and $t = 10$ years.

2. For the horses in Exercise 1, suppose the third age group is an open-ended age group containing all horses older than 10 years. Suppose also that about 8% of horses in this open-ended age group survive beyond the end of each projection step. Draw an arrow diagram showing the permitted transitions between the age groups under this new specification. Using data from Exercise 1, find the population vector at $t = 10$ years.

3. Using lifetable person-years lived entries for the cohort of U.S. women born in 1934 from Table 4.2, calculate subdiagonal entries for a Leslie matrix with 5-year-wide ($n = 5$) age groups. Assume $_5f_{50} = 0$ and $_5L_{50} = 4,421$.

4. Using age-specific fertility rates for the cohort of U.S. women born in 1934 from Table 4.2, calculate entries in the first row of a Leslie matrix with 5-year-wide ($n = 5$) age groups.

5. The matrix A shown below is a Leslie matrix for projecting the female population of Argentina. There are three age groups, each 18 years wide. The starting population for 1992 includes 3.9 million girls aged 0 to 18, 3.3 million women aged 18 to 36, and 2.8 million women aged 36 to 44.

$$A = \begin{pmatrix} 0.551 & 0.556 & 0.037 \\ 0.962 & 0 & 0 \\ 0 & 0.909 & 0 \end{pmatrix}$$

(a) How long is the interval of time covered by a single projection step?

(b) What is the total population of women up to age 54 after one projection step?

(c) What is the total population of women up to age 54 after three projection steps? To what year would this total apply?

(d) At what rate would the population of Argentina be growing according to this projection over three projection steps?

6. The first row of a 10 by 10 dimensional Leslie matrix with 5-year-wide age groups for projecting the population of Honduras in 1965 forward in time contains elements

$$0, 0, 0.152, 0.466, 0.629, 0.607, 0.521, 0.331, 0.125, 0.022$$

The first 13 elements in the $_5L_x$ (person-years lived) column of the women's life table with a radix of 100 are

$$474, 458, 452, 447, 441, 435, 426, 416, 405, 391, 374, 352, 322$$

Write out the Leslie matrix A. What is the matrix product of A with the vector whose elements are the first 10 values of $_5L_x$?

* 7. Consider an increment-decrement lifetable with only two states with an interval length $n = 1$. Assume equal rates of flow in both directions between states, so that the off-diagonal elements of the U matrix defined in Section 5.6 are both equal to $-u$, where u is a small positive constant. Express the transition matrix A in terms of u, and show that u can be calculated from the net flow A_{21} by the formula $u = (-1/2)\log(1 - 2A_{21})$, a formula pointed out to Keyfitz and Caswell (2005, p. 457) by the demographer Jan Hoem.

* 8. Suppose a strict government, determined to maintain a stationary population, issues licenses for childbirth and prevents those without licenses from giving birth. A license is issued to some couple each time there is some death in the population, so the number of births equals the number of deaths. Write down an equation for the number of births in year t as a function of the numbers of births in prior years and of relevant life table entries. What does the Euler–Lotka equation tell us for such a population?

6

Period Fertility

6.1 Period Measures

It is now time to take an important step forward in the kinds of measures that we calculate. Up to now, we have been studying *cohort* measures like the *NRR* and the expectation of life at birth, based on observations of the life experience of cohorts. Now, we shall consider how to calculate versions of these measures based on *period* data. Alongside a "cohort *NRR*" we shall have a "period *NRR*". Alongside a "cohort lifetable" we shall have a "period lifetable".

The concepts of all these measures are fundamentally cohort concepts. They describe features of the life course of individuals. When we move to period versions of our measures, the concepts do not change, but the kinds of data do change.

Our motivation for calculating measures based on period data is timeliness. We cannot, strictly speaking, determine a cohort's *NRR* until the last member of the cohort has completed childbearing, and we cannot determine a full cohort lifetable until the last member of a cohort has died. The most recent cohort *NRR*'s now available belong to cohorts born before the parents of many readers of this book. The most recent complete cohort lifetables belong to cohorts born at the close of the nineteenth century. Clearly, the fertility of our parents' and grandparents' generation is not very relevant as a description of today's and tomorrow's childbearing. The lifetime mortality experience of the cohorts to which people now in their nineties belong is not a good description of the risks of dying that most of us face. Cohort measures are out of date long before they are complete.

To fill in the picture of fertility or mortality before we have the full story requires making assumptions. One way of doing so is to make forecasts of future fertility and mortality and fill in the future life experience of recent cohorts on the basis of guesses. There is no unique right way of doing this. After all, most of today's young people have not made up their minds about childbearing, and none of us know whether risks of dying will be worse or better when we are old. In the face of this uncertainty, demographers adopt a neutral assumption, the assumption that today's rates will stay the same, rather than going up or down. This assumption provides a baseline. More complicated forecasts can always also be calculated, but the assumption of unchanging rates gives common ground on which to start.

Our neutral assumption, even though events eventually prove it wrong, allows comparisons from place to place and time to time which are easily understood. We do not have to read the fine print every time we see a measure in a demographic publication.

When we calculate a period measure, we are always playing a *Game of Pretend*. We pretend that the age-specific rates we see today for different age groups continue unchanged into the future. The concept is illustrated on the Lexis diagram in Figure 6.1. For purposes of the diagram, "today" is taken to be "Y2K", the year 2000, the period marked off by the vertical bar on the left. Dashed horizontal lines single out the age group of 20-to-25-year-olds. Events of birth and death and counts of person-years found in the small rectangle where the period strip intersects the age-group band determine the period age-specific rates. In our Game of Pretend, these rates carry forward in time unchanged.

Thus when a newborn cohort whose lifelines are found on the path up the diagonal in the diagram reach ages 20 to 25, we pretend that their age-specific rates of fertility and mortality are the same as the rates of the 20-to-25-year-olds in our period Y2K. In childhood, they have the rates that children faced in Y2K. When they reach their 80s, they have the rates of the octogenarians of Y2K. In our Game of Pretend, we are creating an imaginary cohort whose life experience is pieced together from the experiences of different people found at different ages in one period of time—in this case, our period Y2K. We call this imaginary cohort the

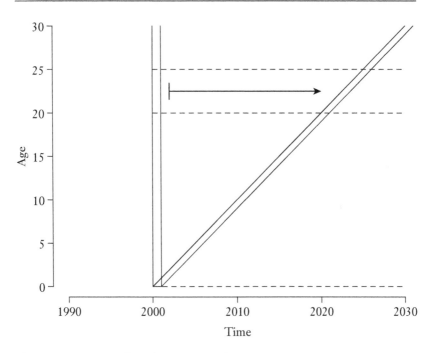

Figure 6.1 From period to cohort on a Lexis diagram

"synthetic cohort". The Greek root *syn* means "together" and *thetic* means put or pieced: "synthetic" = "pieced together". The age-specific cohort rates of the synthetic cohort are the age-specific period rates of the period population. The concept of a synthetic cohort is central to demography. It is explored in more depth in Chapter 10.

The rule for calculating a period measure is a simple one: Take the formula for the cohort version of the measure. Replace all the cohort age-specific rates with period-age specific rates. Then evaluate the formula. In the TV quiz show *Jeopardy*, the emcee speaks a phrase that is the answer, and the contestants have to come up with the question to which this phrase is the answer. Suppose the emcee says, "Period *NRR*". That's the answer. What's the question? The question is, "What would a *cohort* have for an *NRR* if the *period's* age-specific rates persisted forever?" We can replace the words "period *NRR*" with any other period measure. The answer is "Period Lifetable"; what is the question? The question is, "What would a *cohort* have for a lifetable if the *period's* age-specific rates persisted forever?" The definition of a period rate has the word cohort in it. This may sound

surprising, but it is essential. The concepts are still cohort concepts. What
changes is the source of data. Age-specific rates for periods are substituted
for age-specific rates for cohorts.

6.2 Period Age-Specific Fertility

As we have seen, cohort age-specific fertility $_n f_x$ is defined to be a quotient
whose numerator is the count of babies born to the cohort between ages x
and $x + n$ and whose denominator is cohort person-years lived. Period age-
specific fertility $_n F_x$, written with a capital "F", is defined to be a quotient
whose numerator is the count of babies born in the period to population
members between ages x and $x + n$. Its denominator is the period person-
years lived by people between ages x and $x + n$ in the period. With some
period in mind, we write $_n B_x$ for the count of births and $_n D_x$ for the count
of deaths and $PPYL$ for the person-years lived for women (or men) aged x
to $x + n$ in the period. Our period $ASFR$ is $_n F_x = {_n B_x}/PPYL$ and we have
a period age-specific mortality rate $_n M_x = {_n D_x}/PPYL$. When desired, we
can make such rates specific for parity or marital status or other categories
by restricting both the numerators and denominators in ways described in
Chapter 4.

For these period calculations, the width n of the age group is not generally
the same as the duration T of the period. Often n is 5 and T is 1. Period rates,
in which n and T typically differ, are unlike Leslie matrices, in which the
age-group width and the length of the projection step have to be the same.
With period rates, the events in the numerator and the person-years in the
denominator are both being counted inside a rectangle like the rectangle in
Figure 6.1 with height n and base T. With cohort rates, events and person-
years are instead counted inside a parallelogram with diagonal sides on the
Lexis diagram, as described in Sections 2.4 and 2.6. Thus a period $_n F_x$ is only
approximately equal to the cohort $_n f_x$ for the cohort born x years before
the period. Highly refined estimates distinguish each of the triangles like
those in Figure 2.3 that make up rectangles and parallelograms on a Lexis
diagram. But for most purposes these refinements can be foregone.

Our usual estimate of period person-years lived, $PPYL$, is the mid-period
population times the period length, the product $_n K_x \, T$. With a period 1 year
in length, period person-years has the same numerical value as the mid-

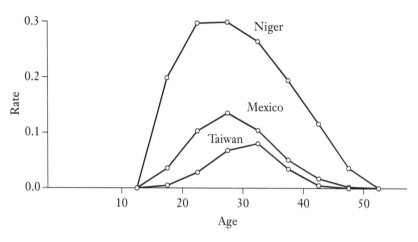

Figure 6.2 Typical age-specific fertility schedules

year population, but units of person-years instead of units of people. With a period of a whole decade, *PPYL* would be about 10 times the mid-period population, but there would also be about 10 times as many babies born over 10 years for the numerator, so the ratio $_nF_x$ would be roughly the same. Similarly, doubling the width of the age group would increase both the numerator and denominator and produce a similar value for the ratio, not a value twice as big. Like the cohort $_nf_x$, the period $_nF_x$ is a *rate* with units of 1/time. In principle it can be bigger than 1, but rarely so.

A set of values $_nF_x$ for all reproductive age groups is called a "fertility schedule". Like lifetable functions, fertility schedules have typical shapes illustrated in Figure 6.2 with estimates for 2013 from the IDB. Niger has a *TFR* of 7.0, the highest in that dataset. Taiwan has the lowest *TFR*, 1.1, an extreme example of below-replacement fertility. Mexican fertility has dropped considerably over several decades and is seen in the middle with a *TFR* of 2.2. Notice how dramatic are the contrasts in fertility levels still found across the globe. The lower-fertility examples show a slower start to childbearing. At later ages the schedule for Niger is bulging out as it bends downward, whereas the schedules for Mexico and Taiwan flatten out like a children's slide. This contrast is also found in graphs of marital fertility and is important for the measures of family limitation in Section 6.8.

Our period age-specific rates are the building blocks for our main period measures, the period *NRR* and *GRR* and *TFR*. Table 6.1 illustrates the

Table 6.1   Age-specific rates for India, 2000

x	$_nB_x$	$_nK_x$	$_nF_x$	$_nD_x$	$_nK_x$	$_nM_x$	$_nL_x$
15	2,430	48,407	0.050	65	48,407	0.00134	4,442
20	9,258	42,371	0.218	115	42,371	0.00270	4,398
25	7,128	39,708	0.180	97	39,708	0.00245	4,341
30	3,593	36,036	0.100	112	36,036	0.00311	4,281
35	1,632	31,880	0.051	88	31,880	0.00276	4,219
40	627	27,725	0.023	104	27,725	0.00376	4,151
45	183	23,125	0.008	98	23,125	0.00424	4,069

Source: Author's calculations from WPP (2003).

calculation of $_5F_x$ on the left and $_5M_x$ on the right for Indian women for the 1-year period Y2K. The mid-year count $_5K_x$ is our estimate of *PPYL* for this 1-year period. It is repeated in the table, because the same numbers supply the denominators for $_nF_x$ and for $_nM_x$. For example, in the first row $_5F_{15} = 2,430/48,407 = 0.050$ and $_5M_{15} = 65/48,407 = 0.00134$. Our $_nF_x$ values from such a table are used directly in calculations of *NRR*'s, *GRR*'s, and *TFR*'s. But our $_nM_x$ values are only a stepping stone toward the period lifetable $_nL_x$ values (with a radix of 1,000), which are shown in the table but whose calculation will not be explained until Chapter 7.

6.3 Period *NRR*, *GRR*, and *TFR*

The ingredients for calculating a period *NRR* and other period measures are the period $_nF_x$ values and the $_nL_x$ values from the period lifetable, both computed by pretending that the age-specific rates of the period continue unchanged forever. Pending the explanations in Chapter 7, we take the $_nL_x$ values as given and enter them directly into our formulas.

The formula for the period *NRR* is exactly the same as the formula for the cohort *NRR* presented in Chapter 4, except that period age-specific fertility rates $_nF_x$ replace cohort age-specific fertility rates $_nf_x$ and period lifetable $_nL_x$ values replace cohort lifetable $_nL_x$ values:

$$NRR = \sum {}_nF_x \, {}_nL_x \, f_{\text{fab}}/\ell_0$$

Table 6.2 takes the building blocks, period $_nF_x$ and $_nL_x$ values, from Table 6.1 and illustrates the calculation of the period *NRR* for women

Table 6.2   Calculating the NRR, India, 2000

x	$_5F_x$	$_5L_x$	Babies	$x+n/2$	Product
15	0.050	4,442	222	17.5	3,885
20	0.218	4,398	959	22.5	21,578
25	0.180	4,341	781	27.5	21,477
30	0.100	4,281	428	32.5	13,910
35	0.051	4,219	215	37.5	8,063
40	0.023	4,151	95	42.5	4,037
45	0.008	4,069	33	47.5	1,567
Sum	0.630		2,733		74,518

in India in the year 2000. The column headed "Babies", the product of the $_5F_x$ and $_5L_x$ columns, shows the babies that would be born to the imaginary synthetic cohort under our Game of Pretend, not at all the same as the real babies in the period population shown in Table 6.1. We add up these imaginary babies, divide by the radix, and multiply by the default fraction female at birth to obtain the period NRR equal to $(2{,}733/1{,}000) *$ $(0.4886) = 1.335$.

A salient point to understand about the calculation of the period NRR is that the person-years that go into it are $_nL_x$ values from the period lifetable, not Period Person-Years Lived. We repeat, not PPYL! We use PPYL values to find the age-specific rates $_nF_x$ and $_nM_x$, and then we throw the PPYL values away. From that point on, the age-specific rates are all we need. We go on to compute a period lifetable, which is a cohort lifetable for the synthetic cohort, and every further computation uses quantities for the synthetic cohort. If we made the mistake of using PPYL instead of period lifetable $_nL_x$ values, our answers would depend on how many people happen to be found at various ages in the period population. Dividing births and deaths by PPYL gets rid of this effect of current age structure and lets us construct period measures that express the life experience implied by the age-specific rates.

When we compute a period NRR in the fashion illustrated in Table 6.2, it takes ony a little extra work to find out how young or old, on average, the mothers are at the babies' births. Since our data are grouped into 5-year-wide intervals, we do not know the exact ages of mothers, but we can use the middle age in each age group as an approximation. We have

222 babies whose mothers are about 17.5 years old at their births, so the sum of their mothers' ages is the product $222 * 17.5 \approx 3{,}885$. Adding up such contributions from all the rows, the sum of mothers' ages for all babies is about 74,518. Dividing by the 2,733 babies results in a mean age of 27.266.

This quotient calculated from the last column of Table 6.2 is the average age of mothers from the synthetic cohort at their babies' births. It is called the "synthetic cohort mean age at childbearing" and often denoted by the Greek letter μ (mu), which resembles the letter "u" but is in fact the original form of our letter "m". In most countries and periods μ is around 27. Women in countries with early marriage also tend to continue to bear children late in their reproductive span, leading to average ages that are not very different from countries with late marriage but substantial fertility control.

$$\mu = \sum (_nF_x)(_nL_x)(x + n/2) / \sum (_nF_x)(_nL_x)$$

The period Total Fertility Rate and Gross Reproduction Ratio can also be calculated from the data in Table 6.2. As with the period NRR, the formulas for period TFR and GRR are the same as the formulas for cohort TFR and GRR, with period $_nF_x$ replacing cohort $_nf_x$ and with the rate $_nF_x$ applying to n full years of risk in each age group, since the TFR and GRR assume survival through all ages of childbearing:

$$\text{Period } TFR = \sum (_nF_x)(n)$$

$$\text{Period } GRR = \sum (_nF_x)(n)(f_{\text{fab}})$$

There are some logical relationships among our indices. The NRR is always less than or equal to the GRR (since mortality can only decrease the net total of daughters), and the GRR is always less than or equal to the TFR (since daughters are a subset of sons and daughters).

In our example in Table 6.2, every age group is 5 years wide, so we can add up $_nF_x$ values before multiplying by n, rather than vice versa as in the formulas. We find a period TFR of 3.150 equal to five times the sum 0.630 of the second column and we find a period GRR of $3.150 * 0.4886 = 1.539$. When age-group widths differ, we have to compute the products of $_nF_x$ and n row by row and add up the results to find the TFR and from it the GRR.

The *TFR* is one of the most widely cited measures in demography. Total Fertility Rates can change rapidly and can signal major shifts in demographic experience. In the United States, as reported in the Human Fertility Database (HFD), the period *TFR* rose from 2.380 in 1945 to 3.161 in 1947 at the onset of the Baby Boom. It peaked at 3.738 in 1957, dropped to 2.467 by 1968, and fell as low as 1.792 in 1984. The period *TFR* was around 1.928 in 2010. We must remember that the period *TFR* is an abstraction calculated for a synthetic cohort. Real cohorts of U.S. women did not experience such large swings in total fertility. The period *TFR* is affected by changes in ages of childbearing as well as by changes in completed cohort parity through influences called "tempo effects", discussed in Section 6.6.

Like the period *TFR*, the period *NRR* is an abstraction. It is a useful abstraction that tells us what the long-term implications of present-day fertility and mortality would be for population growth. But in the real world, age-specific fertility and mortality do not remain constant as they are assumed to do in our Game of Pretend. The long-term implications of short-term rates expressed in the *NRR* are not telling us about the real future. In 2010 the period *NRR* for the United States was a little below 1. If the age-specific rates of 2010 continued unchanged forever, eventually the size of the U.S. population (excluding net immigration) would begin to decline. Newspapers often misunderstand this conclusion and publish articles that suggest that a period *NRR* less than 1 means that population growth has ceased. That is a serious mistake. In fact, in the United State births exceed deaths by a substantial amount, and when net immigration is added into the picture, the United States has the fastest growing population of any large country in the developed world.

* 6.4 Log(*GRR*) Plots

The Net Reproduction Ratio, which is a measure of generational growth, as we have said, summarizes the combined effects of fertility and mortality. In trying to understand the course of population change, it is often valuable to decompose a change in growth rates into the contributions of changes in fertility and changes in mortality. The full story involves different changes at different ages and may be complex. But there is a decomposition which lets us grasp an overall picture in a vivid way.

This decomposition leads to plots called "Log GRR Plots" which plot the logarithm of the GRR on the vertical axis against an index of survivorship on the horizontal axis. The index is chosen so that the contours of constant growth on these plots are straight lines.

To introduce this technique, we first define the "net maternity function". Set $n = 1$ for 1-year rates, and plot daughters-only age-specific fertility rates $(_1F_x)$ (f_{fab}) as a function of x. The area under this curve is the GRR. Now plot $(_1F_x)(f_{\text{fab}})(_1L_x)/\ell_0$ on the same plot against x. This new curve lies below the old one. The area under the new curve is the NRR. This curve whose area defines the NRR is called the "net maternity function". Assume a radix of 1.0. Then we get the bottom curve by multiplying the top curve by a factor $_1L_x$ which is roughly equal to ℓ_x. The average adjustment factor over mothers of all ages is close to the adjustment at the average age μ of mothers, which is the proportion ℓ_μ. We expect then that the NRR will be approximately equal to the product $(GRR)(\ell_\mu)$. When we take logarithms this becomes a linear relation:

$$\log(NRR) \approx \log(GRR) + \log(\ell_\mu)$$

$$\log(GRR) \approx \log(NRR) + (-1)\log(\ell_\mu)$$

$$\text{fertility index} \approx \text{intercept} + (\text{slope})(\text{mortality index})$$

Suppose we have a set of combinations of fertility and mortality that keep the same rate of generational growth, that is to say, the same NRR. Then, when we plot of $\log(GRR)$ against $\log(\ell_\mu)$, we obtain a straight line whose slope is -1 and whose intercept is $\log(NRR)$. In other words, the "contour" of points representing combinations with this level of growth is a straight line. When we change the NRR, we obtain another line parallel to the first. The contours of growth form a grid of diagonal lines sloping from upper left to lower right. Equal separations on this plot correspond to unit changes in the logarithm of the NRR, not in the NRR itself. In Chapter 10 we shall see that they can be labeled by values of the quantity called Lotka's r. In practice, we generally have measurements of GRR and NRR, and we plot the log of the GRR on the vertical axis against $\log(NRR/GRR)$ on the horizontal axis. This helps us to decompose the changes in growth rates into the relative contributions of changes in fertility and mortality.

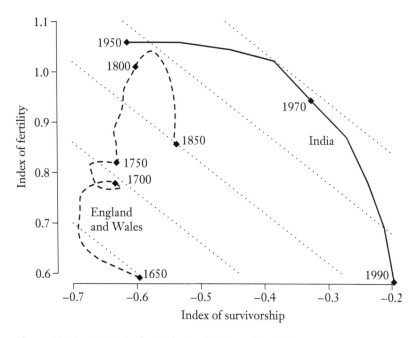

Figure 6.3 Log *GRR* plot for England and Wales and for India

The classical picture of demographic transition envisions a reduction in mortality followed by a reduction in fertility. Such a transition is illustrated in Figure 6.3 by the solid line for India between 1950 and 1990. The movement to the right, reflecting improvements in survival, takes the population up the "ski slope" toward higher growth, and the movement downward, reflecting drops in fertility, brings the population back over the contours to lower growth.

The dashed line on the figure shows the more complicated story for England between 1650 and 1850 as it led the world into the Industrial Revolution. The estimates are based on *The Population History of England* by Wrigley and Schofield (1981). Movement upward, reflecting increases in fertility, are mainly responsible for taking the population across the diagonal contours to higher growth, although simulateous improvements in survival play some role before declines in fertility set in. The changes in overall fertility are understood to be driven largely by changes in marriage ages and marriage rates. This evidence shook the old belief that England and other European countries had gone through a demographic transition similar in nature to that which Third World countries began to experience after World War II.

6.5 Age-Standardized Rates

The period measures we have been studying, like the period *TFR*, *GRR*, and *NRR*, are preferred to simpler period measures like the *CBR* mainly because they are not influenced by the age distribution of the population. Bringing twenty-year-olds into a population will raise the number of births and raise a crude measure like the *CBR* but will leave the period *TFR*, *GRR*, and *NRR* unchanged, provided that the age-specific rates remain unchanged. It is sometimes desirable to keep the simplicity of a crude rate while removing the effects of the observed age distribution. We can do so by calculating "age-standardized" rates. Such rates serve for quick comparisons among contrasting countries or areas. To calculate age-standardized rates, we pick one special population to define our standard. Here, we base our standard on the population of the whole world in 2000 as estimated by the United Nations WPP for 2001, on page 38 of the printed volume. There are other popular standards, including a European standard. For comparing countries, we take each country, multiply its age-specific rates by the standard population counts, add up the products, and divide by the total standard population to obtain our age-standardized rate.

Table 6.3 shows the calculation of an age-standardized birth rate for France in 2000. The standard population counts (in millions of person-years) in the third column are multiplied by the French age-specific rates in the fourth column to give the implied number of babies (in millions) in the last column. Since ordinary age-specific fertility rates credit all the births to women, we multiply the count of men by zero. Adding up the columns, we find that 88.819 million babies would be produced by the 6,057 million people in our standard population, for a standardized crude birth rate of $88.819/6,057 = 0.014539$. The process of age standardization has raised the observed *CBR* of 0.013228 by about 10%. When we turn to a new country, for instance, Senegal, we keep the same standard population counts but we replace the rates from France by the rates from Senegal. The results give us simple comparisons of fertility levels freed from direct effects of age structure.

Table 6.3   An age-standardized birth rate

	x	n	Standard $_nK_x$	France $_nF_x$	Product (babies)
	0	15	882	0	0
W	15	5	270	0.008	2.107
O	20	5	248	0.056	13.864
M	25	5	245	0.134	32.726
E	30	5	232	0.118	27.483
N	35	5	209	0.050	10.531
	40	5	182	0.012	2.108
	45	5	164	0.000	0
	50	∞	574	0	0
M					
E	0	∞	3,051	0	0
N					

Source: United Nations World Population Prospects (2001).

A similar calculation with period age-specific mortality rates $_nM_x$ applied to standard counts leads to an Age-Standardized Death Rate. Age-specific marriage rates applied to standard counts leads to an Age-Standardized Marriage Rate, and so forth. The most widely used of these measures is the Age-Standardized Death Rate, because age structure has so much influence on the *CDR*. The *CDR* in the United States is about 9 per thousand, and the *CDR* for the whole world is about 9 per thousand. Does it follow that the United States has no better mortality than the world average? Hardly. The United States has lower age-specific mortality rates at every age than the world as a whole. But the U.S. also has a much higher percentage of its population in older, high-risk age groups. The favorable mortality rates are disguised by the effect of the risk-prone age structure. Turning to age-standardized rates removes the false impression. This point is worth repeating: the highest Crude Death Rates are not found in countries with the most severe mortality, but the highest Age-Standardized Death Rates are.

The kind of standardization which we have been studying is called "Direct Standardization". The rates come from the countries under study. The counts of people at risk come from the standard population. A less common kind of standardization is "Indirect Standardization", in which rates come from a standard population and counts of people at risk come from the populations under study. Indirect standardization is the basis for indices of family limitation called "Princeton Indices", presented in Section 6.7.

We can use the idea of standardization to gain insight into the meaning of the Total Fertility Rate. We pick our standard population to be an artificial population with the same constant number k of women in every 1-year-wide age group at every instant of time. The number k, which we can choose at will, plays the same role for period measures as the radix ℓ_0 for cohort measures. Every square box on a Lexis diagram which covers 1 year of age and T years of time includes kT woman-years from this standard population. The period *TFR* times kT is the number of babies that would result from applying the period's age-specific fertility rates to this standard population.

We could obtain a similar result by taking a sample of the same fixed size k in every 1-year-wide age group, a sample drawn from the $_1K_x$ women in the observed period population. We give each sampled woman 1 person-year of exposure and treat births to these women in the period as a standardized sample of childbirths. We could plot each such childbirth as a point on a Lexis diagram with x equal to the mother's age at giving birth and t equal to the time of giving birth. A period of length T corresponds to a vertical box on the Lexis diagram rising from a base of length T. If we count the childbirths from our standardized sample within the box and divide by kT, we obtain the period *TFR*.

* 6.6 Tempo and Quantum

As we have seen in Section 6.5, the period Total Fertility Rate is a measure of fertility standardized for the number of women at risk of childbearing. It is often interesting to take standardization a step further and calculate a measure which is standardized for average ages of childbearing. Choose a fixed width T for our periods, and write $TFR(t)$ for the period Total Fertility Rate in the period from t to $t + T$. Imagine that we also know the average age of childbearing $A(t)$ implied by the age-specific fertility rates for each instant of time, as a continuous function of time. In practice, each value of $A(t)$ needs to be estimated from fertility rates in some short (e.g., 1-year) period centered on t.

We begin by choosing some standard age $A^{(s)}$—say, $A^{(s)} = 25$. The particular choice turns out not to matter to the answer. We take a standardized

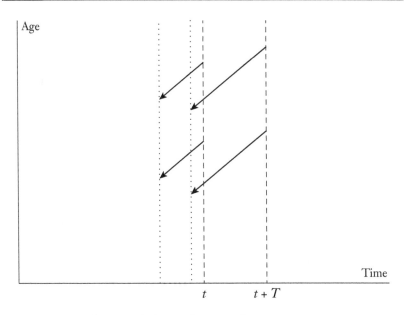

Figure 6.4   Birth age standardization for tempo adjustment

sample of births as described at the end of Section 6.5 reflecting the whole
set of age-specific fertility rates over time. Each childbirth in our sample
occurs at some time t to a mother at some age x. We shift this birth forward or backward along its mother's diagonal lifeline on the Lexis diagram
by the difference $A(t) - A^{(s)}$. A birth that takes place at mother's age x at
time t is reassigned to take place at mother's age $x - A(t) + A^{(s)}$ at time
$t - A(t) + A^{(s)}$. Some such shifts are shown in Figure 6.4.

As long as our choice of $A^{(s)}$ is sensible enough to avoid negative ages,
these diagonal shifts leave every cohort *TFR* unchanged. All the births
originally belonging to a given cohort of mothers still belong to the same
cohort of mothers. However, the average age of the mothers for births
originally at time t is changed by the shift and ends up equal to $A(t) -$
$(A(t) - A^{(s)}) = A^{(s)}$. In other words, after the shift average ages are all
constant and equal to our choice of standard age, as we wanted them to be.

What does the shift do to the period *TFR?* We see the effect in Figure 6.4.
All the births originally occurring in the period box between t and $t + T$
end up in a box between a starting time $t - (A(t) - A^{(s)})$ and an ending
time $t + T - (A_{t+T} - A^{(s)})$. (Our construction depends on $A(t)$ changing
slowly and smoothly enough that births between the endpoints stay between

the endpoints.) The width of the new box is found by taking the difference between the new endpoints. It equals $T - (A_{T+t} - A_t)$. Thus, when we calculate the *TFR* in the shifted box by the sample-based method of Section 6.5, our count of births in the numerator remains the same but the width of box in the denominator changes from T to T times $1 + (A_{T+t} - A_t)/T$. The Total Fertility Rate $TFR^{(s)}$ in the shifted box equals the original *TFR* divided by this factor:

$$TFR^{(s)} = \frac{TFR(t)}{1 - (1/T)(A(t + T) - A(t))}$$

If $A(t)$ is smooth and T is tiny, the fraction in the denominator is close to 1 minus the derivative of $A(t)$ with respect to time.

This form of age standardization removes the effects of the thinning out in time that occurs when women are postponing births later and later in their lives. France provides an example. The Human Fertility Database reports a *TFR* for French women in the period 1980 to 1985 of 1.878, below replacement levels. In this 5-year period the average age at childbearing was rising from $A(1980) = 26.82$ to $A(1985) = 27.48$. The factor $1 - (A(1985) - A(1980))/5$ is $1 - (27.48 - 26.82)/5 = 0.868$, implying a $TFR^{(s)}$ standardized for birth age of $1.878/0.868 = 2.163$. Had ages at childbearing not been rising, the level of fertility would have been seen to be above replacement. Trends in standardized or "adjusted" Total Fertility Rates are often taken to be a better guide to trends in cohort fertility than period *TFR*'s on their own. The choice and interpretation of indices are important, sometimes entering into political controversies.

When ages at childbearing are falling, births are compressed in time, the factor in the denominator is greater than 1, and $TFR^{(s)}$ is smaller than the period *TFR*. The chosen standard age $A^{(s)}$ does not affect the standardized rate; it merely serves as a device in our construction. Its effects on location of our shifted box are essentially arbitrary, and we suppress them, always attributing $TFR^{(s)}$ to the same period as $TFR(t)$.

This kind of birth-age standardization can be applied separately to groups of births. For instance, births can be separated out by birth order, into first births, second births, and so forth, a version of $A(t)$ can be calculated for each birth order, a standard age chosen for that order, and births of that order shifted to make that $A(t)$ equal that standard age. An overall

standardized *TFR* can be obtained by summing the standardized *TFR* values
for the birth orders. For this process, the groups need not be groups defined
by birth order. They could be defined, for instance, by mother's level of
education. In effect, only the numerators of age-specific rates are being
split up into terms that can be added back together, implicitly keeping
denominators that cover all the groups.

A measure very close to the standardized $TFR^{(s)}$ just described was introduced by Bongaarts and Feeney (1998). They separate out births by birth
order and, using 1-year-wide age groups, estimate $A(t+1) - A(t)$ by half
the difference between the average age in the year following $t+1$ and the
average age in the year preceding t. Their formula has the same denominator, and their measure is called a "Tempo-Adjusted *TFR*".

Demographers use the word "tempo" in general to refer to the timing
of births (or other events) within a person's lifecourse, and "quantum" to
refer to the lifetime number of births (or other events). The distinction
was brought into prominence by Norman Ryder (1964), who emphasized
cohort-based changes in fertility. In recent years, major swings in fertility
have tended to respond to chronological period influences, cutting across
cohorts. Adjustments for changing ages at birth are meaningful, because
there is something we care about that is left invariant by the adjustment—
namely, the cohort quantum of fertility. Despite some proposals to the
contrary, tempo adjustments for mortality do not make sense, because the
quantum of mortality does not vary, since every person dies exactly once.
Mortality is entirely a matter of "tempo", that is, of the timing of deaths
in the life course. Changing ages at death reflect real changes in mortality,
whereas changing ages at childbirth may not reflect real changes in the total
numbers of children that individuals have.

6.7 Princeton Indices

We return now to the study of measures of fertility limitation begun in
Chapter 4. Some of the widely used measures, although they could be used
with cohort data, are commonly used with period data and fit better into
this chapter.

The best parity data available today come from sample surveys. The best
parity data for the past come from information recorded in church registers

of baptisms, marriages, and burials, analyzed with the aid of methods of family reconstitution described in Section 4.5. Neither of these kinds of sources supply detailed geographical coverage. In the 1970s, under the leadership of Ansley Coale, a large project was organized to study variations in the onset of fertility limitation province by province across Europe. Known as the European Fertility Project, this set of studies originally aimed at identifying relationships that held up across place and time between fertility limitation and aggregate economic indices of modernization and industrialization.

These studies required indices of fertility limitation which could be calculated with data widely and uniformly available at a provincial or local level across Europe from the mid-1800s on. Such demands rule out any indices that require relating births to ages or parities of mothers or tabulations of person-years. Two forms of data are, however, widely available. First are counts of births at local levels broken down by the marital status of mothers. Second are counts of women by age and marital status. The former are available from birth registration systems, the latter from national censuses.

At Princeton, Ansley Coale developed four indices that can be computed from such administrative data. They are called I_f, I_g, I_h, and I_m and are known as the Princeton Indices. Their chief virtue is that they can be computed for many different local areas and thus allow comparisons at a fine-grained level of geography. They are also designed to measure how favorable the patterns of age at marriage are to high fertility, and to separate out the effects of changing ages of marriage from changes in fertility within marriage, as they both affect overall fertility.

The Princeton indices are a form of indirect standardization. For direct standardization, we would need age-specific fertility rates for all the places of interest, and that is what we do not have. Instead, we take a standard schedule of age-specific fertility rates. Ansley Coale chose to use rates for the Hutterites, members of a Protestant religious group founded by Jacob Hutter in the 1500s, a small number of whom migrated to North America and founded communities in the area of North Dakota and central Canada. The Hutterites put a high value on large families, and they make communal provisions for childrearing which spread the burdens of looking after the young. They have some of the highest sustained fertility rates ever measured, and their numbers have increased phenomenally over the last century. They have been studied intensively by anthropologists.

Table 6.4   Calculating I_f and I_g for Berlin in 1900

Age x	Hutterite Rates	Overall Women	Implied Babies	Married Women	Implied Babies
15	0.300	91,358	27,407	1,538	461
20	0.550	114,464	62,955	28,710	15,791
25	0.502	99,644	50,021	55,417	27,819
30	0.407	88,886	36,177	62,076	25,265
35	0.406	75,729	30,746	55,293	22,449
40	0.222	66,448	14,751	47,197	10,478
45	0.061	54,485	3,324	36,906	2,251
Sum		591,014	225,381	287,137	104,514

The Princeton Indices I_f, I_g, and I_h all compare the number of births that a population actually has in a period with the number that the population would have had if their fertility rates had been equal to the Hutterite rates. Since Hutterite rates are among the highest known, this procedure amounts to comparing the number of births a population does have to the maximal number it could have.

The index I_f is an index of overall fertility, regardless of marital status. In the numerator is the total $B^{overall}$ of births to all women observed in the actual population. In the denominator is the hypothetical total of births implied by multiplying actual counts of women $_nK_x$ by standard Hutterite rates.

$$I_f = \frac{B^{overall}}{\sum (_5K_x)(_5F_x^{Hutt})}$$

The companion index I_g is an index of marital fertility. In the numerator are births $B^{marital}$ to married women in the actual population. In the denominator are hypothetical births within marriage implied by multiplying actual counts of married women by the same standard Hutterite rates.

$$I_g = \frac{B^{marital}}{\sum (_5K_x^{married})(_5F_x^{Hutt})}$$

The calculation is illustrated in Table 6.4 with counts for women in the German Kaiser's capital of Berlin in 1900. There is one set of rates along with two sets of population counts. The rates, the same for every I_f and I_g calculation, are the Hutterite rates. The counts in the third column are for all women, those in the fifth column just for married women. In both cases we multiply rates by counts to obtain implied births and add up the implied births. The other pieces of data we need are observed birth totals. In this population 49,638 births were registered in 1900, of which 42,186 were within marriage.

Had they been reproducing at Hutterite rates, the 591,014 women in the table would have had 225,381 babies, the sum of the fourth column in the table. In fact, they only registered 49,638 babies. The value of I_f, the ratio of the number they had to the number they would have had, is $I_f = 49,638/225,381 = 0.220$. For marital births and married women, $I_g = 42,186/104,514 = 0.404$. The low I_f value, one-fifth of Hutterite levels, indicates that fertility limitation overall was well advanced by 1900 in the German capital, but the middling value of I_g indicates that low fertility within marriage was not wholly responsible. Proportions marrying, as we shall shortly see, also played a role. Values of I_f and I_g are never negative and usually less than 1, although nothing prevents values greater than 1 in populations with even higher fertility than the Hutterites.

We use the same Hutterite rates for our overall and our marital fertility calculations. The Hutterites had high proportions marrying at young ages, so there would be little point in having a separate standard for marital fertility.

Complementing I_f and I_g is the Princeton Index of Marriage, I_m. It measures how conducive the marriage pattern is to high fertility. To calculate it, we take the denominator from I_g and divide it by the denominator from I_f. The quotient shows how many births the married women could have had compared to the number of births married plus unmarried women could have had under Hutterite rates. I_m is never greater than 1 but often higher than 0.70 or 0.80. For Berlin in 1900 it comes out to be to be $I_m = 104,514/225,381 = 0.464$, a low value confirming that low proportions marrying contribute strongly to the low levels of overall fertility.

There is also a Princeton Index of Non-Marital Fertility, I_h, for which the numerator equals observed births out of wedlock and the denominator equals the hypothetical births that unmarried women in the population would have had at Hutterite rates. The index I_h is rarely employed, but it enters into an easily proved identity:

$$I_f = (I_g)(I_m) + (I_h)(1 - I_m) \approx (I_g)(I_m)$$

When illegitimate fertility is a small part of overall fertility, as it often is or was, the term involving I_h can be neglected, and I_f is close to the product of I_g with I_m. Through this approximate multiplicative relationship, the Princeton Indices help us distinguish the role of lower fertility within marriage from the role of later or less frequent marriage in promoting lower overall fertility. Postponement of marriage can be a powerful contributor to fertility reduction, as it was in China in years preceding the One-Child Policy. It is often informative to plot values of I_m versus I_g for different places and periods. On such a plot, pairs of I_m and I_g values that yield the same value of I_f are found along the kind of curve called an hyperbola, and points for different places at the same time often form clusters in the shape of ellipses. In Coale and Watkins (1986), the story of fertility decline in Europe through the nineteenth and twentieth centuries is vividly displayed with plots that show a march of ellipses across a grid of hyperbolas.

6.8 Coale and Trussell's *M* and *m*

In the 1970s, in tandem with the development of the Princeton Indices, Ansley Coale and James Trussell introduced a pair of indices of fertility limitation for calculation from schedules of age-specific marital fertility rates. They are often but not always computed from period data. These indices require more in the way of data than I_f, I_g, and I_m, but less than indices based on parity combined with age. The indices are called M and m or "big M" and "little m". They arise as parameters in a model for age-specific marital fertility rates introduced by Coale et al. (1974). Because the indices do not make any use of parity-specific information, they are, at best, rather indirect tools for detecting the presence of parity-specific fertility control or of deviations from "natural fertility" in Louis Henry's sense of the word. However, they have the virtue of simplicity, and they are widely used, especially among historical demographers.

Following our customary approach from Chapter 1, after describing the ingredients of the model, we first show how to work forward from parameters to predictions and then show how to work backward from observed data to estimates of the parameters. The quantity Coale and Trussell are modeling, the "leader", is the age-specific marital fertility rate $_5F_x^{\text{marital}}$ defined in Chapter 4. The model has two parameters M and m and two sets of age-specific constants, or "spines", called $n(x)$ and $\nu(x)$, where

Table 6.5   Coale–Trussell spine constants

Age x	15	20	25	30	35	40	45
$n(x)$	0.360	0.460	0.431	0.396	0.321	0.167	0.024
$v(x)$	0.000	0.000	0.279	0.667	1.042	1.414	1.670

v is the Greek letter "nu", which looks like "v" but is the precursor of our letter "n". Here is the model formula:

$$_5F_x^{\text{marital}} = M\, n(x)\, e^{-mv(x)}$$

Two parameters govern the level and shape of marital fertility:

- M sets a background level of natural fertility;
- m sets the strength of parity-specific fertility limitation.

There are two spines:

- $n(x)$ is an assumed schedule for age-specific marital fertility under conditions of natural fertility;
- $v(x)$ is an assumed set of weights for the impact of fertility limitation on the rates for age x.

Values for $n(x)$ and $v(x)$ are given in Table 6.5 and do not change from application to application. These values, taken from Coale and Watkins (1986, p. 12), differ slightly from Coale and Trussell's original constants. The $n(x)$ values are very like the Hutterite rates, which could have been used instead. They are averages from ten populations believed to showcase natural fertility in Louis Henry's sense. The $v(x)$ values were fitted to a larger set of marital fertility schedules.

We begin by working forward from parameters to predictions. The index M is typically less than 1.0, although it does not have to be so. Values close to 1.0 indicate natural fertility near maximum levels. In the absence of parity-specific control, with m values near zero, marital fertility rates may still be well below maximum, reflecting breast-feeding practices and other influences. For example, in Bangladesh in the early 1970s M was about 0.70 with m at zero. The model predicts a marital fertility rate for women 30 to 35 of

$$_5F_{30}^{\text{marital}} = (0.70)\, n(30)e^0 = (0.70) * (0.396) = 0.277$$

This prediction is closed to the observed value. For industrialized countries M values as low as 0.40 are common.

The index m is usually between 0 and 3, although it does not have to be so. Values less than about 0.20 are interpreted as indicating the absence of fertility control. Values above 1.00 indicate active control. Among Taiwanese women, the m index had already grown to 1.03 by 1978, according to graphs in Knodel (1983, p. 67), with a M value of 0.79. The fitted value for age-specific marital fertility for women 30 to 35 comes out at

$$_5F_{30}^{\mathrm{marital}} = (0.79) * (0.396) * \exp(-1.03 * 0.667) = 0.157$$

It is important to bear in mind that this model is a model for *marital* fertility. Numerators for rates are births to married women. Denominators are person-years lived in the married state. At young ages few person-years are person-years-married, making these denominators small and making marital fertility rates higher than overall fertility rates. At older ages shapes of schedules of marital fertility and overall fertility tend to differ less. Above age 25 the graph of overall fertility for Niger in Figure 6.2 is very close to marital fertility and to a Coale-Trussell model with $M = 0.70$ and $m = 0$. The graphs of overall fertility for Mexico and Taiwan show the flattening characteristic of Coale-Trussell models with values of m greater than 1.

We now turn to the process of working backward from observed marital fertility rates to estimates of parameters, following the steps introduced in Section 1.4 with Moore's Law. First, we transform the formula for the Coale–Trussell Model into an equation for a straight line by taking logarithms:

$$\log\left(\frac{_5F_x^{\mathrm{marital}}}{n(x)}\right) = \log(M) - mv(x)$$

We write Y for the values on the left-hand side, which we plot on a vertical axis, and X for the values $v(x)$, which we plot on a horizontal axis, and we arrive at an equation of the form $Y = (\text{intercept}) + (\text{slope})X$ with intercept equal to $\log(M)$ and slope equal to $-m$. As in Chapter 2, we find best-fitting values of intercept and slope using our recipe for linear regression.

We illustrate the estimation of M and m with data in Table 6.6 from the 2007 Demographic and Health Survey (DHS) for Bangladesh. The

Table 6.6 Coale–Trussell M and m for Bangladesh 2007

Age	$n(x)$	$v(x) = X$	ASMFR	Y	$X * X$	$X * Y$
15	0.360	0.000	0.1982	−0.597	0.000	0.000
20	0.460	0.000	0.1814	−0.931	0.000	0.000
25	0.431	0.279	0.1396	−1.128	0.078	−0.315
30	0.396	0.667	0.0734	−1.685	0.445	−1.124
35	0.321	1.042	0.0430	−2.009	1.086	−2.094
40	0.167	1.414	0.0144	−2.451	1.999	−3.466
45	(0.024)	(1.670)	NA	NA	NA	NA
mean		0.567		−1.467	0.601	−1.167

empirical observations are found in the column labeled "ASMFR" for Age-Specific Marital Fertility Rates. We divide by the column for $n(x)$ and take logarithms to obtain the column labeled Y. Entries in the last row for ages over 45 are often unstable and often excluded, as we do here. Taking X to be $v(x)$, we compute columns for $X * X$ and $X * Y$, find the column means that we need, and plug them into the regression formulas:

$$\text{slope} = \frac{\text{mean}(X * Y) - \text{mean}(X) * \text{mean}(Y)}{\text{mean}(X * X) - \text{mean}(X) * \text{mean}(X)}$$

$$= \frac{(-1.167) - (0.567) * (-1.467)}{(0.601) - (0.567) * (0.567)} = -1.199$$

$$\text{intercept} = \text{mean}(Y) - (\text{slope}) * \text{mean}(X)$$

$$= (-1.467) - (-1.199) * (0.567) = -0.787$$

Since our intercept is the log of M, we have $M = e^{-0.787} = 0.455$ and since our slope is minus little m, we have $m = 1.199$.

The data points and the best fitting line are shown in Figure 6.5. The intercept where the line crosses the Y-axis falls between two data points both with $X = 0$, data points for the two youngest age groups for which the impact of fertility limitation is assumed negligible. Between $X = 0$ and $X = 1$ the fitted line drops a little more than one unit, consistent with $m = 1.199$. This sizable value of little m indicates that parity-specific fertility limitation has spread through Bangladesh, a dramatic change since the 1970s and a remarkable outcome in the face of persistent poverty. The low value of big M suggests that births at all parities are being spaced apart.

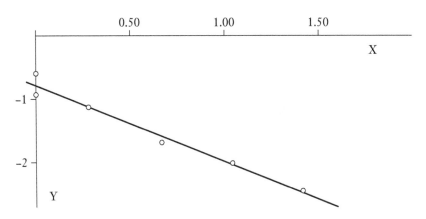

Figure 6.5   Fitting the Coale–Trussell model

The Coale–Trussell model relies on women at later ages being mainly at higher parities, since it uses the shape of a curve by age to give clues to the pattern of fertility by parity. The assumptions built into the model are often but not always reasonable ones. When marriage is concentrated at early ages and childbearing is concentrated early in marriage, the model works well. When significant numbers of couples marry in their thirties or postpone childbearing into their thirties and forties, age groups over 35 will have women at low parity still in the process of family formation. Everyone may be using contraception and everyone may have low total desired family sizes, but the high marital fertility for the older low-parity women will tend to fool the Coale–Trussell model. The present-day United States is an example in which the model does not function particularly well.

Historical series in which modest family limitation comes into prominence during periods of falling age at marriage also tend to strain the model, and changes in m may be confused with changes in M. In such settings M and m should always be interpreted with caution. The M and m measures are often used with data from family reconstitution of parish registers, but family reconstitution typically provides direct measures of parity-specific age-specific fertility rates. In that case, exclusive use of M and m is hard to justify, since M and m make no use of the parity-specific information.

At the time when I_f and I_g and M and m were gaining acceptance, Louis Henry's focus on parity-specific control was shared by most demographers. Over recent decades, it has become more common to emphasize child-spacing as a form of family limitation alongside parity-dependent, target-driven stopping behavior and new methods been developed, but none has come into general use.

HIGHLIGHTS OF CHAPTER 6

- The strategy for defining period measures.
- The period *NRR*, *GRR*, and *TFR*.
- Age-standardized rates
- Quantum and tempo
- Princeton I_f, I_g, and I_m
- Coale and Trussell's M and m

KEY FORMULAS

Period $NRR = \sum (_nF_x)(_nL_x)(f_{fab})/\ell_0$

Period $TFR = \sum (_nF_x)(n)$

Period $GRR = \sum (_nF_x)(n)(f_{fab})$

$\log(NRR) \approx \log(GRR) + \log(\ell_\mu)$

$$I_f = \frac{B^{\text{overall}}}{\sum (_5K_x)(_5F_x^{\text{Hutt}})}$$

$$I_g = \frac{B^{\text{marital}}}{\sum (_5K_x^{\text{married}})(_5F_x^{\text{Hutt}})}$$

$_5F_x^{\text{marital}} = Mn(x)e^{-mv(x)}$

FURTHER READING

A main source on quantum and tempo is Bongaarts and Feeney (1998), building on ideas of Ryder (1964), with further discussion in Wachter (2005). Application of demographic methods to the historical study of fertility limitation may be found in Coale and Watkins (1986).

EXERCISES FOR CHAPTER 6

1. Calculate the period *NRR*, *TFR*, *GRR*, and synthetic cohort mean age at childbearing μ from data in Table 6.7 for women in the African

Table 6.7   Period data for women in Togo for 1961

x	$_nB_x$	$_nD_x$	$_nK_x$	$_nL_x$
15	7,150	578	48,564	337,775
20	21,910	502	67,096	321,570
25	25,305	1,034	80,746	306,003
30	14,825	659	53,670	287,031
35	9,935	638	51,975	270,049
40	3,625	441	32,022	253,276
45	1,420	638	32,307	232,925

Source: Keyfitz and Flieger (1968, pp. 74–75).

country of Togo in 1961 from Keyfitz and Flieger (1968). It is rare to have such data from Africa from the 1960s, epitomizing high mortality and fertility unaffected by fertility decline. The period lifetable radix is 100,000, the total female population is 813,295, and 41,315 babies in 1961 were boys and 42,855 were girls.

2. Period age-specific death rates for women from Togo in 1961 in broad age groups include $_5M_0 = 0.063014$, $_{10}M_5 = 0.007884$, $_{35}M_{15} = 0.012225$, and $_\infty M_{50} = 0.046653$. Taking the world population counts for the year 2000 from Table 6.3 as a standard, calculate an age-standardized death rate for women in Togo in 1961 (ignoring men).

3. Taking the population counts from Table 6.3 as a standard, calculate an age-standardized birth rate for Togo in 1961. Calculate an age-standardized birth rate for the Hutterites using the rates in Table 6.4. Compare the two answers.

4. About 126 million babies were born into the world in the year 2000. Calculate a value of the Princeton Index I_f for the whole world based on population counts by age in Table 6.3. Hypothetical proportions married in 5-year age groups from 15 upward were 0.20, 0.70 0.85, 0.90, 0.94, 0.92, and 0.90, and, at a rough guess, perhaps 90% of these births were within marriage. Calculate implied values of I_g and I_m. How close is I_f to the product of I_g and I_m?

* 5. Values of the NRR and GRR for the People's Republic of China from Keyfitz and Flieger (1990, p. 213) are shown in Table 6.8. Plot log(GRR) on the vertical axis against log(NRR/GRR) on the

Table 6.8   *GRR* and *TFR* from China

Date	1950	1960	1970	1980	1990
GRR	3.030	2.880	2.310	1.148	1.044
NRR	1.890	2.100	2.040	1.054	0.991

Table 6.9   Portuguese fertility 1930 and 1960

Age	15	20	25	30	35	40	45
1930 Portugal	0.452	0.398	0.291	0.222	0.176	0.084	0.015
1960 Portugal	0.415	0.350	0.245	0.160	0.111	0.051	0.005
Hutterite	0.300	0.550	0.502	0.407	0.406	0.222	0.061

horizontal axis. Explain what your plot suggests about the course of China's fertility transition.

6. Table 6.9 shows age-specific marital fertility rates for Portugal in 1930 and in 1960 from Livi-Bacci (1971). Estimate the Coale–Trussell indices of marital fertility level M and family limitation m using data from all age groups. Are your answers evidence for the presence of family limitation?

7. Period *TFR*'s in France were 1.746 in 1995 to 2000, 1.878 in 2000 to 2005, and 1.968 in 2005 to 2010 according to the HFD. Average ages at childbirth based on period $_nF_x$ values were $A(1995) = 28.98$, $A(2000) = 29.38$, $A(2005) = 29.71$, and $A(2010) = 30.03$. Compute values of $TFR^{(s)}$ standardized for birth age for each period and compare these tempo-adjusted values to the original period *TFR*'s.

8. The Princeton Marriage Index I_m for Berlin in 1900 is about 0.463. In the same year, Frankfurt had $I_g = 0.497$ and $I_m = 0.454$. Muenster had $I_g = 0.764$ and $I_m = 0.396$. Trier had $I_g = 0.766$ and $I_m = 0.342$. From this information, what is your best guess as to the ordering of Berlin, Frankfurt, Trier, and Muenster in terms of overall fertility as measured by the Princeton Index I_f?

9. If the fertility rates for Hutterite women shown in Table 6.4 were interpreted as age-specific marital fertility rates, what would be the values of Coale and Trussell's M and m?

7

Period Mortality

7.1 Period Lifetables

Our approach to building period lifetables is essentially the same as our approach to period fertility measures. We make the assumption that the age-specific rates for the period continue unchanged into the future. We work out the lifetable that an imaginary cohort of newborn babies would experience under this idealized, neutral assumption about the future. This imaginary cohort is our *synthetic cohort*.

With fertility measures, the age-specific rates enter directly into the calculations, and we simply substitute the period rates for the cohort rates in the formulas. The situation with lifetables is a bit more challenging, because we have not been building up our lifetables directly from the age-specific rates. Instead, we have been constructing cohort lifetables by starting with the observed survivorships ℓ_x. From ℓ_x we have been computing $_nq_x$, and from these two columns we have been constructing the other columns, including $_nd_x$ and $_nL_x$. From $_nd_x$ and $_nL_x$ come the age-specific mortality rates $_nm_x$, which are the quotients $_nd_x/_nL_x$. These age-specific mortality rates have not been prominent up to now and have come late in the process of building the lifetable.

For a period lifetable, however, we want to be able to start with the age-specific rates, because it is the age-specific rates that we are assuming to continue unchanged into the future. The solution is to use algebra to solve for $_nq_x$ in terms of $_nm_x$. Then we can substitute the period age-specific mortality rates $_nM_x$, written with capital "M", into the formula in place of $_nm_x$ and so obtain our period $_nq_x$ values. We can go on and calculate all the other columns from $_nq_x$, ending up with the whole period lifetable.

The formula expressing the q's in terms of the m's is derived at the end of this section. Here, what matters is the answer. After substituting $_nM_x$ for $_nm_x$, we have the formula

$$_nq_x = \frac{(n)(_nM_x)}{1 + (n - _na_x)(_nM_x)}$$

Let us review again why we need to take this different route to the construction of the lifetable. For a period, we do not have information on lifetime cohort survival, as we do in principle for cohorts. What we have are period counts of deaths and counts of people. Contrast the sort of data we had for the cohort life table for the children of King Edward III. For every person, we had a death and an age at death. With period data, there will be many people for whom dates at death are not available, because many people will not die in the period. The data that will be available are, first, deaths in the period, and, second, a mid-period count of people by sex and age. We know that multiplying the mid-period count by the length of the period gives an estimate of period person-years lived (*PPYL*). This *PPYL* is not to be confused with cohort person-years lived for any real cohort nor with cohort person-years for the synthetic cohort, which will turn out to quite different, and which will supply our $_nL_x$ column for the period lifetable.

Given deaths $_nD_x$ between ages x and $x + n$ in the period and mid-period counts of people $_nK_x$, we are in a position to compute an age-specific death rate $_nM_x$ for each age group:

$$_nM_x = \frac{_nD_x}{_nK_x\, T}$$

Usually, the length T of the period is 1. The period lifetable formula for $_nq_x$ contains not only $_nM_x$ but also $_na_x$, the average years lived per person by people dying in the interval. For most age intervals, we can substitute the approximate value $_na_x = n/2$. But for the first few age groups and the last one, there are better options.

Special formulas for $_na_x$ come from empirical work by Keyfitz and Flieger (1968, p. 138). For the first year of life the $_1a_0$ value depends on $_1M_0$:

$$_1a_0 = 0.07 + 1.7\,(_1M_0)$$

For very low mortality, the average is about 1 month, or 0.07 of a year. For the United States, about half of all babies who die do so in the first month of life. It requires an age-specific rate almost as big as $_1M_0 = 0.200$ to imply an average $_1a_0$ near 6 months.

For a 4-year-wide age group from age 1 to age 5, we use the following value:

$$_4a_1 = 1.5$$

For the last interval, we use

$$_\infty a_x = 1/_\infty M_x$$

In a period lifetable the last interval is open-ended. It is infinitely long (∞ is the symbol for infinity) since it includes everyone who dies after the last age x in the table. Everyone alive above age x does die above age x, so we already know that the probability $_\infty q_x$ is 1. (Our rule for $_\infty a_x$ does make $_\infty q_x$ come out to be 1.) Even though we do not need $_\infty a_x$ for our probabilities, we do need it for person-years lived and life expectancies.

Table 7.1 gives raw counts of deaths and population for U.S. males and females for 2010. We illustrate our period lifetable calculations using the males.

We start with infants and calculate the observed period age-specific mortality rate for the 1-year-wide period. It comes out to about 7 per thousand per year:

$$_1M_0 = {_1D_0}/{_1K_0} = 13{,}703/2{,}029{,}308 = 0.006753$$

How early in the interval do those who die in it die?

$$_1a_0 = 0.07 + 1.7 \; _1M_0 = 0.07 + 1.7 * 0.006753 = 0.081480$$

The fraction 0.081 of a year is just about 1 month. Infant boys who do die live about 30 days. This information gives us a refined estimate of the probability of dying in the first year after birth:

$$_1q_0 = \frac{(1)(_1M_0)}{1 + (1 - _1a_0)(_1M_0)} = \frac{0.006753}{1 + (1 - 0.081480) * (0.006753)}$$

$$= 0.006710$$

Table 7.1　U.S. raw mortality data from 2010

		Male		Female		
Age x	n	$_nD_x$	$_nK_x$	$_nD_x$	$_nK_x$	Age x
0	1	13,703	2,029,308	10,884	1,942,651	0
1	4	2,460	8,281,720	1,856	7,932,129	1
5	5	1,325	10,372,176	1,005	9,939,790	5
10	5	1,729	10,583,108	1,220	10,104,857	10
15	35	139,372	74,583,451	76,052	73,789,207	15
50	20	365,912	34,559,040	244,524	37,013,053	50
70	5	120,193	4,277,145	97,007	5,069,352	70
75	5	143,016	3,187,811	130,346	4,135,105	75
80	5	168,836	2,306,217	183,485	3,451,358	80
85	5	157,711	1,290,434	221,744	2,357,755	85
90	5	88,592	428,765	170,943	1,033,640	90
95	5	25,975	80,683	78,713	288,017	95
100	∞	3,607	7,883	18,223	43,621	100
Male		$_{35}a_{15} = 22.247$		$_{20}a_{50} = 11.874$		
Female		$_{35}a_{15} = 23.996$		$_{20}a_{50} = 12.201$		

Source: Human Mortality Database (HMD) [accessed 29 June 2013].

A common mistake is to use $_na_x$ instead of $n - {_na_x}$ in the denominator. The denominator itself is always close to 1.

For our next interval, we have $x = 1$ and $n = 4$. Half of $n = 4$ would be 2, but our rule places deaths half a year earlier on average, putting $_4a_1 = 1.5$ and $1 - {_4a_1} = 2.5$. This factor 2.5 arises with a 4-year interval. Later the same factor arises in a different way as half of a 5-year interval. From our factor and from $_4M_1 = 2,460/8,281,720 = 0.000297$, we find

$$_4q_1 = \frac{4 * 0.000297}{1 + 2.5 * 0.000297} = 0.001187$$

A common mistake is to omit the factor of n in the numerator. Doing so would spoil all the rest of the lifetable.

From school age onward, deaths are fairly evenly spread and we rely on the usual approximation $_na_x = n/2$ for all 5-year-wide intervals. However, Table 7.1 has an interval 35 years wide and one 20 years wide. Normally, accuracy would be lost, but in this table we are also given $_{35}a_{15}$ and $_{20}a_{50}$ based on data for 5-year intervals not shown in the table. With this information we can calculate precise $_nq_x$ values for the broad intervals. For example,

$_{35}q_{15}$ is $(35)(_{35}M_{15})/(1 + (35.000 - 22.247)_{35}M_{15})$ equal to 0.063881. For the open-ended interval, we have $_{\infty}a_{100} = 1/(3{,}607/7{,}883) = 2.185$ years.

For period lifetables, we go on to build all the other columns from the $_{n}q_{x}$ column, not from the ℓ_{x} column as we did for cohort lifetables. We choose a radix ℓ_{0}, and calculate $\ell_{1} = (1 - _{1}q_{0})\ell_{0}$ and $\ell_{5} = (1 - _{4}q_{1})\ell_{1}$ and so on through the whole table. Bearing in mind that our period lifetable is the cohort lifetable for the synthetic cohort, we go on to use all the familiar formulas from Chapter 3 to find $_{n}d_{x}$, $_{n}L_{x}$, T_{x}, and e_{x}. As a bonus, we have a chance to check our calculations, since $_{n}m_{x} = _{n}d_{x}/_{n}L_{x}$ has to come out equal to the period age-specific rates $_{n}M_{x}$ with which we start.

We now turn to the derivation and explanation of our period lifetable formula for $_{n}q_{x}$, which is obtained by substituting period $_{n}M_{x}$ values for synthetic cohort $_{n}m_{x}$ values after reexpressing $_{n}q_{x}$ as a function of $_{n}m_{x}$ in the synthetic cohort lifetable. The n-year probability $_{n}q_{x}$ has to be about n times as big as the per-year rate $_{n}m_{x}$, so we write

$$_{n}q_{x} = \frac{(n)(_{n}d_{x})}{(n)(\ell_{x})} \quad \text{and} \quad (n)(_{n}m_{x}) = \frac{(n)(_{n}d_{x})}{_{n}L_{x}}$$

The numerators are the same. We examine the denominators. The product $(n)(\ell_{x})$ represents person-years that would be lived by cohort members alive at age x if no one died in the interval. These person-years are the sum of the $(n)(\ell_{x+n})$ person-years lived by members surviving the interval plus the $(_{n}a_{x})(_{n}d_{x})$ person-years lived by those dying in the interval plus $(n - _{n}a_{x})(_{n}d_{x})$ person-years lost because of death by those dying in the interval. The sum of the first two terms is $_{n}L_{x}$, so we have shown that $(n)(\ell_{x}) = _{n}L_{x} + (n - _{n}a_{x})(_{n}d_{x})$, implying

$$_{n}q_{x} = \frac{(n)(_{n}d_{x})}{_{n}L_{x} + (n - _{n}a_{x})(_{n}d_{x})} = \frac{(n)(_{n}m_{x})}{1 + (n - _{n}a_{x})(_{n}m_{x})}$$

Thus the journey from $_{n}m_{x}$ to $_{n}q_{x}$ is being taken by adding back into the denominator person-years lost to death.

7.2 Gaps and Lags

One of the greatest human achievements of the last two centuries has been the reduction in risks of mortality and the extension of life. The pace of gains has been remarkably steady. The pattern is especially simple in terms of a measure called "best-practice life expectancy", the period life expectancy in each year in the country with the highest life expectancy for that year. Different countries have held the record in different years. It has been found by Oeppen and Vaupel (2002) that best-practice life expectancy has been increasing at about the rate of 2.5 years per decade for 150 years and the trend is continuing.

When mortality is falling, life expectancy in the period lifetable for a given year is lower than life expectancy in the cohort lifetable for the cohort born in that year. The newly born cohort will have the advantage when it arrives at older ages of experiencing reduced mortality compared to present-day older people. The relationship between period and cohort life expectancy can be expressed in terms of "gaps" and "lags", discussed by Goldstein and Wachter (2006). The gap at time t equals cohort life expectancy $e_0^C(t)$ minus period life expectancy $e_0^P(t)$. The lag at time t equals the smallest number of years λ back in time for which $e_0^C(t - \lambda) = e_0^P(t)$, that is, for which earlier cohort life expectancy equals present period life expectancy. The lag is not necessarily well defined, but in practice such a λ can usually be found. Since we do not know with certainty what cohort life expectancies will be for cohorts which still have living members, gaps and lags are generally calculated using forecasts of future mortality rates.

Figure 7.1 shows period and cohort female life expectancy for the United States based on forecasts by the actuaries of the U.S. Social Security Administration. The gap has narrowed over time and now amounts to about 4 years. Present-day female period life expectancy corresponds to the cohort life expectancy of U.S. women born about 40 years ago. Period life expectancy is subject to large swings in the face of mortality crises, illustrated by the sharp drop in 1918 during the worldwide influenza pandemic. However, this short-term shock was spread across cohorts living at the time and only represented a temporary episode in the experience of each one of the cohorts. The curve of cohort life expectancy is less affected by crises than the period curve.

Period life expectancy $e_0^P(t)$ summarizes current mortality conditions, and (projected) cohort life expectancy $e_0^C(t)$ for the newly born cohort summarizes expected future mortality conditions. It is also valuable to have a measure that summarizes the past mortality risks to which members of the

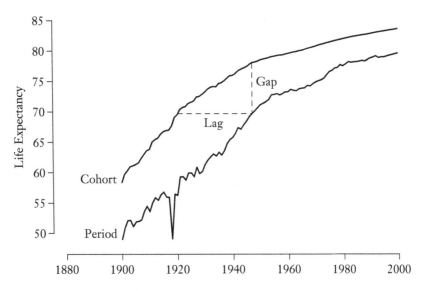

Figure 7.1 U.S. gaps and lags

population have been subjected during their lifetimes. The measure *CAL*, the "Cross-Sectional Average Length of Life" developed by Guillot (2003) building on work by Nicolas Brouard, supplies this need.

The measure *CAL* is easy to compute. At time t, for each age x, we look at a cohort lifetable (with unit radix) for the cohort born at time $t - x$. We take the proportion surviving to age x for this cohort, and we sum up these proportions over all ages x. The sum, $CAL(t)$, is the size of the population that would survive to time t, given the past history of mortality, if every past cohort had had unit size at birth. In the presence of falling mortality, $CAL(t)$ is lower than $e_0^P(t)$, summarizing the effects of the higher mortality of the past. Under some conditions, *CAL* turns out to be a weighted average of recent values of period life expectancy.

7.3 The 1660s and Laws of Mortality

The lifetables we have been constructing so far have been lifetables based on complete empirical data. We have information for all ages on deaths and populations at risk, so we can base our lifetable entries for each age on data for that age. For many applications, that is not the case, and we only have partial information from which to build our table. We may only have information about certain ages, or the information for certain ages may be more reliable than that for other ages, or we may only have general ideas about the level of mortality, but we may need a full lifetable to make projections. In these situations, we seek to fill in the missing parts of a lifetable from whatever empirical information we do have using mathematical formulas. A lifetable constructed from mathematical formulas in this way is called a model lifetable.

The first of all lifetables, published under the name of John Graunt, Citizen of London, in 1662, was in fact a model lifetable. The author used two pieces of empirical information based on observations of survivorship and he filled in the rest of the lifetable with a formula. This practice is only going to work if mortality rates do tend to obey some formula. Is the pattern of mortality by age sufficiently similar in different societies and environments that a few pieces of information are enough to tell the whole story? Model lifetables had a heyday in the 1960s and 1970s, lost their glamor in the 1980s because of overuse and misuse, and today are back in cautious favor. In the 1970s one could practically define the community of demographers by the presence of Coale and Demeny's *New Model Lifetables and Stable Populations* on the bookshelf or in the briefcase.

To understand the fascination and the limitations of model lifetables, we go back to the year of the first model lifetable, set out in Graunt's *Natural and Political Observations Mentioned in a following Index and made upon the Bills of Mortality*. A mystery surrounds the question of whether this founding work of demography was actually written by John Graunt or by his friend Sir William Petty. For a detective story, see Le Bras (2000). The year of the *Observations* is 1662. Two years earlier, in 1660, the Royal Society had been founded by King Charles II. Four years later, the year 1666 was called the "*Annus Mirabilis*", or "Marvelous Year".

The Great Fire of London occurred in 1666, following an outbreak of plague which was the last of the great periodic outbreaks of plague in London. These outbreaks had been the motive for the collection of the Bills of Mortality. London merchants wanted early warnings, and they paid a subscription to have the numbers of burials collected from parish registers and published each week. When they saw a sharp rise in burials, they stopped adding to their inventories, shut their shops, and took their families out into the country. These weekly reports collected with interruptions since 1592 formed the data base for the *Observations*.

During the plague the universities closed, and Isaac Newton, who was a student at Trinity College, Cambridge, went home to Lincolnshire. As the story goes, he was sitting in the garden when an apple fell on his head, and he said to himself, "F equals GMm over r-squared," letters that express the universal law of gravitation. This is the picture to have in our minds when we think about the origins of model lifetables. Demography was beginning during the years when Newton and his friends were developing the theory of gravitation, the science of mechanics, and the calculus. They were finding laws given by simple mathematical formulas which would describe phenomena as diverse as apples falling from trees, moons circling Saturn, and tides rising and falling in the ocean.

The formulas that Newton discovered about physics were taken to be rules that God had programmed into the world to make it work when He created it. In those days, no distinction was usually made between the physical and the human world. The planets and the human body were both seen as part of the same creation. Thus the successes of simple mathematical formulas in physics suggested that there might be simple mathematical formulas with which God had also programmed the processes of life and death in the human body and the social world. This world view leads naturally to a search for simple formulas for lifetables, laws of life and death which parallel laws of falling bodies. Model lifetables are still called "Laws of Mortality".

As time has gone on, the unity of creation has become less a part of our intellectual credo, and the hope for simple mathematical formulas for demographic processes has waned with the discovery of more empirical diversity. Nonetheless, faith in simple formulas for lifetables is deeply ingrained. The idea of Laws of Mortality for older ages is having a resurgence through mathematical formulas describing genetic influences shaped by evolution, the centerpiece of the field of biodemography. It is partly a matter of philosophical preference whether one resists the temptation to reduce the variety of empirical variation among mortality patterns to a set of mathematical curves or whether one feels that mathematical formulas reveal something real about the way living beings are put together.

7.4 Graunt's Model Lifetable

The Graunt lifetable is found in the *Observations* in Section 9, page 62 of
the original, reprinted in facsimile in Laslett (1973) and extracted in Smith
and Keyfitz (2013, pp. 19–20):

> Whereas we have found, that of 100 quick Conceptions about 36 of
> them die before they be six years old, and that perhaps but one survivith
> 76 . . .

What is a "quick Conception"? The "quickening" of the fetus, when it first
moves in the womb, is taken in medical and religious tradition as the start
of life. "Quicken" is derived from *kviker* in old Norse, which is ultimately
connected to the Latin *vivus* for "alive". Here, no distinction is being made
between quick conceptions and live births. The number 100 is the initial
size of the cohort, the radix ℓ_0 for the lifetable.

Notice carefully the two pieces of empirical information on the basis of
which other entries are filled in. These are the parameters of the model.
They are strategically chosen. One, the number dying before 6 years old, or,
equivalently, the number surviving to 6 years, reflects the severity of infant
mortality. The other, the number surviving to 76, reflects late adult lifespan.
These are the two aspects of mortality which vary most from time to time
and place to place, good choices which have their counterparts in most
model lifetables. The model formula is described in the following words:

> . . . we, having seven Decads between six and 76, we sought six mean
> proportional numbers between 64, the remainder, living at six years,
> and the one, which survives 76, and find that the numbers following
> are practically near enough to the truth; for men do not die in exact
> Proportions, nor in Fractions: from whence arises this table following,
> Viz . . .

Numbers surviving are reproduced in Table 7.2, along with calculated values for $_nq_x$.

What does Graunt mean by "six mean proportional numbers"? One
interpretation would be that ℓ_{x+n} stays proportional to ℓ_x as x changes,
or, what is the same thing, that $_{10}q_x$ stays nearly constant. Examination of

Table 7.2 The Graunt lifetable

x	ℓ_x	$_nq_x$	x	ℓ_x	$_nq_x$	x	ℓ_x	$_nq_x$
0	100	0.360	26	25	0.360	56	6	0.500
6	64	0.375	36	16	0.375	66	3	0.667
16	40	0.375	46	10	0.400	76	1	1.000
						80	0	NA

Table 7.2 shows that to be roughly true, making allowances for the warning in the text that fractional values of ℓ_x are being avoided. The exact formula has to be more complicated, and it appears to have been discovered in the course of his historical detective work by Hervé Le Bras (2000). For our purposes, the chief point is that the author was coming close to assuming constant $_{10}q_x$ between the ages pinned down by the two parameters. In other words, he was nearly assuming the same rule to build his table as the rule we use to calculate $_nq_x$ in the absence of information.

The *Observations* only presents a lifetable for one choice of parameter values, chosen to apply to London in 1662. But the model has all the ingredients familiar from earlier chapters (except for spines). It has a leading column, parameters, and a formula, and it can be applied to other times and places with other choices for parameter values. The leading column can be taken as $_nq_x$. The parameters can be written $\alpha = \ell_6$ and $\beta = \ell_{76}$, where α and β are "alpha" and "beta", the first two letters of the Greek alphabet. It takes seven 10-year intervals to go from age 6 to age 76, so $\beta/\alpha = (1 - {}_{10}q_x)^7$, and the formula can be written

$$_{10}q_x = 1 - (\beta/\alpha)^{1/7}$$

As applied to London in 1662, $\alpha = 64$ and $\beta = 1$, and the probability comes out close to 0.448, overstating the early entries and understating the later ones in the table in the text.

There is more to mention about the 1662 model lifetable. Note that the author insisted on whole numbers. He was not comfortable with entries in a table representing means or statistical expectations, just as fractional numbers in Leslie matrix projections still take some getting used to. Note also that probabilities of dying, although "more or less" constant, are less constant further down the table. They tend to rise, partly because rounding has more effect when denominators are smaller, and partly because the exact rule behind the table is more realistic than our approximation, turning out to allow for some rise in mortality by age. Note finally that the table does not end with an open-ended interval but with $\ell_{80} = 0$, probably based on the limit of 80 or "four score" years mentioned in *Psalm 90* and quoted in Chapter 3.

7.5 Coale–Demeny Model Lifetables

Onward from 1662 model lifetables have had a lively history. We encountered the 1825 model of Benjamin Gompertz and the 1860 model of William Makeham in Chapter 3. Popular model lifetables from the United Nations were published in 1955. Model lifetables have many uses: to fill in a whole lifetable from partial information; to identify suspicious data clashing with model expectations; to supply standard assumptions for projections; to pinpoint regularities for the invention of indirect measures; and, in a technique called "inverse projection", to reconstruct rates from historical counts of births and deaths.

The most famous model lifetables are those originally published by Ansley Coale and Paul Demeny in 1966 and extended from age 85 to age 100 in Coale and Demeny (1983). Our examples of model lifetable applications mainly employ the Brass family presented in Section 7.6, but familiarity with the broad features of Coale and Demeny tables is part of demographic culture.

Like Graunt's model lifetable family, the Coale–Demeny model is fundamentally a two-parameter family. There is a parameter for mortality level and a parameter for the shape of mortality rates as a function of age. But the parameter for shape takes only four values. It indexes four subfamilies, which could be called #1, #2, #3, and #4, but which Coale and Demeny had the inspiration to call "North", "South", "East", and "West".

The names of the Coale–Demeny families convey to readers a comfortable familiarity. One might expect that China, being in the Far East, would call for the East family and Zimbabwe, in the southern hemisphere, would call for the South family. However, in fact the Coale–Demeny families are based almost entirely on data from Europe and areas of European settlement, the only sources of reliable data at the time. The East family is based on places like Austria, Hungary, and Poland; the South on places like Italy and Portugal. The West family is a grab bag of tables left over from other families, including France, Israel, New Zealand, and whites in South Africa, among others. Africa and Latin America have no role in the South family, and Asia no role in the East.

Some foolish demography was done by users who did not read the fine print, and sometimes measurements from continents like Africa were branded as "bad data" when they did not fit Coale–Demeny tables, even though we now understand that differences between African patterns of mortality and European ones are real. Despite their limitations, the Coale and Demeny tables were a great step forward. Originally, they came in a weighty printed volume with sections for subfamilies, a whole lifetable for a single C–D level for males or females on a separate page. Demographers would estimate the C–D level parameter by paging through the book till they found a match to some lifetable quantity for which they had a measurement. Some confusion lurks in the fact that the higher the C–D level parameter, the lower the level of mortality. In the tables C–D level runs from 1 to 25, corresponding to values of female life expectancy from 20 years to 80 years in steps of 2.5 years.

The leading column of the Coale and Demeny lifetables is the probability of dying $_nq_x$. The parameters have just been described. The Coale–Demeny model is an example where the spines, sets of age-specific constants, are all-important. For each model family and each sex there are four spines, written A_x, B_x, A'_x, and B'_x (pronounced "A-prime" and "B-prime"), along with constants that define an intermediate parameter ϵ (roughly equivalent to e_{10}) from the C–D level parameter L. The formula is complicated and mathematically awkward but provides good fits. Coale and Demeny define two subformulas, here called "plain" with $_nq_x^o = A_x + B_x\epsilon$ and "prime" with $_nq_x' = \exp(\log(10)\,U)/10{,}000$, where $U = A'_x + B'_x\epsilon$. For any age group, as ϵ increases, $_nq_x$ itself starts plain, shifts to the mean of plain and prime when plain and prime first cross, and shifts to prime when they cross again. In applications, the West family is the one most often recommended. An example is given in the exercises.

7.6 Brass Relational Logit Models

The model lifetable system featured in applications in this book is the Brass Relational Logit System, introduced by William Brass (1974). The

Table 7.3   Spines for Brass general standard

x	Y_x	x	Y_x	x	Y_x	x	Y_x
1	0.83659	10	0.54619	35	0.24966	60	−0.21003
2	0.71963	15	0.51316	40	0.18157	65	−0.37459
3	0.66572	20	0.45500	45	0.10741	70	−0.58184
4	0.63295	25	0.38287	50	0.02120	75	−0.86730
5	0.61005	30	0.31502	55	−0.08319	80	−1.28571

ingredients for the Brass model are easily described. The leading column, the object specified by the model, is the survivorship column ℓ_x based on a radix $\ell_0 = 1$. There are two parameters, as before called α (alpha) and β (beta). Alpha is a level parameter and beta is a shape parameter. There is one set of age-specific spine constants Y_x. The formula expresses ℓ_x in terms of parameters and spines:

$$\ell_x = \frac{1}{1 + \exp(-2\alpha - 2\beta Y_x)}$$

Table 7.3 shows spine constants for a version of the Brass General Standard revised by Ewbank et al. (1983). Spines are the same for males or females. Differences by sex are accommodated by choices of parameter values.

The Brass parameter α is very like the C–D level parameter. Positive α means higher survivorship and weaker mortality at all ages; negative α the reverse. The Brass parameter β is somewhat like a continuous version of the differences between Coale and Demeny's North, South, East, and West subfamilies. It governs the balance between infant and old-age mortality; higher betas favor the young. The model with $\alpha = 0$ and $\beta = 1$ serves as a standard case, but a case with high mortality by twenty-first-century standards, roughly comparable to C–D level 10 of the Coale–Demeny West model family.

These effects are illustrated in Figure 7.2. In both panels the heavy solid lines denote ℓ_x values for the standard case with $\alpha = 0$ and $\beta = 1$. On the left, the dashed line shows the better survivorship for $\alpha = 0.5$, and the dotted line the poorer survivorship for $\alpha = -0.5$, both keeping β at 1. On the right, a crossover is evident. The dashed line shows poorer infant and better old-age survivorship for $\beta = 0.5$, and the dotted line the reverse for $\beta = 1.5$, both keeping α at 0. When crossovers like the contrast between $\beta = 0.5$ and $\beta = 1.5$ occur in empirical data, they often invite controversy. Apparent

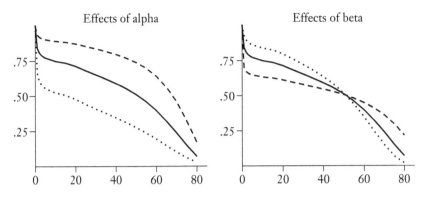

Figure 7.2 Shapes of Brass model lifetables

crossovers in survival statistics for U.S. black males compared to U.S. white males have sparked long debate as to the relative contributions of errors in age reporting versus possible effects of the selection of less frail individuals into older age groups in cohorts experiencing heavier child mortality.

Following our usual approach, we begin by working forward from parameter values to model predictions. Suppose that $\alpha = +0.60$ and $\beta = 0.95$ are settings proposed for women in India in 2000. What is the implied level of childhood survival ℓ_5? We locate $Y_5 = 0.61005$ in the table of spines and plug in alpha and beta:

$$\ell_5 = \frac{1}{1 + \exp(-(2)*(0.60) - (2)*(0.95)*(0.61005))} = 0.9136544$$

The answer is a plausible match to an estimate in the Census Bureau International Data Base.

We now turn to the task of working backward from pieces of empirical information to estimates of parameters. As before, the strategy is to transform the model into an equation for a straight line. We write $Z_x = \alpha + \beta Y_x$ so that the Brass formula becomes $\ell_x = 1/(1 + \exp(-2Z_x))$. Taking reciprocals of both sides yields $1/\ell_x - 1 = \exp(-2Z_x)$, so $-\log((1 - \ell_x)/\ell_x) = 2Z_x$. Simplifying the logarithm, we find

$$(1/2) \log(\ell_x/(1 - \ell_x)) = Z_x = \alpha + \beta Y_x$$

The function of ℓ_x on the left-hand side has a name. It is called the "logit", one of those special functions like cosines, exponentials, and tangents that have their own names. Not all authors include the factor $1/2$ in the definition. The appearance of this logit function is the reason that Brass's system

Table 7.4   Estimation of Brass parameters

| x | Observed Values | | Model |
	ℓ_x	Z_x	Y_x
20	0.70	+0.42365	+0.45500
60	0.40	−0.20273	−0.21003
Difference		−0.62638	−0.66503

is called a "logit" system. (The adjective "relational" in front of "logit" will be explained shortly.) We must bear in mind, however, that the logit function does not appear in the formula for the Brass model itself. It appears when we work backward and solve for $\alpha + \beta Y_x$.

We see that we can take observed values of ℓ_x, calculate $Z_x = \text{logit}(\ell_x)$ (that is, $(1/2) \log(\ell_x/(1 - \ell_x))$) and draw a plot with Z_x on the vertical axis and the spine constants Y_x on the horizontal axis. According to the model, points should lie along a straight line with intercept α and slope β. When we have observations of ℓ_x at a bunch of ages, we can follow our earlier approach and fit a straight line by linear regression. Sometimes we only have observations at a pair of ages. Two points determine a straight line, so we can still find a slope and intercept.

We work through an example of estimation for such a two-point case. Partial information on Afghan women in 2005 suggests that about 70% survive to age 20 and about 40% to age 60. We want to guess the level of infant mortality using a Brass model lifetable. Table 7.4 illustrates the computations. We start with ℓ_x and compute Z_x. For example, $\ell_x = 0.70$ gives $Z_x = (1/2) \log(0.70/0.30) = 0.42365$. We subtract the first row of the table from the second to find the rise −0.62628 in Z_x and the run −0.66503 in Y_x. The slope, the rise over the run, is $\beta = 0.941882$, only a little below 1. For the intercept α we can solve the equation $Z_x = \alpha + \beta Y_x$ for α given β and Z_x and Y_x from either row of the table. The answer is $\alpha = -0.004906$, close to zero. The fitted table for Afghan women is close to the standard table. For an estimate of ${}_1q_0$, we consult the table of spines, find $Y_1 = 0.83659$, and evaluate

$$\ell_1 = \frac{1}{1 + exp(-(2) * (-0.004906) - (2) * (0.941882) * (0.83659))}$$
$$= 0.827231$$

We calculate $_1q_0 = 1 - \ell_1 = 0.172769$, one of the highest probabilities in the world of dying before a first birthday.

Up to now, we have treated the Brass family of model lifetables like the Coale–Demeny family or any other fixed family specified with constants like Y_x. But there is a telling difference. In other families, no particular level is singled out. The Coale–Demeny level 16 is no more special than level 7. In the Brass family, however, $\alpha = 0$ and $\beta = 1$ pick out a special, standard table. If we start with ℓ_x values for this table, we can get the Y_x values back by taking logits. The spine constants Y_x are the logits for a special choice of lifetable.

Nothing prevents us from starting with some other favorite lifetable and creating a new set of Y_x values from the logits of those survivorships. With our new Y_x values, the standard case with $\alpha = 0$ and $\beta = 1$ corresponds to our new favorite table in place of Brass's old one. As we change α and β, we create a whole family of lifetables related through the logit transformation to our favorite table. In this way, the Brass approach provides a way of relating other lifetables to any one favorite life table from which we build our standard. The tables are related to each other through the logit function. This is the reason for calling the Brass system "Relational Logit Model Lifetables".

An appealing application is to take the present-day lifetable of a country as the standard and tabulate Y_x values from that one. The lifetable for each earlier time t for the country can be represented by parameter values α_t and β_t in relation to the present-day lifetable. We can plot α_t and β_t as functions of t. When we are lucky, the alpha points may lie along a straight line, and we can fit the straight line and use it to project alpha into the future. Similarly, the beta points may lie along their own straight line and allow us to project beta into the future. (When straight lines are poor fits, other simple curves may serve the same purpose.) The resulting projection is specially tailored to the mortality pattern of the country of interest. In this way the Brass approach supplies a method for taking historical mortality data and projecting lifetables into the future.

* 7.7 Lee–Carter Models

In the early 1990s Ronald D. Lee and Larry Carter introduced a versatile method for forecasting mortality using a model lifetable family of their own, presented in Lee and Carter (1992). The authors were primarily interested in modeling changes over time in the mortality of a single country or population rather than differences among countries. They dispensed with any general set of spine constants pretabulated for use. Instead, they put forward procedures for generating sets of spine constants from historical data country by country, so that the system is entirely relational.

The Lee–Carter model has the usual ingredients. The leading column is the age-specific death rate $_nm_x$. There is only one parameter, k, a level parameter which is usually regarded as a function of time and written k_t. For each application there are two sets of spine constants a_x and b_x. The formula is essentially the same as the Coale and Demeny prime subformula, but with $_nm_x$ in place of $_nq_x$:

$$_nm_x(t) = \exp(a_x + b_x\,k_t)$$

In other words, $\log(_nm_x)$ is a linear function of the parameter k, and on a logarithmic scale a_x specifies a baseline age-specific schedule and b_x specifies the strength of the response of age group x to changes in overall mortality indexed by k.

When a_x and b_x are available, working forward from values of the parameter k to predictions of mortality rates is accomplished in the usual way. Working backward from data to estimates involves new approaches. Lee and Carter begin with a whole matrix of log mortality rates. The rows of the matrix are age groups; the columns are time periods. A row-specific additive contribution is subtracted away from the matrix (supplying a_x values in the process), and a matrix transformation called a Singular Value Decomposition is performed. This decomposition is beyond the scope of this book. It leads to estimates for the b_x values along with a historical set of parameter estimates k_t. These k_t values can be plotted as a function of time. A straight line often offers a good fit and can be used to project k_t and thence $_nm_x(t)$ into the future.

For example, a Lee–Carter fit to U.S. female mortality rates from the HMD from 1950 to 2007 turns out to give, among other values, $a_{70} = -3.899304$ and $b_{70} = 0.039981$ with $t = 0$ in 2007 and $k_0 = 0$. A straight line with slope -0.291282 per year gives good fit to the trend in k_t. A forecast for 2000 with $t = 13$ is $k_{13} = (13) * (-0.291282)$, or -3.786666.

For the age group from 70 to 75 we predict $_5m_{70} = \exp(a_{70} + b_{70}k_{13})$, which is 0.017410.

The foremost contribution of the Lee–Carter approach is the treatment of random variability that accompanies it. The parameter values k_t are regarded as a time series, and the past fluctuations of k_t around their trend yield indicators of the range of uncertainty in forecasts of the future. This approach depends on results from probability for processes called random walks which also play a role in studies of migration. They are introduced in Chapter 11 and we return to measures of uncertainty for Lee–Carter forecasts in Section 11.4.

HIGHLIGHTS OF CHAPTER 7

- Period lifetables
- Laws of mortality
- Coale–Demeny model lifetables
- Brass Relational Model tables
- Lee–Carter forecasting

KEY FORMULAS

$$_nM_x = \frac{_nD_x}{(_nK_x)(T)}$$

$$_nq_x = \frac{(n)(_nM_x)}{1 + (n - _na_x)(_nM_x)}$$

$$\text{Brass } \ell_x = \frac{1}{1 + \exp(-2\alpha - 2\beta Y_x)}$$

$$\text{Brass } \alpha + \beta Y_x = (1/2)\log(\ell_x/(1 - \ell_x))$$

$$\text{Lee–Carter } _nm_x(t) = \exp(a_x + b_x k_t)$$

FURTHER READING

The original papers reprinted in Smith and Keyfitz (2013), Part IV, still make good reading. For applications of model tables to forecasting, see Tuljapurkar et al. (2000). For applications to inverse projection, see Barbi et al. (2004) and Wachter (1986).

EXERCISES FOR CHAPTER 7

1. Calculate all the columns of a period lifetable for U.S. females in 2010 from Table 7.1 for the age groups given in the table. What is the expectation of life at birth?

2. Suppose you believe that deaths under age 1 in Table 7.1 are under-reported and the entries for $_1D_0$ for males and females need to be multiplied by 1.10. By how much would female life expectancy be reduced by the correction?

3. According to Keyfitz and Flieger (1968), the Austrian census of 1965 counted 65,607 boys and 63,083 girls less than a year old. Deaths below this age totaled 2,056 for boys and 1,617 for girls. Counts at mid-year 1962 for the country then called Ceylon and now called Sri Lanka showed 229,000 boys and 224,000 girls age 0 to 1. During the year, 10,561 boys and 8,581 girls under age 1 were reported to have died. What are the ratios of $_1q_0$ for males to $_1q_0$ for females in Austria and in Ceylon?

4. For Coale and Demeny's West model family for females, spine constants for young age groups include

$$A_0 = 0.53774; \quad B_0 = -0.008044; \quad A'_0 = 5.89920; \quad B'_0 = -0.05406$$

$$A_1 = 0.39368; \quad B_1 = -0.006162; \quad A'_1 = 7.45760; \quad B'_1 = -0.088344$$

   C–D levels 16, 17, and 18 correspond to ϵ values of 55.83396, 57.16346, and 58.54585, respectively. Find values of $_1q_0$ for these levels by taking means of the plain and prime formulas. What C–D level would make $_1q_0$ come closest to a reported value of 0.064 for girls in India in 2000? Calculate $_4q_1$ for this level and work out the implied value of $_5L_0$.

5. An estimated lifetable for Chinese women in the early 1990s is a reasonable fit to a Brass model with parameters $\alpha = 1.25$ and $\beta = 0.93$. Estimate the proportion of women dying before age 60 and the lifetable person-years lived between 60 and 70.

6. The United States Internal Revenue Service publishes a lifetable called Table 90CM for calculations affecting gift taxes and inheritance taxes. The table in force around 2001 has $\ell_{55} = 0.89658$ and $\ell_{80} = 0.47084$. Fit a Brass model using these two pieces of information. What are your

estimates of α and β? What value of $_1q_0$ would you predict with the Brass model you have fitted?

7. In the Internal Revenue Service lifetable from Table 90CM, we have $\ell_6 = 0.98850$ and $\ell_{76} = 0.57955$. If the 1662 Graunt model is fitted to these modern data, what would the prediction of ℓ_{56} be?

8. Accurate full lifetables for contemporary Bangladesh are not available. However, about 89% of all babies are now surviving to the age of 1, and about 75% of women survive to age 35. Find values of the Brass α and β parameters to make the Brass model fit these two ℓ_x values.

9. Use your estimates from Exercise 8 to predict the proportion of women surviving to age 65 in Bangladesh today.

* 10. Show by your own algebraic manipulations that the formula

$$_nq_x = \frac{(n)(_nM_x)}{1 + (n - {_na_x})_nM_x}$$

implies $_nM_x = {_nm_x}$.

* 11. Consider the 1962 data from Ceylon for boys in Exercise 3. Calculate two estimates of $_1q_0$, one by the usual period lifetable formula and the other by assuming that the hazard rate h_x for ages between 0 and 1 equals the observed value of $_1M_0$. Is there any value of $_1a_0$ which would make these estimates agree? (For extremely old ages, setting the hazard rate equal to $_nM_x$ often gives better values for $_nq_x$ than the usual formula with the unrealistic value $_na_x = n/2$.)

8

Heterogeneous Risks

8.1 Heterogeneity

Most of the methods in earlier chapters have been applied to one population at a time with interest in one outcome at a time. We take, for example, a cohort of men or of women, making no distinctions among the different cohort members, and we study the outcome "death", making no distinction among different kinds of deaths. Or we take women of a given age and study the outcome of next childbirth, making no distinction among different women and no distinction among different kinds of births. We assume a homogeneous population and a homogeneous outcome. When data are plentiful, we can adopt a strategy of "divide and conquer", splitting our population into homogeneous subpopulations, studying each one separately, and studying each kind of outcome separately, one at a time. When data are limited or when we care about finer and finer distinctions, we need methods that take account of differences, that is to say, methods addressing heterogeneity.

Initially, in this chapter, we study heterogeneous outcomes; the prime example is the study of deaths from different causes. There are multiple sources for the decreases, or "decrements", in numbers of survivors, leading to "multiple decrement" lifetables presented in Section 8.2 They are based on a theory of "competing risks" in which different risks like cancer and heart disease compete, as it were, to carry a person off from life. The approach described in Section 8.3 was first worked out by the great Swiss mathematician Daniel Bernoulli. Today, the mathematics behind competing risks is expressed in terms of hazard functions, as in Section 8.4.

Similar mathematics can be applied to study risks of a single outcome when the risks vary from individual to individual within a population. A great deal of research is devoted to studying the effects of measured variables like education, ethnicity, or blood pressure on survival, that is to say, on the duration of life. The same ideas are useful for studying the duration of other states like marriage or residence in some city or country. Especially powerful methods are available when it is reasonable to make an assumption of "proportional hazards", described in Section 8.7. The resulting approach, invented by Sir David Cox in 1972 and used throughout demography, is presented in Sections 8.6 and 8.7.

Risks that vary from individual to individual due to effects of variables that have been measured constitute "observed heterogeneity". No data set can hope to capture and record all relevant differences among individuals. Other differences remain as "unobserved heterogeneity". Although unmeasured, they may leave their mark on the statistical distribution of outcomes over time. A model is outlined in Section 8.8.

8.2 Multiple Decrements

In developed societies today, something like two-thirds of deaths are blamed on cancer, stroke, and heart disease, and only a few percent on infectious diseases. A century ago, infections dominated. The reduction in their share of deaths represents one of the triumphs of modern human history. Around the world, however, infections still claim a large proportion of lives, and infections with the HIV virus resulting in deaths from AIDS have become the greatest challenge to public health.

Demographers and epidemiologists track progress against diseases with "Multiple Decrement Lifetables". Multiple Decrement Lifetables are called by this name because the population is suffering losses, or decrements, from a multiplicity of causes. There is only one way of being dead, but many ways of dying.

When a number of causes of death are carrying off members of a population, the deaths observed from a disease like AIDS do not fully reflect the killing power of the disease. Some people who would have died of AIDS

die of something else before AIDS kills them. Similarly, in the presence of
AIDS, other causes will seem less lethal than they are, because AIDS kills
people who would have died of these other causes. The methods of this
section are designed for separating out the effects of causes of death acting
on their own from effects observed when all causes are acting together.

Zimbabwe, in southern Africa, has nearly the highest rate of HIV infections in the world. One United Nations estimate pegged the overall
probability of dying for men aged 30 to 35 in Zimbabwe in 2000 at $_5q_{30} =$
0.113390. About four-fifths of the deaths observed in the age group are
attributed to AIDS.

The probability of dying of AIDS *in the presence of other causes* is four-fifths
of the overall probability of dying. We have $(4/5)(0.113390) = 0.090712$.

We want a formula for calculating what the probability of dying of AIDS
would be *in the absence* of other causes. We write this special probability
with a star on the label for the cause:

$$_5q_{30}^{\text{AIDS}*} = 1 - (1 - {}_5q_{30})^{4/5}$$

$$= 1 - (1 - 0.113390)^{4/5} = 0.091790$$

In this case, the numerical difference between the two kinds of probabilities
is not large, but at older ages it may be heftier. Our formula with stars also
tells us the probability of dying of other causes *in the absence of AIDS:*

$$_5q_{30}^{\text{OTHER}*} = 1 - (1 - {}_5q_{30})^{1/5}$$

$$= 1 - (1 - 0.113930)^{1/5} = 0.023782$$

Notations are not standard. Various authors use various symbols in place of
stars for these probabilities.

These formulas will be derived in Section 8.4. Notice their similarity
to our familiar formulas for $_nq_x$-conversions from Chapter 3. To convert
from a 5-year probability to a 4-year probability and a 1-year probability,
we would calculate

$$_4q_x = 1 - (1 - {}_5q_x)^{4/5}$$

$$_1q_x = 1 - (1 - {}_5q_x)^{1/5}$$

To survive the whole 5-year interval, a person must survive for 4 years AND
for 1 more year. Similarly, to survive the whole battery of causes of death, a

person must survive the four-fifths share of AIDS deaths AND survive the one-fifth share of deaths from other causes. In both sets of formulas, the *survivorships* multiply. For causes of death, the reason for multiplication is an idealized assumption that the causes of death act independently, as discussed in Section 8.3.

To make our formulas fully general, we need some notation. We use letters "A, B, C . . . " for causes of death, and write $_nD_x{}^A$, $_nD_x{}^B$, and so on, for deaths observed from these causes. The essential quantities for our calculations are the *shares* of deaths by cause:

$$s^A = {}_nD_x{}^A/{}_nD_x \quad \text{and} \quad s^B = {}_nD_x{}^B/{}_nD_x \quad \text{etc.}$$

In our example from Zimbabwe, A is AIDS, B is all other causes, $s^A = 4/5$ and $s^B = 1/5$.

Just as we have deaths $_nD_x{}^A$ from cause A, we have death rates $_nM_x{}^A$ for cause A, obtained by dividing the deaths from cause A by the period person-years lived by everyone in the age group. These are "cause-specific death rates" (strictly speaking, cause-, age-, and sex-specific death rates). Since the denominator, the person-years lived, is the same regardless of cause, we can calculate the shares from the death rates or from the deaths and get the same answers. The deaths for all the causes add up to total deaths. The death rates for all the causes add up to the total death rate. The shares add up to 1. We can also reverse the formulas:

$$_nD_x{}^A = (s^A)(_nD_x); \qquad _nM_x{}^A = (s^A)(_nM_x)$$

There is a parallel equation with q in place of D or M:

$$_nq_x^A = (s^A)(_nq_x) = \frac{(n)_nM_x^A}{1 + (n - {}_na_x)(_nM_x)}$$

The numerator on the right is specific to cause A, but the adjustment for person-years in the denominator applies to everyone at risk.

Worldwide standards for classifying deaths by cause, with thousands of detailed categories, are published in the *International Classification of Diseases*. On each death certificate, doctors or hospital assistants generally record one primary cause, sometimes along with some secondary causes. This is a routine process. Scrutiny might often reveal that the true causes of

Table 8.1   Cause-specific death rates for Japan,
ages 80–85 for 1981 to 1990

Cause of Death	Rates	
	Females	Males
Accidents and violence	0.000515	0.001070
Infectious diseases	0.000221	0.000504
Cancers	0.003876	0.008498
Heart disease	0.002021	0.003685
Stroke	0.001920	0.003187
Diseases of other organs	0.000971	0.002127
Remaining causes	0.001370	0.002434

death were other than the apparent causes given on the death certificate. Especially among the elderly, the choice of one of several contributing causes to list as the primary cause may be quite arbitrary. Despite efforts at standardization, diagnostic practices differ from time to time and country to country, and aggregation into broad categories is subject to wide variation. Cause of death data should always be regarded with caution.

Table 8.1 shows cause-specific death rates for ages 80 to 85 for 1981–1990 for Japan, the current world leader in low mortality. Popular rather than medical names for categories of disease are used to avoid lengthy specifications. The row for "Diseases of other organs" includes pneumonia and diseases of the stomach, liver, and kidneys.

Let us calculate what the male probability of dying of other causes would be in the absence of cancer. First, we find the overall value of $_5M_{80}$ by adding up the cause-specific rates in the third column. The sum is 0.021505. The corresponding overall $_5q_{80}$ from the period lifetable formula is $(5)(0.021505)/(1 + (2.5)(0.021505)) = 0.102039$. The share of cancers s^C is $0.008498/0.021505 = 0.395166$, so the share of other causes is 0.604836. The probability of dying of these other causes between ages 80 and 85 in the absence of cancer would amount to as much as $1 - (1 - 0.102039)^{0.604836} = 0.063024$.

A lifetable built up out of such probabilities for every age group is called a "cause-elimination lifetable". It tells us how much progress would be made if a cure for cancer could be found. The progress is a little less than we would expect, because some of the people who would have died of cancer would be dying of other causes in the age interval.

We may also concentrate on causes A, B, C ... by themselves, each in the absence of all the others. We build a lifetable from the probabilities ${}_nq_x{}^{A*}$ for all the age groups, and another from the ${}_nq_x{}^{B*}$, and so forth. We write $\ell_x{}^{A*}$, $\ell_x{}^{B*}$ ... for the survivorship columns of these tables and use similar notation for other lifetable columns. These tables are called "associated single-decrement lifetables", while the table built from the overall ${}_nq_x$ values is the multiple-decrement lifetable. The single-decrement tables describe the effects of causes in isolation from each other, which combine when taken together into the multiple-decrement lifetable.

* 8.3 Competing Risks

Understanding the formulas for associated single and multiple decrement lifetables involves the idea of "competing risks". We think of causes of death A, B, C ... competing to carry off each member of the population. The deaths that would occur from each cause acting on its own differ from those that do occur when all the causes compete together.

Probabilities of dying in the presence of other causes add together, whereas probabilities of dying in the absence of other causes, written with stars in the formulas, do not:

$$q = q^A + q^B$$
$$q = q^{A*} + q^{B*} - (q^{A*})(q^{B*}) = 1 - (1 - q^{A*})(1 - q^{B*})$$

(We temporarily omit n's and x's for shorter formulas.)

Why must we subtract the product $(q^{A*})(q^{B*})$ from the sum of the starred q's? The answer is "double jeopardy". Figure 8.1 is a Venn diagram. The oval on the left denotes people who would be killed by A acting on its own, the one on the right people killed by B acting on its own. Acting on its own, in the absence of other causes, A would kill some of the same people as B, namely, the people in the shaded intersection, who are counted twice if we simply add the starred q's together and have to be subtracted once to obtain the correct overall probability of dying.

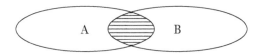

Figure 8.1   Double jeopardy

In principle we cannot observe double jeopardy. We see people die of one thing or another, and we do not know whether, had they been spared, they would have died before the end of the age interval of another cause. Sometimes we do observe something rather like double jeopardy, when medicine succeeds in bringing people back from the brink of death with heroic interventions. Some patients rescued by heart transplants die shortly afterward of lung cancer. But most of the time we are dealing with a mathematical abstraction.

Two separate assumptions are involved. One is the multiplication law for *independent* competing risks. The other is an assumption of *steady shares* of deaths by cause inside each interval over which we observe the totals.

The assumption of independent competing risks is a strong assumption. It is violated whenever people susceptible to dying from some particular cause are at heightened risk of dying of another. Smokers, particularly vulnerable to lung cancer, have higher risk of heart disease. In practice, demographers try to make the independence assumption more nearly valid by restricting calculations to subpopulations which are as much alike as possible with respect to known risk factors. For instance, the formulas may be applied separately to smokers and nonsmokers. For advanced work, complex models for dependent competing risks are also available, including stochastic risk factor models developed by demographer Kenneth Manton and others.

The assumption of steady shares is a sensible expedient. When we have no information about changes in shares inside an interval, we assume shares are constant. It is the same kind of assumption we have made for converting $_nq_x$ values for different n. When we have no extra information, we assume constant rates within intervals.

We gain insight into the working of competing risks from an analogy inspired by the trials of medieval knights who had to "run the gauntlet" down a row of adversaries striking at them from both sides. Imagine the adversaries as devils, A-devils and B-devils and C-devils competing to claim victims for their causes. Hundreds of them line up along the gauntlet, scattered so that the shares of each kind of devil are much the same in every part of the line. Each devil strikes out once on its own as the knight runs by, each with the same chance of hitting him. The knight has to run the whole gauntlet, getting up and moving on whenever he is hit. He may be hit more than once, by an A-devil, by a B-devil, by another A-devil, by a C-devil. The first devil who succeeds in hitting him has the right to claim him in the end for that devil's cause. But he may not be hit. The knight, fortified with grace, may dodge all the devils and come safely through the gauntlet, a survivor.

The way the devils strike out separately on their own is the assumption of independent competing risks. The constant mix of devils down the line is the assumption of steady shares. With hundreds of devils, each step is too short to worry about double jeopardy at any single step. Double jeopardy occurs when the knight is hit by more than one devil in the line. Take away the A-devils, we have a cause-elimination lifetable. Take away all devils but the A-devils, we have the single-decrement lifetable for A. The chance that at least one A-devil hits the knight somewhere along the line is the probability of dying of A in the absence of other causes. The probability of dying of A in the presence of other causes is the chance of an A-devil winning the competition, being first to hit the knight. The chance that one or more A-devils hit the knight is not proportional to the number of A-devils; it is more complicated. But if the knight is hit, the chance that the first to hit him is an A-devil *is* proportional to the number of A-devils. That is the important feature of the picture. The shares of devils are the same as the shares of deaths.

∗ 8.4 Calculations with Hazards

The mathematics behind our formulas for competing risks also helps us study differences in risk from person to person in the remainder of this chapter. The basic tool is the hazard function introduced in Chapter 3, also called the "force of mortality". Hazards are natural objects for advanced research, because the hazard functions for different groups are often found to be proportional to each other, a simple and powerful relationship.

We recall that the hazard function h_a at age a is the slope of minus the logarithm of the survivorship function ℓ_a, in this chapter always with a radix of 1. We can go back from hazards to survivorships in three steps. First, we take the area under the hazard function from 0 to x, which is called the cumulative hazard function, written H_x with a capital "H". In calculus, finding areas is the reverse of taking slopes. Second, we multiply H_x by minus one;

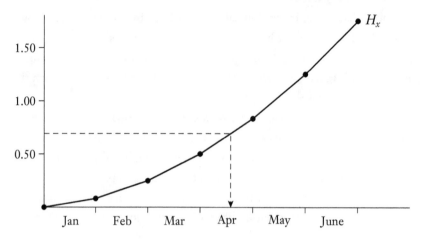

Figure 8.2   Cumulative hazard and median duration

more hazards mean less survival. Third, we undo the logarithm by applying the exponential function, forming $\exp(-H_x) = e^{-H_x} = \ell_x$. Here, the letter "a" in h_a is standing for ages inside an interval and "x" in H_x is standing for age at the interval endpoint.

For example, with $a = 0$ on New Year's Day, suppose hazards measured in units per year are equal to 1 in January, 2 in February, 3 in March, up to 6 in June. The hazard h_a is a step function with a unit step at the start of each month. The cumulative hazard at the end of January is the area of a rectangle with height 1 and base $1/12$ of a year, an area of $1/12$. Each month we add the area from the next rectangle. By the end of February we have $(1 + 2)/12$; by the end of June, $(1 + 2 + 3 + 4 + 5 + 6)/12 = 21/12$. (We pretend each month lasts exactly $1/12$ of a year.) In lifetables, age refers to time since birth and hazards are hazards of death, but our example could refer to other kinds of entrances and exits—for instance, a cohort of enthusiasts entering a training program in January and exiting when they pass their fitness tests. In our example, $\exp(-21/12) = 0.17$ of the cohort would still be training at the end of June.

Plotting the cumulative hazard as in Figure 8.2 helps us calculate the median time to exit. Half the cohort have departed when x is such that $1/2 = \ell_x$, implying $-\log(1/2) = -\log(\ell_x) = H_x$. The dotted line on Figure 8.2 at a height of $-\log(1/2) = 0.6931$ meets the H_x curve partway into April.

For more precision, we use linear interpolation. First, we pick the interval (here, the month) in which the median will be found by comparing 0.6931 to the height of H_x at the start and end of each interval. We have $H_x = 6/12 = 0.50$ at the start of April and $H_x = 10/12 = 0.83$ at the end of April, so April is our month. Second, we find the slope of H_x for April. The slope of the cumulative hazard is the hazard itself, 4 per year in April. Slope is rise over run, so a run of δ beyond April Fools' Day gives a rise of 4δ, bringing H_x up from $6/12$ to $6/12 + 4\delta$. We reach our target of 0.6931 if we choose $\delta = (0.6931 - 6/12)/4 = 0.0483$, just short of half a month. Since 1 April is $3/12$ of a year, our median completion time is $365 * (3/12 + \delta) = 109$ days into the new year.

In place of the median, we can ask for any percentile. How soon do the first 10% finish the program, leaving 90% at their exercises? Our target is $-\log(0.90) = 0.1054$, which falls in February, where the slope is 2. So our 90% point matches $\delta = (0.1054 - 1/12)/2 = 0.011$, or about $365 * (1/12 + \delta) = 35$ days into the new year.

Such calculations with percentiles are important for two reasons. First, they help us make up or "simulate" random samples from a population with any given lifetable. Second, they help us judge the practical significance of factors that produce differences between groups in their lifetables.

For our first goal of making up samples, the point about percentiles is that they are evenly distributed. Exactly 90% of the exit times should be beyond the 90th percentile, 50% beyond the 50th percentile, 10% beyond the 10th percentile. So if we draw, say, 1,000 uniformly distributed random numbers $U_1, \ldots U_{1,000}$ with a random number generator in the computer, we can calculate a target $-\log(U(i))$ for each of them and find the exit time $x(i)$ for which $H_{x(i)}$ equals our target. The result will be a sample of a thousand random exit times for the lifetable whose cumulative hazard function is H_x.

For our second goal of drawing comparisons, consider a group of novices entering the training program with a hazard function for completion only half as strong at every x as the "baseline" group of enthusiasts from Figure 8.2. What is the median exit time for novices? The area under $(1/2)h_x$ is half the area under h_x, so cumulative hazards for novices are half as high. If one drew the novice curve onto a plot like Figure 8.2, it would not cross a horizontal line for $-\log(1/2)$ until June. The crossing point would be a time δ into June given by

$$\delta = (0.6931 - (1/2) * (15/12))/(6/2) = 0.0227$$

That would be $365 * (5/12 + \delta) = 160$ days into the year. The practical effect of having half the hazard in this case is to extend the median time in training by $160 - 109 = 51$ days. It is easier to think about 51 days than to think about half the hazards. Our comparison of enthusiasts and novices is an introductory example of *proportional hazard models* featured in Section 8.6.

Before treating proportional hazards in detail, we write down some formulas. The cumulative hazard is an area, expressed as an integral; the hazard itself is a slope, expressed as a derivative:

$$H_x = \int_0^x h_a \, da; \qquad h_x = \frac{d}{dx} H_x$$

Survivorship ℓ_x is e^{-H_x}. The density of deaths at age x is the product $h_x \ell_x$; we multiply the hazard of dying h_x by the proportion ℓ_x still alive and so at risk of dying. For lifetable deaths in the whole interval between x and $x + n$, we integrate:

$$_n d_x = \int_x^{x+n} h_a \, \ell_a \, da = \int_x^{x+n} h_a \, e^{-H_a} \, da$$

These formulas bring us the bonus of a better understanding of competing risks, when quantities from Section 8.3 are rewritten in terms of hazards. With independent competing risks, the overall hazard h_a is written as a sum of hazards from different causes. For example, $h_a = h_a^A + h_a^B + h_a^C$. As we know, probabilities of dying come in two kinds, $_n q_x^A$ for dying of A in the presence of other causes and $_n q_x^{A*}$ for dying of A in the absence of other causes. But there is only one kind of hazard. We do not need stars on hazards. What differs between measures is the pool of survivors on which the hazards act; we have the same hazards, different pools. In the presence of other causes, deaths from A come from a pool of survivors reduced by the action of all the causes together. In other words, survivors are calculated from a cumulative hazard which is the sum of the cumulative hazards from all the causes:

$$_n d_x^A = \int_x^{x+n} h_a^A \, e^{-(H_a^A + H_a^B + H_a^C \cdots)} \, da$$

In the absence of other causes, deaths from A come from a pool of survivors reduced only by the cumulative hazard for cause A alone:

$$_n d_x^{A*} = \int_x^{x+n} h_a^A \, e^{-(H_a^A)} \, da$$

Our assumption of independent competing risks reappears as the assumption that hazards for competing causes add, implying that cumulative hazards H_x^A, H_x^B ... add, implying in turn that survivorships $\exp(-H_x^A)$, $\exp(-H_x^B)$ ... multiply, as probabilities for independent statistical quantities ought to do. Our assumption of steady shares reappears as the requirement that within a single interval of age each cause-specific hazard is a fixed proportion of the overall hazard, so that $h_a^A = s^A h_a$, $h_a^B = s^B h_a$, and so on.

Key formulas for independent competing risks are now easily derived. In the presence of other causes, lifetable deaths are given by

$$_n d_x^A = \int_x^{x+n} h_a^A \, e^{-H_a} \, da = \int_x^{x+n} s^A \, h_a \, e^{-H_a} \, da = s^A \, _n d_x$$

In the absence of other causes, survival probabilities are given by

$$1 - {}_n q_x^{A*} = \frac{\exp(-H_{x+n}^A)}{\exp(-H_x^A)} = \frac{\exp(-s^A H_{x+n})}{\exp(-s^A H_x)}$$

$$= \left(\frac{\exp(-H_{x+n})}{\exp(-H_x)} \right)^{s^A} = (1 - {}_n q_x)^{s^A}$$

* 8.5 Lifeluck, Risk, and Frailty

With multiple decrement lifetables we study differences among causes of death that all impinge on the same person. We now turn our attention to differences among people. The mathematics is similar, but the purpose is new.

Table 8.2   Lifeluck, risk, and frailty

Student:	R	D	B	J	L
Lifeluck $\mathcal{L}$	0.800	2.843	1.527	1.761	4.042
Risk $\mathcal{R}$	1.528	1.000	1.528	1.528	1.000
Frailty $\mathcal{Z}$	0.515	1.411	0.126	0.860	1.788
Cumulative H_T	1.016	2.015	7.931	1.340	2.261
Age at death	77.5	85.7	102.0	80.8	87.0

An ordinary lifetable lumps everyone in some cohort together. The lifetable itself does not separate out people by their characteristics or the dangers that they run. When we want to distinguish among groups of people, one alternative is to build separate lifetables group by group. We can build separate lifetables for women and men, for villagers and cityfolk, for drinkers and teetotalers, for female village teetotalers and all the combinations in between. But if we do build separate tables for small groups, we may have unstable answers. We would also be failing to take advantage of similarities in age patterns of mortality from group to group.

The favorite approach to group-by-group differences in demography is called "proportional hazards". It takes advantage of empirical discoveries that groups defined in terms of many common variables have hazard functions that are proportional to each other over broad ranges of age. Before presenting these models, we work through an example which shows how they fit into a larger picture of heterogeneity in times till death.

Table 8.2 shows a prediction of age at death for five imaginary twenty-five-year-old students, R, B, and J being men and D and L being women. The row labeled curvy $\mathcal{L}$ is called lifeluck. Each student's lifeluck is chosen by generating a uniform random number U and setting $\mathcal{L} = -\log(U)$. Like the uniform random numbers in Section 8.4, U picks out the percentile at which the student's death occurs within the student's own lifetable. The row labeled curvy $\mathcal{R}$ is called risk. It depends on each student's observed characteristics, in this case, male or female. It is the effect from the proportional hazard model to be studied in Section 8.6. The row labeled $\mathcal{Z}$ is called frailty (written curvy $\mathcal{Z}$ rather than curvy $\mathcal{F}$ for historical reasons). It is another kind of random number studied in Section 8.8 which reflects those unobserved characteristics of a student affecting survival which remain relatively unchanged throughout life.

We take lifeluck and divide it by risk and by frailty. The quotient $\mathcal{L}/(\mathcal{R}\mathcal{Z})$ is shown in the row labeled Cumulative H_T. We are comparing the quotient to a particular cumulative hazard function written as a function of duration till death t. Our prediction of duration till death is the value $t = T$ such that

$$\mathcal{L}/(\mathcal{R}\mathcal{Z}) = H_T$$

If risk and frailty were both equal to 1, we would be repeating calculations familiar from Section 8.4. Here, the students' own values for risk and frailty affect T and so affect age at death. For these twenty-five year olds, predicted age at death is $25 + T$, shown in the final row of the table.

Our calculation rests on a simple fact. When $\mathcal{L}$ divided by $\mathcal{R}$ and $\mathcal{Z}$ equals H_T, then $\mathcal{L}$ itself equals the product of $\mathcal{R}\mathcal{Z}$ times H_T. In other words, the student's time till death comes from a cumulative hazard which is *proportional* to H_T. The constant of proportionality is $\mathcal{R}\mathcal{Z}$. The function H_t is our "baseline cumulative hazard", also written $H_t(0)$; its slope is the baseline hazard $h_t(0)$. The baseline is a standard version to which other hazards are compared.

In this example the baseline comes from a Gompertz model with slope parameter $\beta = 0.0835$ and modal age at death 77.2. Usually we need graphs or interpolation to find T, but in this case we can find T and $x = 25 + T$ from the Gompertz formulas of Chapter 3. The calculation of T from H_T is spelled out in the next section. Here, the answers can be checked (up to rounding) by finding values of T from the table and plugging them into the formula $H_T = (\alpha/\beta)(\exp(\beta T) - 1)$. Lifeluck, risk, and frailty all contribute to the variability in predicted time to death. However, lifeluck contributes the lion's share.

* 8.6 Proportional Hazards

We now focus on the risk multiplier $\mathcal{R}$ and consider general proportional hazard models. These models exploit individual-level data when there are measurements of background variables (called covariates or cofactors) associated with lower and higher risk but when the shape of the age pattern of mortality is likely to be common to everyone. We label individuals with identification numbers $i = 1$, $i = 2$, and so on. We write $h_t(i)$ for the hazard function and $H_t(i)$ for the cumulative hazard function for the ith individual. We let $i = 0$ stand for an imaginary individual whose hazards are the baseline hazards.

Our proportional hazard model is given by the equation

$$h_t(i) = h_t(0)e^{\beta_1 X_1(i) + \beta_2 X_2(i) + \beta_3 X_3(i)...}$$

When we add up areas under the hazard curve to obtain cumulative hazards, we obtain an equation of the same form for $H_t(i)$ in terms of $H_t(0)$. Each β_j is a parameter giving the size of the effect for the jth covariate and $X_j(i)$ is the value of that covariate for the ith individual. The observed covariates, the X's, may be indicator variables (e.g., 1 if male, 0 otherwise) or discrete variables like parity or continuous variables like income. Values for the parameters have to be estimated from data on survival. As usual, we first describe going forward from parameter values to predictions, the subject of this section. Then, in Section 8.7, we describe going backward from data to parameter estimates.

In our model the factor multiplying $h_t(0)$ is the risk curvy $\mathcal{R}$ introduced in Section 8.5. The risk is written as the exponential of a sum in order to make the method as similar as possible to linear regression. The logarithm of $h_t(i)/h_t(0)$ is a linear combination of the covariates; the model is a "log-linear" model. Bear in mind that the exponential of a sum is the product of exponentials:

$$\mathcal{R} = e^{\beta_1 X_1(i) + \beta_2 X_2(i)\cdots} = \left(e^{\beta_1 X_1(i)}\right)\left(e^{\beta_2 X_2(i)}\right)\cdots$$

Effects from the different covariates multiply.

The multiplicative relationships in the model mean that the effects are assumed to be independent of duration and of each other. The assumption that they are independent of duration is a serious restriction, but the assumption that they independent of each other is not. If the effects of two variables depend on the levels of each other—for example, if the effect of smoking depends on whether the individual is a man or a woman—we can define a combined variable or "interaction". For instance, we can define a

Table 8.3 Proportional hazard parameters

Covariate:	Starting age	Sex	Race	Education
Coefficient:	0.078	0.424	0.301	−0.056

new variable that takes the value 1 for male smokers and 0 for everyone else. The art of defining interactions, adding or deleting variables, and testing for statistical significance is a subject treated in books on statistical demography. In such respects, proportional hazard models are very like ordinary linear regression models.

Here, we concentrate on drawing demographic implications out of proportional hazard models. Table 8.3 shows a set of parameter values for a proportional hazards model with four covariates pertaining to recent older U.S. adults. The estimates are derived from the U.S. Health and Retirement Study (HRS) using the methods to be described in Section 8.7. As mentioned in Chapter 5, the HRS is a longitudinal survey. The same respondents are followed across time, interviewed over and over again in successive "waves". Estimates are based on 11,903 respondents from the first wave in 1992 followed to the tenth wave in 2010. This example is stylized for the sake of illustration. A full study would have more covariates and other refinements.

The four covariates in Table 8.3 are age at the first wave minus 50 years, sex (1 for males; 0 else), race (1 for minorities; 0 else), and years of education minus 12. Duration t is measured as time since the first survey wave, not age. Age enters through the first covariate. If respondent i dies at duration t, he or she dies at age $50 + X_1(i) + t$. The baseline group are nonminority women with a high school education 50 years old at the first wave. The baseline hazard as a function of duration turns out to be a good fit to a Gompertz model with slope parameter $\beta_0 = 0.0835$ and modal duration to death of 27.2 years, corresponding to $\beta_0/\alpha = 9.691$.

When we are furnished with parameter estimates, the first and easiest application is to plug in values and find the overall risk factors $\mathcal{R}$ for different groups. We find, for instance, that minority males age 52 at the first wave with a college education have predicted hazards whose ratio to the baseline hazard at every age equals

$$\mathcal{R} = e^{0.078*(52-50)+0.424*(1)+0.301*(1)-0.056*(16-12)} = 1.929$$

The advantage of education does not overcome the disadvantages of being male and minority.

A second application combines risk factors with hazards for predictions of survival ratios. The cumulative hazard for the baseline Gompertz model is

$$H_t(0) = (\alpha/\beta_0)(e^{\beta_0 t} - 1) = (1/9.691)(e^{0.0835t} - 1)$$

At duration $t = 15$, $H_t(0) = 0.258$. For the minority males with risk factor $\mathcal{R} = 1.929$, the probability of surviving a duration of $t = 15$ years from age $10 + X_1(i) = 52$ to retirement at age 67 is given by

$$\ell_{67}/\ell_{52} = \exp(-\mathcal{R} \, H_{15}(0)) = \exp(-1.929 * 0.258) = 0.608$$

A third application compares groups in terms of median survival times. As in Section 8.4, the median survival time for the baseline group is the value T solving the equation $-\log(1/2) = H_T(0)$. In other words, the median survivor has lifeluck $\mathcal{L} = \log(2)$. Usually we interpolate to find T, but with a Gompertz model we can solve directly. From $H = (\alpha/\beta_0)(e^{\beta_0 T} - 1)$ we have $T = (1/\beta_0)\log(1 + H\beta_0/\alpha)$, the promised formula from which the ages at death in Table 8.2 were obtained. Here, we plug in for $\beta/\alpha = 9.691$ and $H = \log(2)$, to find

$$T_{\text{median}}(0) = (1/0.0835)\log(1 + \log(2) * 9.691)) = 24.473$$

Among our slightly older minority male college graduates with risk factor $\mathcal{R} = 1.929$, the median survivor i has $\mathcal{L}/\mathcal{R} = \log(2)/1.929 = H_T$, implying

$$T_{\text{median}}(i) = (1/0.0835)\log(1 + (\log(2)/1.929) * 9.691) = 17.966$$

The higher risks for this group reduce the median duration till death by $24.473 - 17.966 = 6.507$ years.

The relationship between time and age in our model deserves attention. Any proportional hazard model which includes age at first survey wave as a covariate like our X_1 is assuming an exponential dependence of hazards on this component of age. But the exponential (Gompertz) dependence of baseline hazard on duration of time since the first wave just happens to be what we find in our HRS data set. It is not an assumption. Dependence on duration could be quite different. In our case it turns out that the coefficient

β_1 on the starting-age X_1 and the slope parameter β_0 governing duration dependence are both close to the same value, 0.080. Probably $\beta_0 \approx \beta_1$ in this case because the underlying dependence of hazards on age in this population happens to follow a Gompertz model. Being a year older at the start has the same effect as growing 1 year older since the start. Such a pattern is seen often, but far from always.

For the sake of brevity, our example of a proportional hazard model with data from the Health and Retirement Study has been highly stylized. Longitudinal surveys like the HRS allow a rich array of characteristics and behaviors to be tracked for individuals across the lifecourse and incorporated into hazard models and more sophisticated statistical frameworks. Work of demographers like Burton Singer and others with these kinds of data are stimulating a new appreciation of relationships among social connectedness, personal resilience, health, and physiological and cognitive status to which the methods of this chapter can be applied.

* 8.7 Cox Regression Estimation

The method in use for working backward from survival data to parameter estimates in proportional hazard models is due to Sir David Cox and is one of the leading breakthroughs in statistics. We explain the concept with a simple example of interest in its own right with a single covariate and five individuals. The covariate is sex. The five individuals are the five longest-lived human beings with well-documented lifespans up to the turn of the millenium.

Table 8.4 shows the five longest lifespans from a particular collection of carefully validated data published by Robine and Vaupel (2001). We want to see how to marshal this information along with the assumption of proportional hazards to estimate β, the effect of being male.

The key idea behind Cox regression is to separate the estimation of coefficients from the estimation of the baseline hazard. Imagine a competition in which we start at age 115 and see which of our five individuals is the first to die. Early in this chapter we had a competition among causes of death, which we could describe loosely as a competition among organs of the body as to which is to be the first to fail. Here, instead, we have a competition among individuals of a population as to which is to be first to die. The

Table 8.4   Record lifespans

Name	Sex	Date of Birth	Date of Death	Lifespan
J. Calment	F	21 Feb. 1875	4 Aug. 1997	122.4
M. Meilleur	F	29 Aug. 1880	16 Apr. 1998	117.6
C. Mortensen	M	16 Aug. 1882	25 Apr. 1998	115.7
C. Hughes	F	1 Aug. 1877	17 Mar. 1993	115.6
A. Jennings	F	12 Nov. 1884	20 Nov. 1999	115.0

picture is different, but the mathematics is the same. With causes of death, the probability that A comes first is given by the ratio of h_x^A to the sum $h_x^A + h_x^B + \ldots$. With individuals, the probability that i dies first is given by the ratio of $h_x(i)$ to the sum $h_x(1) + h_x(2) + \ldots$. Under the assumption of proportional hazards, this ratio does not depend on age x but only on the effects of the covariates—in this case, on β.

Just as before, in Sections 8.3 and 8.4, two assumptions are involved. The first is an assumption of independent competing risks. This time that assumption is fairly innocent. The deaths of different individuals are to be independent of each other. The assumption would be violated if the population included members of the same families or the same mountain-climbing teams, but for large populations or randomly selected samples it is easy to accept. This time the second assumption, of steady shares—proportional hazards—is the strong assumption.

When we run our competition with the data in Table 8.4, the model says that the chance of Mrs. Jennings dying first is

$$\frac{h_x(0)}{h_x(0) + h_x(0) + e^\beta h_x(0) + h_x(0) + h_x(0)} = \frac{1}{4 + e^\beta}$$

The numerator has the female hazard. The denominator adds hazards for four females and one male. In fact, Mrs. Jennings dies first. The chance the model assigns to the event that actually occurs is called the "likelihood". This likelihood is a function of the unknown parameter β, so we have a "likelihood function" of β.

After Mrs. Jenning's death, we are left with four survivors, three women and one man. Total hazard amounts to $(3 + e^\beta)h_x(0)$. We run our competition again. Each of the women has a chance $1/(3 + e^\beta)$ of being the next to die, and our man has a chance $e^\beta/(3 + e^\beta)$. It is a woman who dies. The likelihood is $1/(3 + e^\beta)$. At the next round, two women and one man remain. The man, Mr. Mortensen, dies. The likelihood is $e^\beta/(2 + e^\beta)$. At the next round, the likelihood is $1/2$. At the final round, one woman remains, Madame Jeanne Calment. She dies, with likelihood 1. The process is like a game of musical chairs, with one fewer place for a survivor at each round. In reality, it is no game. But it is happy to dwell on the remarkable survival of these five individuals. Madame Calment may be the oldest human being who has ever lived. Her story is told by Allard et al. (1994).

The different rounds are independent of each other. The death of each of these individuals has no effect on the survival of the others. Since probabilities of independent events multiply, we take the product of the likelihoods from each round. This product is called a "partial likelihood" because it only takes into account the order of deaths and not the ages at death. Sir David Cox realized that the partial likelihood is all we need for estimating the effects of covariates. We look for the value of the parameter β which maximizes the partial likelihood, that is, which makes the observed order of deaths as likely as possible under the model. Hunting maxima usually requires computers, but in our simple example we can plug in trial values for β and choose the one that gives the highest value for the partial likelihood

$$\lambda = \frac{1}{4 + e^\beta} \frac{1}{3 + e^\beta} \frac{e^\beta}{2 + e^\beta} \frac{1}{2} \frac{1}{1}$$

Figure 8.3 shows the partial likelihood for 36 trial values of β. At first the numerator increases more rapidly and later the denominator, so that the partial likelihood attains a maximum—in this case, close to $\beta = 0.353$. The outcome means that the hazard function for men at these extreme ages is estimated to be about $e^\beta = 1.423$ times the hazard for women. With only five data points, we would not expect this estimate to be reliable, but in fact ratios like 1.4 are often seen at older ages. Estimates of the male disadvantage at ages around 100 from larger data sets given by Hill et al. (2000) range between 1.1 and 1.3.

Computers can find a maximum for the partial likelihood and thus find estimates of effects even when many covariates and many cases are involved. Often ages at death are "censored", that is, unseen because a person is still

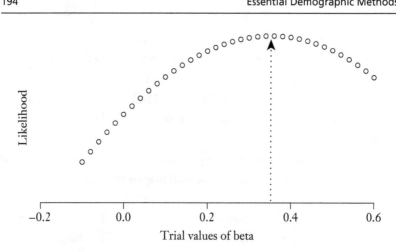

Figure 8.3   Partial likelihood

alive when the period of observation ends. Cox's method handles these cases easily. The person enters into the denominators of the partial likelihood for all deaths that occur while the person is still in observation and could have been next to die. The person contributes no factor of his or her own to the likelihood, because he or she is never seen to be the next to die. For instance, suppose we had only known that Mrs. Hughes was still alive in March 1993 and did not know her age at death. Then we would remove the factor $1/(3 + e^\beta)$ from the likelihood. We would search for a value of β to maximize the product of the four remaining factors corresponding to observed ages at death.

∗ 8.8 Frailty Models

Many characteristics of individuals which are not directly observed must also influence their risks of dying. Variations across the population introduce what is called "unobserved heterogeneity". Some sources of variability reflect factors that could be measured in surveys or medical examinations but are not measured. No study measures everything. Other sources, like the genes which an individual carries, have long been unobservable but are starting to be observable. Still other sources remain unobservable, given our present state of knowledge. Many complicated and somewhat independent influences presumably combine to affect risk, with total effects that may vary rather randomly across the population. It seems reasonable to treat unobserved heterogeneity by assuming random probability models that describe variations across the population, in the absence of knowledge about which levels of risk apply to which individuals.

Demographers generally follow an approach introduced by Vaupel et al. (1979) already outlined in the section on lifeluck, risk, and frailty. In this approach the effects of unobserved heterogeneity are summed up by a single random variable Z called "frailty" acting within the framework of a proportional hazard model. An individual's unknown, randomly distributed nonnegative value of Z multiplies the individual's age-specific hazard function at all ages. The higher an individual's frailty, the higher the hazard function, and the more likely a death. This process, called "demographic selection", gradually culls individuals with high Z values from the population of survivors, leaving a population enriched with robust individuals and lower hazards. As we have seen, frailty can be combined with lifeluck and risk in large proportional hazard models with subjects from various cohorts. Here, for simplicity, we take frailty to be the only proportional factor, acting on a baseline hazard function expressed as a function of age shared by all members of a single cohort.

The frailty Z which changes a baseline hazard h_a into the product $Zh(a)$ also changes the cumulative hazard into the product ZH_x. Drawing on the relationship between cumulative hazards and logarithms of survival proportions, we have e^{-ZH_x} for the proportion surviving to age x among those cohort members with frailty Z. High Z makes the proportion fall off more quickly as age x and cumulative hazard H_x increase.

Suppose half a cohort had frailties of $Z = 0.4$ and half had $Z = 1.6$, averaging out to 1. At an age when only 10% would survive under the baseline hazard, H_x would equal $-\log(0.10) = 2.30$. The proportion surviving among the less frail members would be $\exp(-0.4 * 2.30) = 0.398$, or nearly 40%. But only $\exp(-1.6 * 2.30) = 0.025$, or less than 3%, of the more frail members would survive. The percentages of less frail and more frail would shift from fifty-fifty to $0.398/(0.398 + .025) = 0.940$, or 94% versus 6%. This process is called "demographic selection". The survivors are a group selected for low-level hazards. The hazard function for the whole cohort, mixing everyone together, is called the "aggregate hazard". In this example, $(1/2) * (0.398) + (1/2) * (0.025) = 0.212$, or 21%, of the whole cohort would survive, about twice as many as under the baseline hazard. Average frailty would drop from 1 at the start to $(0.94) * (0.40) + (0.06) * (1.60) = 0.47$. The aggregate hazard would be only 47% of the baseline hazard at our target age.

When cohort frailties range over many possible values, not just two, we describe them with a probability density function $p(z)$ for the random variable $\mathcal{Z}$. The aggregate proportion of cohort survivors is obtained by averaging over the random values of frailty represented in the cohort:

$$\ell_x = \int e^{-zH_x} \, p(z) \, dz$$

This form of integral is called the Laplace transform of $p(z)$ evaluated at H_x, and it has been studied for 200 years.

Since frailty is unobserved, $p(z)$ is unknown and cannot be estimated directly from empirical data. It is customary to choose $p(z)$ from the family of "gamma" probability distributions. Random variables from the gamma family are always nonnegative (as factors multiplying the hazard have to be), and gamma distributions come in a convenient variety of shapes. Choosing a gamma distribution for initial frailty turns out to make the distribution of frailty among survivors at later ages stay within the gamma family. A gamma distribution is determined by two parameters, a shape parameter κ and a scale parameter θ (Greek "kappa" and "theta"), with mean given by θ/κ and variance θ/κ^2. Its Laplace transform is known to imply the aggregate survival function

$$\ell_x = \left(\frac{\theta}{\theta + H_x} \right)^{\kappa}$$

To normalize average frailty to 1, we set $\theta = \kappa$. A typical value might be $\kappa = 5$, corresponding to a standard deviation of 0.447. For the age considered in our last example, at which 10% would survive under the baseline hazard, aggregate survival in the presence of heterogeneous frailty would be given by

$$\ell_x = 5^5/(5 + \log(10))^5 = 0.150$$

The aggregate hazard among cohort survivors to age x is given by the derivative of $-\log(\ell_x)$. The average frailty among survivors comes out to be 0.684 in this case, given by the formula $\kappa/(\kappa + H_x)$.

For these frailty-based calculations, we have not had to specify the shape of the hazard function itself, only the value of baseline survival that interests us. We may, however, choose a baseline hazard function—for instance, a Gompertz hazard above some age like 40—and then we can solve completely for the aggregate cohort ℓ_x. It turns out that Gompertz baseline with gamma frailty leads to a logistic hazard curve.

If we knew the baseline hazard, we could estimate the frailty distribution from aggregate survival data. Vice versa, if we knew the frailty distribution, we could estimate the baseline hazard. But aggregate survival data are not sufficient for us to estimate both together, without imposing arbitrary restrictions or bringing extra information to bear. Nonetheless, frailty models can be highly informative, because they give a quantitative sense of how much of a tapering off of hazards at advanced ages could be explained by the process of demographic selection.

The model of Vaupel, Manton, and Stallard which we have been describing is a model for fixed frailty. The value of the random variable $\mathcal{Z}$ which applies to an individual remains with the individual throughout life, multiplying the age-specific hazard at all ages. Other approaches allow for frailty or "vitality" variables whose values change across the lifecourse, in accordance with one or another probability model, often from the family of Markov models. These models for heterogeneous risk are prominent today in the field of biodemography.

HIGHLIGHTS OF CHAPTER 8

- Probabilities of dying of a cause A in the presence and in the absence of other causes.
- Competing risks and double jeopardy.
- Cumulative hazards and median durations
- Lifeluck, risk, and frailty.
- Proportional hazard models
- Demographic selection

KEY FORMULAS

$$_nq_x^A = (s^A)(_nq_x)$$

$$_nq_x^{A*} = 1 - (1 - _nq_x)^{s^A}$$

$$H_x = \int_0^x h_a \, da; \qquad h_x = \frac{d}{dx} H_x$$

$$h_x(i) = h_x(0) \exp\left(\beta_1 X_1(i) + \beta_2 X_2(i) \dots\right)$$

$$\mathcal{L}/(\mathcal{R}\mathcal{Z}) = H_T$$

$$t = T_{\text{median}} \quad \text{when } H_t = -\log(1/2)$$

FURTHER READING

The book on lifetables by Namboodiri and Suchindran (1987) has good coverage. Our formulas for competing risks were developed by Chiang (1968) at U.C. Berkeley. Mathematical aspects of frailty models are treated by Yashin et al. (2000). Lifeluck, risk, and frailty appear in Wachter (2014).

EXERCISES FOR CHAPTER 8

1. Data from the World Health Organization (WHO) for 2010 for Sierra Leone show $_5q_0$ close to 0.185. Shares of these childhood deaths from leading causes include HIV with 0.01, diarrhoea with 0.12, malaria with 0.23, pneumonia with 0.17, injuries with 0.03, prematurity with 0.10, neonatal conditions with 0.17, and residual causes with 0.16. What is the probability of dying of malaria in the presence of all other causes? What would be the probability of dying of other causes in the absence of malaria?

2. Suppose that $_5q_{90}^{A*} = 0.097$ and $_5q_{90}^{B*} = 0.132$, where A stands for cancers and B for all other causes. What is the overall probability $_5q_{90}$ and what are the shares s^A and s^B of deaths by cause?

* 3. By analogy with the devils' gauntlet of Section 8.3, here is a lineup for two competing risks A and B: $BABABAAABBBAABAABBBAAA$. The order has been generated at random under the assumption of steady shares. Throw a pair of dice once for each letter in the lineup. The

victim is hit if the dice come up with two aces (that is, 1 and 1, or "ambsace"). In your random experiment, which risk turns out to win the victim by being the first to land a hit? Either by repeating the experiment or by combining appropriate formulas under the assumption of steady shares, find the probability of a win for A in the presence of B, the probability of a hit for A in the absence of B, and the probability of double jeopardy, that is, at least one hit for both A and B.

* 4. In the fitness training example of Section 8.4, what would be the median time to completion for a group with hazards $7/4$ as high as the baseline hazards? How much difference to the median would it make if the cumulative hazard H_x were a continuous function of x given by $H_x = (x^2 + x)/24$ rather than having segments of straight lines?

* 5. Write out the hazard rate h_x as a limit for $n \to 0$ of some expression involving ℓ_x, ℓ_{x+n}, and n. Recall that for small values of y, $\log(1 - y) \approx -y$. Find the relationship between h_x and the limits as $n \to 0$ of $_n q_x/n$ and of $_n m_x$.

* 6. In an application of proportional hazard modeling, Hummer et al. (1999) found an association between attendance at religious services and survival rates among U.S. adults. Suppose that the model of Table 8.3 is extended to include coefficients $\beta_5 = 0.13$ on an indicator X_5 of less-than-weekly attendance and $\beta_6 = 0.63$ on an indicator X_6 of never attending, with weekly attendance as the baseline category. Consider a group of nonminority women with college educations who were aged 60 at first survey wave who never attend services. What is the predicted ratio of their hazard to the baseline hazard? What is their probability of surviving for $t = 10$ years after the first wave?

* 7. For the group of women in Exercise 6, what is the predicted median survival time? What is the predicted median for women with the same covariates except for weekly attendance ($X_5 = X_6 = 0$)? A number of factors might lie behind the measured association. Mention a few that come to mind.

* 8. In Table 8.4, suppose Mrs. Hughes had only been known to survive until March 1993 rather than to die at that time, so that her death age were censored rather than observed. Re-estimate the coefficient β for the ratio of male to female hazards in a proportional hazard model.

*   9. Consider a frailty model for which the baseline hazard is Gompertz and the frailty multipliers $\mathcal{Z}$ are drawn from a gamma distribution with shape parameter $\kappa = 5$ and unit mean. At an age x to which only 1 in 10,000 would survive under the baseline hazard, what would the aggregate survivorship ℓ_x be in the presence of heterogeneous frailty?

*   10. With the model of Exercise 9, substitute an expression for the Gompertz cumulative hazard into the expression for aggregate survival ℓ_x. Show that the aggregate hazard rate, minus the slope of the logarithm of ℓ_x, can be put into the form of the logistic function studied in Section 1.6. What choices of κ, α, and β, if any, would lead to an entirely constant aggregate hazard rate?

*   11. Find an expression for the difference in life expectancy between a person with frailty $\mathcal{Z}$ and a person with frailty 1 when $\mathcal{Z}$ is very close to 1. Relate your expression to the measure called disparity in Chapter 3.

9

Marriage and Family

9.1 The Complexity of Marriage

Marriage is full of complexities, not only for humans who enter into it, but also for demographers who study it. Not all models of population growth and change include marriage as a component. There is no explicit mention of marriage in the Balancing Equation. But marriage enters implicitly into all models through its impacts on other processes. Marriage obviously affects fertility, initiating exposure to significant risks of childbearing for many. Marriage also affects mortality. Married people live longer than nonmarried and never-married people. It remains a question whether this effect occurs primarily because marriage enhances chances of survival by providing nurturance and support or because healthier people with better life chances are more likely to find spouses, marry, and remain married.

Not only does marriage affect other demographic processes, but it is affected by them. Becoming widowed, for example, is a change in marital status determined not by marriage rates but by mortality rates impinging on a spouse. Whenever we study a process, it is easier to begin by studying the process as far as we can on its own in isolation from other processes. With marriage we shall not be able to get far with our models before we have to bring other demographic processes into the picture.

Transitions into and out of marriage are significant, not just for their own sake, but for what they mean for the nature of the family. It is in the study of marriage that demography has its closest ties to sociology and psychology and newsworthy relevance to debates over family values.

Fundamentally, of course, we are interested in marriage because it is a lifecycle event that happens to most of us. It is a process over which we have some control and about which we can make informed choices. We had no choice about being born, and we have limited control over dying. But entering or leaving marriage is always partly up to us.

The subject of marriage is called "nuptiality", from a Latin word for the wedding ceremony. Nuptiality is a complicated subject, not only because of its interactions with fertility, mortality, and the sociology of the family, but also because of problems of definition. What is a "marriage"? Should consensual unions be treated as marriages for demographic purposes? Should any or all cohabiting couples be treated among the married or among the single? All demographic processes are subject to some fuzziness of definition. Are brain-dead patients with beating hearts dead or alive? If a fetus is moved from its mother's womb to life-support systems, has it been born? But with marriage, the fuzziness in definitions is more intrusive than with death and birth.

Should couples who are separated but not divorced be counted as married? Should same-sex unions be counted as marriages? Should couples in historical data who were betrothed be counted as married prior to the wedding ceremonies? Legal definitions of marriage are poorly suited in many respects to the needs of demographers. On the other hand, having a different definition for every different purpose is an invitation to confusion, and there is no consensus on how far the legal definitions should be broadened in demographic usage.

Nuptiality is also complicated because marriage and divorce rates are volatile. We often pretend that demographic rates are unchanging when we devise methods for calculating measures from period data. Rates of marriage formation and dissolution change rapidly. In the past their changes were sensitive regulators of population growth.

The nature of marriage is especially in flux in recent times. Within a few decades in countries like Sweden and Austria cohabitations went from being rarities to being something like a new norm. Within two generations in the United States, divorce and remarriage burgeoned and anthropologists began to write about "serial polygamy"—having several spouses, one after the other, rather than all at the same time. Transformations in the timing and role of marriage have been spreading throughout the newly developed countries of East and Southeast Asia. Demographers are continually compelled to come to grips with social change.

There are also technical reasons that nuptiality in general is harder to quantify than, say, mortality. A person can have several events of marriage formation and dissolution along his or her lifeline, and these events divide the lifeline into successive episodes of being married and being not-married whose duration generally matters to the rates of transition. No person has successive episodes of being dead and being alive. Duration of life is the same as age, whereas duration of marriage is different from age for either partner. There are multiple ways of exiting from the state of marriage, through being divorced, through being widowed, or through dying.

In the face of all this complexity, we focus first and foremost in the next sections on the one eminently tractable part of the subject, the process of entry into first marriage.

9.2 First Marriage by Analogy

First marriage is the transition from being never-married to being ever-married, and it can happen at most once. We use the word "single" in this chapter to mean "never-married". In our terminology, those previously married are either widowed, divorced, or married, but not single again. Being single in this sense is a state that, once left, can never be regained. In this respect, first marriage is like death. An analogy can be drawn between exiting out of singlehood and exiting out of life itself. This analogy gives us demographic measures for first marriage that are close counterparts of familiar lifetable measures.

There is a legend that marriages in medieval and Renaissance Florence were actually recorded in death registers, "Books of the Dead", and the registers were kept beside records of baptisms in the Baptistery, the glorious building with the "Doors of Paradise" sculpted by Lorenzo Ghiberti next to the Duomo, the cathedral in Florence. Developing our analogy between first-marrying and dying means spelling out what about marriage corresponds to what columns of the lifetable. All members of a cohort start out single. In this section we restrict attention to members who remain alive

Table 9.1   First marriages for the U.S. cohort of 1930

Age x	Number Single in Cohort	Cohort First Marriages
0	661	0
10	661	280
20	381	315
30	66	29
40	37	3
50	34	0
60	34	0

Source: Female respondents to the U.S. Current Population Survey (1990).

through all ages of interest—for example, to cohort members still alive and able to respond to a survey taken when they are in late middle age. For more advanced analysis, marrying and dying can be treated as competing risks with the techniques presented in Chapter 8.

Table 9.1 shows numbers still single by age for those members of the cohort of U.S. women born in 1930 who were alive in 1990 and responded to the Marriage and Family Supplement of the Current Population Survey (CPS). There were 661 such respondents. These women grew up in the Great Depression and had their first marriages in the late 1940s and 1950s, creating a marriage boom accompanying the Baby Boom.

From the number of cohort members single at age x we can find the proportion single at age x by dividing by the initial cohort size 661. This step is like choosing a radix of 1 for a cohort lifetable. The proportion still single at age x in our marriage table then corresponds to the proportion still alive at age x in our lifetable, ℓ_x. The proportion marrying between ages x and $x + n$, that is, the proportion exiting the single state, corresponds to $_n d_x$, the proportion exiting life between ages x and $x + n$. The probability of marrying in the next n years for those still single at age x is like $_n q_x$.

Although the proportion still single at age x is analogous to ℓ_x in its definition, the typical shape of such a curve is different from familiar ℓ_x curves. The proportion single as a function of x is entirely flat during ages of infancy and childhood. It drops rapidly during prime ages of marriage in the late teens and twenties, and flattens out at older ages. The ℓ_x curve typically drops during infancy, flattens through the teens and twenties, and drops again in old age. A graph of cohort first marriages by age typically has a single hump in the twenties, whereas the $_nd_x$ column of the lifetable typically has two humps, one in infancy and one in old age.

There is another notable difference between first-marriage tables and lifetables, between singleness and survivorship. Not everyone eventually marries, whereas everyone does eventually die. When we calculate a measure of timing, like a cohort's mean age at first marriage, the only members who contribute are those who do marry. How early or late in life marriages occur among those who do marry is only part of the story. How many never marry at all is the other part. We distinguish the timing of marriage from its level of universality. For cohorts, the mean age at first marriage among those ever-marrying is the most common measure of timing, and the proportion ever-marrying is the most common measure of universality.

Just as there are model lifetables, there are model schedules for first marriage. Most models take the proportion ever-marrying as one of the parameters and then have one or more parameters for marriage timing which jointly determine the mean age at first marriage. A 1972 model by Ansley Coale and Donald McNeil has three parameters, proportion ever-marrying, minimum age at marriage, and a slope parameter governing the pace of marriage in its prime years. Another 1972 model with three parameters by Gudmund Hernes is described in Section 9.5.

Mean age at first marriage and proportions ever-marrying are mathematically separate measures. But around the world and over history they have been closely associated with each other. In 1965 the English demographer John Hajnal brought a striking demographic contrast to the attention of social scientists. His paper was called "The European Marriage Pattern in Perspective". It is reprinted in Glass and Eversley (1965). Hajnal pointed out that late ages at marriage and high proportions never marrying were found together throughout most of northwestern Europe before the twentieth century. This pattern, has come to be called the "European Marriage Pattern", although it only applies to a part of Europe (the northwestern part) and only to part of European history. It contrasts dramatically with early marriage and nearly negligible proportions never-marrying throughout most of Asia and Africa and in the southern and eastern portions of

Europe up to recent times. Hajnal contrasted 17% never-marrying among Belgian women of 1900 to 1% never-marrying among Bulgarian women in 1900, and he contrasted mean ages at marriage for women of 28.8 in Venice around 1700 to 21.3 years in Serbia around 1900. (Hajnal's mean ages were for all marriages, but similar contrasts in mean ages of first marriages are not hard to find.) Many exceptions to Hajnal's generalization have been pointed out since 1965. Nonetheless, his broad-brush picture, based on two measures studied in the next section, remains a central element of our understanding of what was special about the part of the world in which the industrial and scientific revolutions first took place.

9.3 The *SMAFM*

The letters *SMAFM* are an acronym for the "Singulate Mean Age at First Marriage". This measure is also less properly called the *SMAM*, omitting the letter for the adjective "first" but still referring to first marriages. A cohort's mean age at first marriage is a straightforward concept. When we lack cohort data, the *SMAFM* offers a substitute that can be calculated from period data of a kind frequently available from censuses. John Hajnal (1953) introduced the approach a decade before his work on European marriage patterns.

Hajnal's *SMAFM* is a very popular measure. The only pieces of information required are proportions never-married in each of the age groups in the period population. The word "singulate" in the name has nothing to do with "single" people. "Singulate" is a technical term from statistics. Hajnal's measure has a special form which makes it usable in principle with "singular" statistical distributions. Singular distributions are infinitely jagged on small scales, like the fractal curves popularized by Benoit Mandelbrot, found in books on chaos theory and bandied about by characters in the movie *Jurassic Park*. The distributions at use in demography are not singular, but the name from statistics has stuck.

The *SMAFM* provides a tool for inferring mean age at first marriage when we do not have data on ages *at* marriage but only data on proportions married *by* certain ages. Censuses often do not supply marital histories or ages at marriages but do break the population down by age and marital status. Such a tabulation is ideal for calculating the *SMAFM*.

Like any calculation of a cohort measure from period data, the *SMAFM* requires us to pretend that age-specific values prevailing in a period persist unchanged into the future. Unlike the period measures in Chapter 6, in this setting the values that are to remain unchanged are not age-specific rates but proportions of never-married individuals in age groups. Six assumptions are involved. The first three are general prerequisites for singulate means:

1. Ages are never negative numbers.
2. Being ever-married is a state which, once attained, is never lost.
3. Only the subset of individuals who do eventually attain the state (like the every-marrying subset of the population) are included in the calculation.

The singulate mean is a form of calculation that can be used with processes other than first marriage if these three conditions are met. We can calculate a singulate mean age of college graduation (once a graduate, always a graduate) so long as we restrict ourselves to the subset of those who do eventually graduate. But we cannot calculate a singulate mean bank balance. Sadly, bank balances can be negative as well as positive. Nor can we calculate a singulate mean age over all marriages. Being married, as opposed to being ever-married, is a state which once attained can all too easily be lost.

For practical applications, the *SMAFM* depends on three further assumptions:

4. Proportions married by age have not been changing markedly.
5. Those reported as married, widowed, or divorced are in fact the ever-married.
6. At young adult ages, death rates are independent of marital status.

None of these assumptions is ever strictly true. Proportions married can change quickly. Especially in days gone by, some of the divorced and widowed may report themselves as single and some of the never-married with children born out of wedlock may report themselves as widowed or divorced. Mortality rates do vary by marital status, a bit even among young adults, depleting the population of never-married persons more than the population of the ever-married. Because its assumptions are not strictly met, the *SMAFM* is an imperfect measure, but a helpful one.

Table 9.2   Marital breakdowns for Egypt in 1986

Age x	Total Egyptian Women	Ever-Married Women	PEM_x	$_nS_x$	$(n)(_nS_x)$
0	4,533,002	0	0.000	1.000	5.000
5	3,469,468	0	0.000	1.000	5.000
10	2,153,358	0	0.000	1.000	5.000
15	1,764,959	366,014	0.207	0.785	3.923
20	1,889,617	1,145,262	0.606	0.371	1.853
25	1,824,119	1,573,377	0.863	0.104	0.521
30	1,484,115	1,376,066	0.927	0.037	0.185
35	1,486,419	1,431,268	*0.963	0.000	0.000
40	1,070,386	1,025,612	0.958		
45	1,011,132	983,191	0.972		
SMAFM					21.482

Source: United Nations Demographic Yearbook (1990:894–895).

We illustrate the calculation of the *SMAFM* with an example from Egypt in Table 9.2. Two columns report total women and ever-married women in the census of September 1986. We divide the latter by the former to obtain the next column, the proportion ever-married PEM_x in the age group from x to $x + n$. For the next step in the calculation, we look down the column for PEM_x until we reach the largest value before the first decrease if any. This value is called PEM_{ult}, an estimate of the proportion ultimately marrying. In Table 9.2, $PEM_{ult} = 0.963$, marked with a star and found in the row for $x = 35$. The first decrease crops up with the next value, 0.958. Even though there is an increase afterward, to 0.972, it has no bearing on PEM_{ult}, which is determined by the position of the first decrease. If no decrease occurs, the last value of PEM_x in the table supplies PEM_{ult}.

For the next column, we calculate $_nS_x = 1 - PEM_x/PEM_{ult}$, but only for rows up to the star. Our $_nS_x$ is an estimate of the proportion still single out of those who do ultimately marry within the age group from x to $x + n$. For the last column, we multiply $_nS_x$ by n, and the sum of these products is the *SMAFM*.

The selection of PEM_{ult} is the heart of the calculation. The rule given here is an extension of Hajnal's original procedure. If the PEM_x values had come from cohort rather than period data, then PEM_x would be increasing across all ages and PEM_{ult} would be the last value in the table. However, because we are using period data, the observed proportion ever-married can drop or bounce around as we look over older age groups. Although Hajnal's measure is designed on the basis of an assumption that marriage rates have not been changing, marriage rates do in fact change. The older the ages of people, the more time has generally gone by between their first marriages and the date of a census and the more opportunity there has been for rates to change. At older ages differences in death rates between married and single people also alter proportions before they are observed. Proportions going down as ages go up give out a signal of dubious data. With our choice of PEM_{ult}, we exclude suspect rows from our measure.

In calculating the *SMAFM*, it is imperative to start at age 0. Even though there are no marriages before age 15 in these data, the three age groups below age 15 contribute fully 15 years out of the total sum of around 21.5. If they are omitted, absurd singulate mean ages like 6 or 7 years show up.

The concept behind the *SMAFM* is a cohort concept, even though the estimate is generally based on period data. Singulate Mean Ages at First Marriage for men and women indicate when in the lives of men and women their first marriages occur. These means can be very different from the average ages of grooms and brides marrying for the first time in a population in a given year. The latter statistic depends heavily on the age structure of the population. Even if only a small proportion of women marry at age 15, if a population consists mostly of 15-year-olds, the average age of brides will be close to 15.

* 9.4 The Singulate Mean Formula

The formula for the Singulate Mean exemplifies a general relationship between ways of computing means which is based on a geometric identity. Figure 9.1 is a plot of the $_nS_x$ values for the example in Table 9.2, our estimate of the average proportion still single among those women age x to $x + n$ who do eventually marry. The left side and top of each bar are drawn with heavy lines to remind us that the value $_nS_x$ at the top is labeled by the age x on the left. (The label x on the plot is for $x = 15$.) The area of each

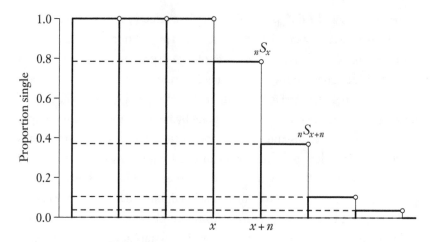

Figure 9.1   The Singulate Mean as an area

bar is the base n times the height $_nS_x$. Adding up the areas of these vertical bars gives the total area under the curve, which is the singulate mean.

We can sum up areas in another fashion, cutting the total area up into the horizontal bands between the dashed lines. Consider the band on the diagram whose top is labeled $_nS_x$ and whose bottom is labeled $_nS_{x+n}$. The length of the base is $x+n$ and the height is $_nS_x - _nS_{x+n}$. Since the whole set of bands cover the same area as the whole set of bars, the sum of the areas of the bands equals the sum of the areas of the bars, the singulate mean:

$$\sum(x + n)(_nS_x - _nS_{x+n}) = \sum(n)(_nS_x)$$

Examine the left-hand side. In each term, the drop in S values measures the increase in proportions married between the age group x to $x+n$ and the age group $x+n$ to $x+2n$, due to women marrying over these ages. The factor $x+n$ is the mid-point age between the two age groups. So we are multiplying the mid-point age by an estimate of proportions marrying around this age. The sum is an estimate of the ordinary mean age at which marriages are taking place. We have thus established an equivalence between a singulate mean age and an ordinary mean age.

Our geometric derivation can be mirrored by an algebraic one. On the left-hand side, the first term is $(n)(_nS_0) - (n)(_nS_n)$, the term for $x = 0$. The next term is $(2n)(_nS_n) - (2n)(_nS_{2n})$ for $x = n$. Minus n plus $2n$ is n itself, so we have n copies of $_nS_n$ just as we have n copies of $_nS_0$. Every pair of terms brings similar cancellation. We have minus $2n$ plus $3n$, minus $3n$ plus $4n$, and so forth, till the S values reach zero and there is nothing more to cancel. We end up as promised with the left-hand side equal to the right-hand side

With true cohort data, it would be possible to express the average proportion $_nS_x$ over the age group x to $x + n$ in terms of proportions s_x still single (never-married) at exact age x. We have $_nS_x \approx (s_x + s_{x+n})/2$. We could draw a version of Figure 9.1 with straight lines between the s_x values, forming a continuous curve in place of a bar graph. Each $_nS_x$ value would be the area of a trapezoid with base n, and we could also cut the area into horizontal trapezoidal bands. The same equivalence holds between singulate means (adding bars) and ordinary means (adding bands), whether we work with averages $_nS_x$ or exact-age values s_x.

We use the *SMAFM* in place of the ordinary mean when our data come in the form of information about vertical bars and we do not have direct information about horizontal bands. Censuses tell us about proportions by marital status observed between the vertical age-group boundaries. When we do have information about the flow of people into marriage, we can dispense with the *SMAFM* and go back to ordinary means.

Figure 9.1 shows the reasons for the requirements on quantities permitting singulate means. A quantity needs to be non-negative, like an age, because our horizontal bands need to have left-hand edges at $x = 0$. A quantity needs to refer to a state which, once attained, is never lost, because each band needs one and only one right-hand edge. Bars getting higher on the right would leave an isolated piece of area that would not be counted in the band. Attention is restricted to individuals who do ultimately attain the state, because the curve needs to meet the bottom edge to give a boundary on all sides.

The analogy between life as a single person and life itself developed in Section 9.2 reminds us that $_nS_x$ is like our lifetable $_nL_x/n$ and s_x like ℓ_x with a radix of 1. Life expectancy e_0, summing up $(n)(_nL_x)/(n)$, is a singulate mean and is equivalent to an ordinary cohort mean age at death $\sum(x + _na_x)(_nd_x)$, where for exact work $_na_x$ takes the place of $n/2$. The *SMAFM* is an estimate of life expectancy for single life.

Mathematically, our geometric argument corresponds to the procedure in calculus called "integration by parts". The formula for integration by parts for two functions $F(x)$ and $G(x)$ is

$$\int_a^b F(x)\frac{dG}{dx}\,dx = F(b)G(b) - F(a)G(a) - \int_a^b G(x)\frac{dF}{dx}\,dx$$

(We assume F and G have well-defined derivatives except at a finite number of steps.) We may set $F(x) = s_x$ and $G(x) = x$, $a = 0$, and $b = \infty$, so that $G(a) = 0$ and $F(b) = 0$ and the formula tells us that $\int s_x\,dx = \int x\frac{-ds_x}{dx}\,dx$. Similarly, with $F(x) = \ell_x$ and $G(x) = x$, we have the identity $e_0 = \int \ell_x\,dx = \int x\, h_x\,\ell_x\,dx$.

9.5 Marity

In traditional marriage vows, bride and groom commit to a union "till death do us part". But for many first marriage is the first of a number of transitions in marital status, not all mediated by death of husband or wife. In the United States in the late twentieth century, something like half of all first marriages ended in divorce. A chain of transitions for an individual starting with first marriage may include first divorce, second marriage, sometimes second divorce, sometimes widowhood, and further transitions until the final absorbing state of death. Methods for studying such chains of transition can be treated somewhat briefly in this chapter, because they have already been introduced for other purposes in earlier chapters of this volume.

Anthropologist and demographer Gene Hammel coined the word "marity" by analogy to parity for the study of successive marriages:

> Marity is the number of marriages into which an individual has entered.

With the methods of Section 4.4, we can define "Marity Progression Ratios", or *MPR*'s. In principle, a table of counts of men or women by completed marity allows their computation. If, as in Chapter 4, $w(j)$ is the count at marity j, then $MPR(j)$ is the sum of $w(i)$ from $i = j + 1$ onward, divided by the sum of $w(i)$ from $i = j$ onward. In practice, cohort data are rarely at hand. Sometimes cross-sectional data include proportions by age in second marriages and higher-order marriages. In such cases, the method of singulate means can be applied to each such table, generating in the process values for proportion ultimately first married (PEM_{ult}) and its generalizations to proportion ultimately second-married—say, $PEM_{ult}(2)$—and so forth. Then $MPR(0) = PEM_{ult}(1)/1$ and $MPR(1) = PEM_{ult}(2)/PEM_{ult}(1)$, and so on. Such estimates may be the only feasible ones, but they must always be treated with caution, because sharp trends in rates of divorce and remarriage along with mortality at older adult ages violate the assumptions on which singulate mean calculations are based.

The most common data for examining marity are marital histories from sample surveys, sometimes compiled from successive waves of a longitudinal survey but often gathered retrospectively in a cross-sectional survey by asking respondents to recall their previous marriages, when they began, and, if they ended, when and how they ended. Such histories may include more states, including cohabitation, consensual union, and separation. Such marital status histories are ideal for applying the methods of multi-state or increment-decrement lifetables treated in Section 5.6. States for the multi-state analysis are labeled by marity—for example, $M1$ for first marriage, $D1$ for divorce from first marriage, $W1$ for widowhood from first marriage, and so on. Some system of labels for cohabitation CH, consensual union CU, and other states may also be devised. From the multi-state transition matrices $A(1)$, $A(2)$, and so on, MPR's and other interesting statistics can be computed.

A limitation of the multi-state approach in its simple form is the observed dependence of rates of divorce on duration of marriage rather than or in addition to age, and of rates of remarriage on duration of divorce. More sophisticated multi-state analysis draws on age-and-stage structured models developed by biologists and biodemographers for understanding the demography of plants and animals in the wild. Another preferred approach is demographic microsimulation, or "agent-based modeling", in which individual life histories are simulated with transitions governed by schedules of rates that may be made to depend on many characteristics of the individual and the population.

Patterns of behavior and priorities with respect to marriage and family formation are shaped by an individual's parents and family of origin and by the attitudes of friends, schoolmates, church members, and relatives early in life. Such patterns tend to run in cohorts, whose members also encounter public events and social trends at the same stages of their lives. Advanced treatments of fertility and family like Kohler (2001) with dynamic models incorporate pathways of influence from peers and feedback from the adoption of new ideas and practices by others. Although a cohort perspective is appropriate, it poses challenges for empirical work, because questions of current interest are being debated while the life experience of cohorts is still unfolding. For this reason, models for forecasting and filling in complete cohort histories from early outcomes play a critical role in the study of marity.

Along with the Coale–McNeil marriage model mentioned in Section 9.2, the 1972 model of Gudmund Hernes may be used for completing cohort histories of marriage and divorce, as in Goldstein and Kenney (2001). Hernes put forward a variation on the logistic model for population growth featured in Section 1.6. Time is measured as duration t from some starting age like 15. The proportion of a cohort ever-married by duration t plays the role of population $K(t)$. However, observed time t is expressed in terms of an artificial time-like coordinate u by setting $t = -(1/\gamma) \log(1 - u)$, where γ is a positive scaling parameter. As a function of u, the proportion ever-married obeys a logistic model. In the notation of Chapter 1, with $c = 1$, we have $K(t(u)) = 1/(1 + f \exp(-g\, u))$. Substituting $u = 1 - \exp(-\gamma\, t)$ along with $a = \exp(-g)$, $b = \exp(-\gamma)$, and $k = \exp(g)/f$, we obtain the model in terms of Hernes' parameters a, b, and k:

$$K(t) = 1/(1 + 1/(k\, a^{(b^t)}))$$

In the Hernes model, the slope of $K(t)$ is proportional to a three-way product $K(t)$ times $1 - K(t)$ times b^t. At early marriageable ages, when $1 - K(t)$ is close to 1, the slope of $K(t)$ is nearly proportional to $K(t)$ itself. More couples already married in a cohort serve as encouragement to other couples to enter into marriage. At later ages, as the pool of the never-married decreases, the factor $1 - K(t)$ drives down the slope. The rescaling of time, expressed in the factor b^t, also slows the occurrence of new marriages as time goes on. Those remaining in the pool of the never-married may be less desirable as partners or they may be or become less inclined toward marriage. The ultimate proportion married settles out at $k/(1 + k)$.

As usual, working forward from parameter values to predictions is straightforward. For example, suppose $a = 0.001352$, $b = 0.840398$, and $k = 14.625$, values roughly appropriate for the U.S. cohort of women born between 1945 and 1950. What is the predicted proportion married by age 20, that is, at duration $t = 5$? We have $b^5 = 0.419$ for the slowing factor, $a^{0.419} = 0.0627$, and a proportion married equal to

$$1/(1 + 1/(14.625 * 0.0627)) = 0.478,$$

nearly 50%, close to the observed value. For the later cohort born between 1960 and 1965, the observed proportion married by age 20 is known to have dropped below one-third.

Working backward from observations to estimates in the Hernes model is less straightforward. Given a guess at the ultimate proportion marrying and thus for the parameter k, it is possible to transform the model formula into an equation for a straight line and estimate the other parameters by linear regression as with models featured in other chapters. However, the ultimate proportion marrying is often the main unknown of interest, and estimation with the more advanced statistical technique of maximum likelihood estimation is preferred.

HIGHLIGHTS OF CHAPTER 9

- Complexities of marriage.
- The European Marriage Pattern
- The Singulate Mean Age at First Marriage
- Marity
- The Hernes marriage model

KEY FORMULAS

$$SMAFM = \sum(n)\left(1 - \frac{PEM(x)}{PEM_{\text{ult}}}\right)$$

$$\int_a^b F(x)\frac{dG}{dx}\,dx = F(b)G(b) - F(a)G(a) - \int_a^b G(x)\frac{dF}{dx}\,dx$$

Hernes $K(t) = 1/(1 + 1/(k\, a^{(b^t)}))$

FURTHER READING

The wider historical role of marriage and family structure is interpreted in Laslett (1977), especially Chapter 1. For methods, the collection edited by Bongaarts et al. (1987) remains a basic source. For trends in marity and marital timing and marriage models, see Goldstein and Kenney (2001).

EXERCISES FOR CHAPTER 9

1. Estimate the *SMAFM* from data on U.S. women in 1990 shown in Table 9.3.

2. Calculate the nearest quantities you can to a singulate mean age at first divorce and a singulate mean age at remarriage from data in Table 9.3. Explain any assumptions beyond the usual ones that would have to hold for either or both of these estimates to make demographic sense.

* 3. Find values of proportions s_x ever-married by exact age x among those ever-marrying which would be consistent with the age-group-wide proportions $_nS_x$ in Table 9.2. Draw a counterpart of Figure 9.1 with s_x plotted against x containing trapezoids in place of rectangular bars and bands. Demonstrate the identity stating that $\sum(x + n/2)(s_{x+n} - s_x)$ equals $\sum(n)(s_x)$.

* 4. The approach using integration by parts which justifies the singulate mean formula can also be applied to the measure called disparity introduced in Chapter 3. Write $F(x) = H(x)$ and $G(x) = \ell_x e_x$, where $H(x)$ is the cumulative hazard function. Show that $\int \ell_x \log(1/\ell_x)\, dx$ equals $\int e_x d_x\, dx$ when d_x is minus the slope of ℓ_x, so long as a particular product vanishes as x goes to infinity. What product has to vanish in order for this derivation to be correct?

* 5. Consider a Hernes marriage model with parameter values $k = 7.772$, $a = 0.002644$, and $b = 0.871$, roughly appropriate for the cohort of U.S. women born between 1960 and 1965. Predict the proportions married by ages 20, 30, 40, and 50. What is the ultimate proportion ever-marrying implied by these parameter values? What is the implied slope of the proportion ever-married as a function of duration at age 20 and age 40?

Table 9.3   Marital status proportions for U.S. women 1990

x	A Ever-Married	B Divorced	C Remarried
15	0.189	0.00	0.00
20	0.625	0.13	0.38
25	0.872	0.19	0.52
30	0.931	0.28	0.60
35	0.955	0.34	0.65
40	0.958	0.36	0.67
45	0.959	0.35	0.66
50	0.958	0.30	0.63

Source: U.S. Census Bureau (1992) "Marriage, Divorce, and Remarriage in the 1990s", Report P23-180. (Age 15 imputed.)

Notes:

   Column A: Proportion ever-married.

   Column B: Proportion of ever-married women divorced after first marriage.

   Column C: Proportion of all divorced women remarried after divorce.

10

Stable Age Structures

10.1 Age Pyramids

We turn now to the study of age structure. There is a very full and satisfactory theory which accounts for the relative numbers of young and old men and women in a population. The basic idea is to obtain formulas for how a population will be distributed by age if the population has been closed to migration and if its birth and death rates have been unchanging for a long time. The actual age distribution of the population naturally differs from this theoretical age distribution. Each of the deviations is explained by reference to particular events of migration and particular changes in rates in the prior history of the population. Thus the age distribution of each population has *general* features which it shares with populations with the same vital rates and *special* features which are derived from its own particular history.

Graphical diagrams of age structure are called "age pyramids" because their shapes may resemble Egyptian or Mayan pyramids. An age pyramid is made up of a pair of bar graphs, one for men and one for women, turned on their sides and joined. The vertical axis corresponds to age. For each age group, the bar coming off the axis to the right represents the number of women in that age group, the bar to the left the number of men. The young are toward the bottom, the elderly toward the top. The open-ended age group at the very top is sometimes drawn with a triangle instead of bars. Demographers tend to use the words "age pyramid", "age distri-

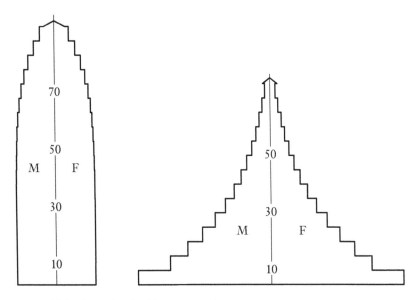

Figure 10.1   Examples of stable age pyramids

bution", and "age structure" interchangeably. The age pyramid represents the distribution of the population by age and sex.

Figure 10.1 shows two examples of the idealized pyramids that occur in closed populations with unchanging vital rates. On the left, tall and slender, is a case for a long-lived population with near zero growth. On the right, quite pyramidal in shape, is a case for a population with heavy mortality and rapid growth. Like these two, any population produced by age-specific rates of fertility and mortality constant over a long period of time is called a *stable population*. Its age pyramid is determined uniquely by its lifetable and its long-term growth rate. The proportions in each age group in a stable population do not change over time. The numbers in each age group may, however, change over time, for the population may be growing or declining in size, depending on what the growth rate happens to be.

In contrast to idealized stable age pyramids, Figure 10.2 shows a pair of observed age pyramids from Keyfitz and Flieger (1968). On the left, France in 1960 shares its overall shape with our low-growth stable case but notches among 20 and 40 years olds disclose a legacy from low births during World Wars I and II. On the right, Mauritius in 1963 shares its overall shape with our high-growth stable case, but indentations at working ages

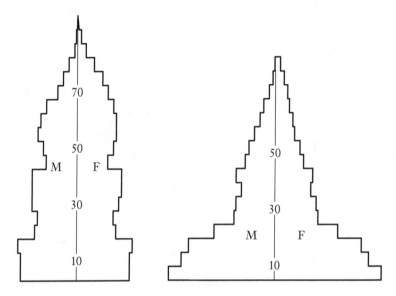

Figure 10.2   Examples of observed age pyramids

hint at changes back around 1945 from increasing growth probably due to gains against infant mortality, and perhaps also hint at out-migration. Stable theory captures the general features well, but each nation's own history of changing rates and movements across borders can be discerned from observable differences from stable shapes.

As mentioned in Chapter 2, demographers are using the word "stable" in a technical sense, distinguishing it from the word "stationary". In a *stable* population, rates stay the same but the population size may change. In a *stationary* population, both rates and population size remain the same. The growth rate is zero. A stationary population is a special case of a stable population which satisfies the extra condition of having "ZPG", zero population growth.

A small point deserves mention. We can imagine complicated cases in which age-specific rates are changing in ways that cancel each other out so that population size remains the same. Sometimes such a population is called stationary, but from here on we reserve the word stationary for cases with unchanging rates as well as unchanging size.

The mathematical analysis of stable age pyramids is called "Stable Population Theory". It is an elegant theory which goes back more than 250 years to the work of Leonhard Euler in 1760, and was extensively developed by Alfred Lotka in the early 1900s and in the last half-century by Nathan Keyfitz and Ansley Coale.

10.2 Stationary Equivalent Populations

Earlier chapters have given several previews of the formulas for stable populations and the ideas surrounding them which we develop in detail in the next sections. The starred Section 5.7 on population renewal pointed out that unchanging age-specific rates along with exponentially growing births imply the equation $k(x, t) = B(t)(\ell_x/\ell_0)e^{-Rx}$. Here, $k(x, t)$ is the density of individuals age x at time t, the height of the Lexis surface introduced in Chapter 2. When cohort survivorship ℓ_x is unchanging, those individuals age x at time t are the survivors $B(t - x)\ell_x/\ell_0$ of the $B(t - x)$ babies born at time $t - x$. When it is also true that births are growing exponentially at rate R, then $B(t - x) = B(0) \exp(R(t - x)) = B(t) \exp(-Rx)$. We shall see in Section 10.3 that unchanging rates do imply exponentially growing births in the long term, so the formula from Section 5.7 is the one we want for a stable population with continuous age in continuous time.

The formula for a stable population with age groups of width n followed across n-year-long steps of time turns out to be $_nK_x(t) = B(t)(_nL_x/\ell_0) \exp(-Rx)$, very like the expression in continuous time with big "L" in place of little "ℓ". The growth rate R in the formula turns out to be a special growth rate which will be written with a small letter "r". Deriving these formulas from Leslie matrix formulas takes a bit of work in the starred Section 10.6. A good starting point is the special case of a stationary population with $R = 0$ and births $B(t)$ equal to an unchanging count B. Then the same reasoning leading from Figure 5.2 to our formula for the subdiagonal elements of a Leslie matrix tells us immediately that, with $R = 0$,

$$_nK_x = B \,_nL_x/\ell_0$$

Total population size for a stationary population is obtained by adding up the sizes of the age groups. Adding up the big-L values and dividing by the radix gives us life expectancy e_0, so the total size is $B \, e_0$. We can divide the size of each age group by the total size to find the proportion in the age group. We avoid having too many letters for too many different quantities by writing $_\infty K_0$ for total size, the whole population from ages zero to infinity. Then the Crude Birth Rate b is $B/(_\infty K_0)$, and the proportion aged x to $x + n$ in a stationary population is

$$\frac{_nK_x}{_\infty K_0} = b \, \frac{_nL_x}{\ell_0}$$

Alternatively, when we divide our formula for counts $_nK_x$ by the formula for total size $B \, e_0$, we come up with proportions equal to $(1/e_0)(_nL_x)/(\ell_0)$. But these two formulas for proportions are the same, thanks to the Stationary Population Identity from Chapter 2, which tells us that $R = 0$ implies $b = 1/e_0$.

Going back to counts, our formula $_nK_x = B \, _nL_x/\ell_0$ looks simple enough, but there is something subtle hidden in it. The units on the left-hand side are people. The units on the right hand side, as written, are people times person-years divided by people, or person-years overall. In other words, the units do not agree. In physics, the first task with any formula is to check the units. When units disagree, it is a disaster.

Here, the disagreement in units is not a disaster but a clue. A correspondence is being established between people and person-years. The big-L column of a lifetable sometimes carries the label "stationary population" instead of or along with the label "person-years lived". (We can choose the radix ℓ_0 equal to B, so that only $_nL_x$ remains on the right-hand side of the stationary formula.) The correspondence springs from the concept of a synthetic cohort.

Chapter 6 started with a period population and ended up with a synthetic cohort, relying along the way on a Game of Pretend. We can try going in the opposite direction, starting with a synthetic cohort and trying to end up with a population in a period. But when we do so, we do not end up with our original period population. Instead, we end up with a stationary population, which shares the same lifetable as our period population but usually has very different age-group counts. The population derived from a synthetic cohort is called a "stationary equivalent population". It is a population equivalent to a cohort.

The stationary equivalent population is constructed by making each year in the life of each member of the cohort match up with a unique member of the population. One cohort person-year is associated with one population person, forcing units to agree. (Interpreting the count of births B in the stationary formula as a density of births *per year* is a formal way of setting up this association.) The size of the cohort is much smaller than the size of the population. On average, each cohort member lives for e_0 years, so a cohort of size ℓ_0 corresponds to a stationary equivalent population of size $\ell_0 e_0$.

This correspondence of ours may be made more vivid by an extended metaphor or mental picture, a little like the "metaphysical conceits" popular among poets of the 1600s like John Donne. In our conceit, we imagine a film director making a monumental epic film portraying the experiences of a selected group of people over the course of a single year, the Millenial Year A.D. 2000, or "Y2K". The director hires a cast of actors from the newborn babies in a hospital and guarantees them life-long employment in the movie. When they are infants, they play the infant roles. Each plays the part of one character for 1 whole year. Then each gets a new role for the next year. As 1-year-olds, they perform the scenes involving experiences of 1-year-olds during Y2K; as 10-year-olds, the experiences of 10-year-olds during Y2K.

The actors are so absorbed in their parts that they live or die at the rates experienced by their characters during Y2K. The actors' lifetable remains the period lifetable of Y2K, whatever happens in the world around them. It takes more than a century for our director and the cast of actors to finish the film. The parts of 80-year-olds are not being filmed until 2080, when Y2K has already become a distant legend for most of the living. Finally, in the twenty-second century, the film debuts, to wonder and acclaim.

The cast of actors is our synthetic cohort, and the characters whose parts they play compose our stationary equivalent population. A cast of a hundred can act out the stories of enough people to fill a small stadium, portraying the joys and sorrows of a single year.

Our metaphor owes much to William Shakespeare, who made his melancholy character Jacques into an impromptu demographer in *As You Like It* (Act II, Scene 7):

All the world's a stage,
And all the men and women merely players:
They have their exits and their entrances;
And one man in his time plays many parts,
His acts being seven ages. At first the infant,
Mewling and puking in the nurse's arms.
And then the whining school-boy, with his satchel,
And shining morning face, creeping like snail
Unwillingly to school . . .

The story goes on, with a lover, a soldier, a justice, and an aged character from comedy called the "lean and slippered pantaloon." Finally,

. . . Last scene of all,
That ends this strange eventful history,
Is second childishness and mere oblivion,
Sans teeth, sans eyes, sans taste, sans everything.

10.3 Consequences of Unchanging Rates

Stable populations are more general than stationary populations, because they may have any growth rate, whereas stationary populations have zero growth. To generalize our formulas, we need to study the effects of keeping age-specific fertility and mortality rates constant at levels for which births do not necessarily balance deaths. We continue to restrict our attention to closed populations either of men or of women. The consequences of unchanging rates can be seen by projecting a population forward over many steps using the Leslie matrices of Chapter 5.

The behavior of the growth rate R in the face of unchanging age-specific rates is illustrated in Figure 10.3. The lines come from projections using a Leslie matrix based on rates for Pakistani women in 2000 from the United Nations WPP (2003). For the solid line, the projection starts with the

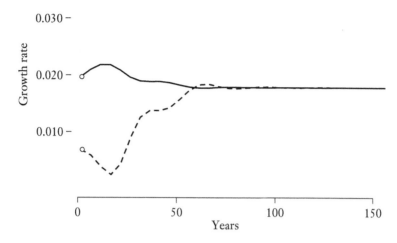

Figure 10.3 Projected growth rates over time

female population of Pakistan in 2000. For the dashed line, the projection starts instead with the female population of Russia in 2000.

The outstanding feature of Figure 10.3 is the flattening out of both lines as time goes by. The growth rates bounce around for a couple of generations, and then they settle down to nearly constant values. What is more, they differ at the start, but they settle down to the same constant value. Under the pressure of constant age-specific rates, the growth rates converge to fixed values, and those values are independent of the choice of the initial population.

In general, populations projected forward with the same constant age-specific rates may differ in their short-term growth rates, but they share the same constant long-term growth rate. This rate has its own symbol, the letter "r". Capital R stands for any growth rate. Little r stands for the special long-term growth rate produced by a long stretch of unchanging demographic rates.

Little r is often called "Lotka's r" after Alfred Lotka, a mathematical biologist working in the United States in the early twentieth century. Its official name is the "intrinsic rate of natural increase". It is "intrinsic" because it is built in to the fertility and mortality schedules, without regard to population numbers, and it is a rate of "natural increase" because it is defined for closed populations without regard to migration. One way to calculate r is to construct a Leslie matrix and project any starting population

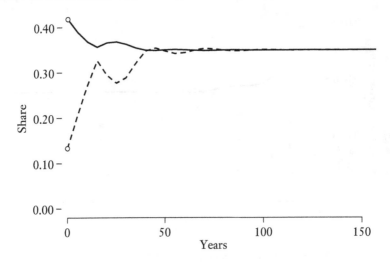

Figure 10.4 An age group share over time

forward until the growth rate settles down to its long-term value, r. There will be an extensive discussion of r later in the chapter, but its first definition is worth stating here:

> Lotka's intrinsic rate of natural increase r is the long-term growth rate of any closed population subject to unchanging age-specific rates of fertility and mortality.

The growth rate is not the only population characteristic which settles down to a fixed value when the population is subject for a long time to unchanging demographic rates. Figure 10.4 shows the share of the group of children under 15 in the population for the same projections as Figure 10.3. Like the growth rates, these proportions bounce around for a couple of generations and then settle down. Like the growth rates, the curves derived from different starting populations differ in the short term and come to coincide over the long term. The same would be true for the proportion in any age group. Under unchanging demographic rates, proportions in age groups stop changing and become independent of the starting population. The population becomes a stable population.

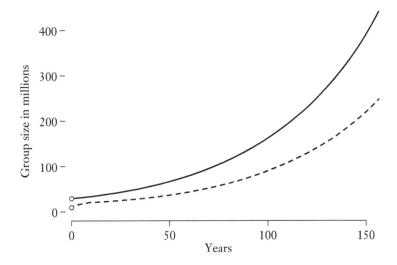

Figure 10.5   Age group size over time

A Stable Population is a population in which the proportions in age groups remain exactly constant over time.

We must always remember that it is the *proportions* in age groups that are constant over time in a stable population, not the *sizes* of age groups. Figure 10.5 shows the sizes of the group of 0- to 15-year-olds over time from the same projections with initial total population sizes equal to each other. The curves do not flatten out. They keep rising, settling into exponential growth. The curves based on the two different starting populations both take on the same shape, but they do not come to coincide. The sizes of the age groups at any time in the future do continue to depend on the starting population. They depend both on initial size and on the initial age distribution. Starting with a thousand young people about to embark on childbearing is bound to produce bigger future populations than starting with a thousand people over 35 with less childbearing in prospect.

The growth rate is the slope of the logarithm of population size over time. When it settles down to r, total population is growing exponentially like e^{rt}. When the proportions in age groups have also settled down to fixed values, each age group, being a fixed fraction of the whole, is also growing exponentially like e^{rt}. The flow of births, reflected in the size of the youngest age-group of new-borns, is growing in the same way.

> In a Stable Population, the size of every age group obeys the formula for exponential growth.

Growth rates and age-group proportions are independent of starting populations, but they are not independent of other inputs to projections. They do depend on the choice of rates that go into a Leslie matrix. It is easy to experiment with projections using Leslie matrices based on different lifetables and fertility schedules and obtain different values for r and for the age-group proportions.

Four main features are manifest in our figures:

A. Growth rates become fixed over time.
B. Growth rates become independent of starting populations.
C. Age pyramid proportions become fixed over time.
D. Age pyramid proportions become independent of starting populations.

These features are consequences of five assumptions which go into the projections:

1. Age-specific rates of giving birth and dying are unchanging over time.
2. The population is closed to migration.
3. The female population can be projected independent of the males.
4. Randomness can be ignored, letting population estimates represent mean or expected values.
5. Children are reckoned in continuous fractions of child.

The first four of these assumptions are familiar from our work with Leslie matrices. The last assumption, although implicit in what we have been doing, has not been spelled out before. Because we are dealing with expected values, the projected numbers of children from any one mother in the population are typically fractions rather than whole numbers. When we are interested in rates of growth or proportions in age groups, this fact is no handicap. But some kinds of statistics only make sense in terms of whole numbers. For example, if we want to project the mean number of sisters for girls under 15, we cannot do so with Leslie matrices in any straightforward way, because numbers of sisters depend on the distribution of family sizes among the possible whole-number family sizes, not simply on mean family size. Stable population theory can be applied to many aspects of family and kinship, but not to all of them.

10.4 Stable Age Pyramids

A stable population grows exactly exponentially, and its growth rate is Lotka's intrinsic rate of natural increase r. These properties have been inferred from observations of the consequences of unchanging rates in projections shown in the figures in Section 10.3. They have not been proved, although they can be proved. What we do prove in Section 10.6 is that the most obvious generalizations of the stationary population formulas are the right ones:

$$\text{Stable Counts: } {}_nK_x = B\frac{{}_nL_x}{\ell_0}e^{-rx}$$

$$\text{Stable Proportions: } \frac{{}_nK_x}{{}_\infty K_0} = b\frac{{}_nL_x}{\ell_0}e^{-rx}$$

The critical new component is the exponential factor e^{-rx}. The minus sign is essential. The formula for exponential growth as a function of time has a plus sign e^{+rt}. Our new formula, as a function of age, has a minus sign e^{-rx}. This sign makes sense. "Up in age" means "back in time" in the sense of "back in time of birth". In a growing population, with $r > 0$, the age pyramid has to shrink as we go up in age, because birth cohorts shrink as we go back in time. In declining populations, with $r < 0$, the effect is reversed. Older people come from larger cohorts from the past. The exponential factor makes for larger numbers of older people, but declining survival with age makes for smaller numbers and eventually wins out.

The three possibilities $r > 0$, $r = 0$, and $r < 0$ lead to three kinds of characteristic shapes for stable age pyramids. With positive growth the shape is broad at the bottom, like the pyramids at Giza or a well-shaped Christmas tree. There are lots of young people and fewer old people. Those born later are more numerous than those born earlier. With zero growth, in stationary populations, the shape is steep like a beehive. The lifetable $_nL_x$ values determine the slope. With negative growth, the base is narrow and the pyramid bulges out like a lightbulb. When an age pyramid is studied, the first step is to assign it to one of these three classes on the overall basis of its shape.

The neat expression for the total size of a stationary population $B\,e_0$ does not have a simple counterpart for stable populations. To find the total size, we have to add up all the age group sizes group by group. We can, however, see that the constant B is the right constant for all stable populations. For the youngest age group, with $x = 0$, e^{-rx} is 1. As we make n very small, like a day or an hour or some other small fraction of a year, we make $_nL_0/\ell_0$ close to n and $_nK_0$ close to Bn. Our age group of newborns comes out, as it should, to B births per year times the corresponding fraction n of a year.

The formula for the stable age pyramid has many applications throughout demography. A good example is the study of dependency ratios and the effects of population growth. In an economy, consumption by children and retired people depends on production by people in prime working ages. A dependency ratio measures the balance between these groups. A child dependency ratio is often defined with the number of children up to age 15 in the numerator and the number in the economically active ages between 15 and 65 in the denominator. A similar old-age dependency ratio has the number over 65 in the numerator along with the same denominator. Adding the two ratios gives an overall dependency ratio. Along with observed dependency ratios based on current counts, we can calculate ratios that would be found in a stable population with the intrinsic growth rate and lifetable for that population. Observed ratios are influenced by migration, prior history, and other special features. The systematic effect of growth is easier to see when we calculate ratios from the stable population formula.

Table 10.1 illustrates a stable population calculation for India. The intrinsic growth rate based on information for 2000 is $r = 0.006$, less than half the current observed growth rate. The first column shows the starting age x for each age group in the numerator of the dependency ratio. The second column shows the observed count for men and women in millions, and the third column the combined-sex lifetable $_nL_x$ values inferred from projection data from the United Nations WPP (2003, p. 493). We multiply

Table 10.1 Stable population data for India, youth, 2000

x	Observed Count (millions)	Lifetable $_5L_x$	Factor e^{-rx}	Product
0	120.878	4.649	1.000	4.649
5	116.296	4.549	0.970	4.414
10	109.984	4.497	0.942	4.235
	347.158			13.298

Table 10.2 Stable population data for India, adults, 2000

x	Observed Count (millions)	Lifetable $_5L_x$	x	Observed Count (millions)	Lifetable $_5L_x$
15	100.852	4.466	60	26.743	3.386
20	88.504	4.426	65	20.861	2.948
25	83.604	4.371	70	14.426	2.381
30	75.671	4.301	75	8.617	1.706
35	66.900	4.228	80	4.250	1.023
40	58.114	4.145	85	1.468	0.477
45	48.176	4.042	90	0.340	0.158
50	39.033	3.900	95	0.047	0.034
55	32.257	3.694	100	0.005	0.005

each $_nL_x$ value by the factor e^{-rx} in the next column to obtain counts. We do not know the factor B in the stable formula, but it will not matter. In ratios the same value of B occurs in numerator and denominator and cancels out. Adding up the counts in the fifth column, we obtain a numerator 13.298 million. A similar calculation with values from Table 10.2 produces a denominator of 33.042 million. The child dependency ratio for the stable population equals $13.298/33.042 = 0.402$, somewhat below the ratio in the observed population $347.158/619.584 = 0.560$.

Dependency ratios for stable populations are revealing because we can compare what we would see with different growth rates. Had India had an intrinsic growth rate equal to its current R of 0.015, with $r = 0.015$ in our formula, we should find a child dependency ratio of $12.740/24.263 = 0.525$, close to the observed ratio. Had India reached sustained zero population growth, with $r = 0$, we should find $13.695/40.959 = 0.334$.

Old-age dependency ratios for stable populations with different choices of r can also be calculated from Table 10.2. They are higher for $r = 0$ and $r = 0.006$ than for $r = 0.015$. Under the current Indian lifetable, it turns out that the reduction in child dependents that accompanies lower growth is nearly balanced by an increase in older-age dependents. The overall dependency ratio is 0.548 with r equal to zero, 0.574 with $r = 0.006$, and 0.648 with $r = 0.015$. By accident, the overall dependency ratio with the current intrinsic rate of $r = 0.006$ is very close to the observed overall dependency ratio of 0.641, although the stable age pyramid is not close to the observed age pyramid, since India's fertility rates have been changing and declining over recent decades.

Economists call these kinds of calculations with stable age pyramids "comparative statics". The word "statics" means the study of things that stay fixed, in contrast to "dynamics", the study of things in the process of movement or change. With our stable population calculations, we are comparing what we would see in a country whose growth rate stayed fixed at one value, compared to what we would see in a country whose growth rate stayed fixed at some other value. If the growth rate of India fell toward zero, the population would not be stable and we would see fluctuations in the dependency ratio for a while. The dynamic story would be more complicated than the static story, and it would depend on the details of changing rates. Comparative statics gives us information that is easier to interpret and which tells us about the underlying impact of alternative rates of growth.

Whenever we apply the stable population formula, it is essential to use age groups that are as narrow as the data permit. If we have data for 5-year-wide age groups, it would be wrong to take $_{15}K_0$ to equal $_{15}L_0 \, e^{0r}$. Instead, we split $_{15}K_0$ into $_5K_0 + {}_5K_5 + {}_5K_{10}$ and add up $_5L_0 \, e^{0r}$ plus $_5L_5 \, e^{-5r}$ plus $_5L_{10} \, e^{-10r}$. If we have separate data for ages 0 to 1 and 1 to 5, we should work out $_5K_0$ with $_1L_0 \, e^{0r}$ plus $_4L_1 \, e^{-1r}$.

Often we want to find ratios, and, when we do, the multiplier B in the stable formula does not matter. For counts rather than ratios we need the value of B. For proportions, we have two options. One option is to add up stable population counts for all age groups and use this total population as a denominator for calculating proportions. Another option is available if we have outside information on the Crude Birth Rate b in the stable population. Then we know that the stable proportion aged x to $x + n$ is given directly by $b \, _nL_x \, e^{-rx}$. For the Indian stable population with $r = 0.006$, we have $b = 0.019$. Referring back to Table 10.1, we calculate a proportion of children under age 15 equal to $(0.019) * (13.298) = 0.253$.

Economists often make more-refined calculations applying age-specific participation rates to counts in stable age groups. Instead of counting everyone above age 65 as a dependent, we can multiply each age-group count by the proportion of the age group who are not in the labor force. To study consumption and production, we can multiply each age-group count by an age-specific consumption rate, do the same with an age-specific production rate, and compare total consumption to total production and their relationship to the underlying rate of population growth as it affects the economy.

For India, as we have seen, reductions in counts at young ages are nearly balanced by increases at older ages, when we look at lower growth rates. The net economic effect depends on the costs and productive output of each age group. Costs include education for the young and medical care for the old, as well as a number of other forms of transfers between age groups and generations. Ronald Lee (1994) has developed frameworks for measuring intergenerational transfers and helped lead an international project on National Transfer Accounts reported in Lee and Mason (2011). A collection edited by Laslett and Fishkin (1992) grapples with issues of justice and fairness that come into play. Calculations with the stable population formula provide the starting point for these studies and for much of economic demography.

10.5 The Many Faces of Lotka's *r*

It is desirable to have a way of finding r without relying on computer projections. There turns out to be a handy approximation:

$$r \approx \frac{\log(NRR)}{\mu}$$

This approximation is easy to understand. Lotka's r is the growth rate of the stable population. We start with our usual formula for a growth rate $R = (1/T) \log(K(T)/K(0))$. The NRR is the factor by which the population grows in one generation, so we can substitute it for $K(T)/K(0)$. The cohort mean age of childbearing μ is, roughly speaking, the length of time it takes for the daughter generation to come along, so we can replace T by μ. We end up with our approximation for Lotka's r. Like r, both the NRR and the mean age μ depend only on $_nL_x$ and $_nF_x$ and the fraction female at birth.

This formula is easy to apply. For instance, at the peak of the Baby Boom around 1960, the NRR for the United States was about 1.7. The mean age μ was around 27. We find $r \approx (1/27) * \log(1.7) = 0.019653$. For 2012, we find $r \approx (1/29) * \log(0.95) = -0.001769$.

Does the negative value for r mean that the population of the United States is declining? By no means! Lotka's r is the long-term growth rate that would occur if the rates for 2012 remained in effect for a very long time. The United States is a good example of a population in which the value of r has been negative while the period growth rate has been strongly positive. The United States does not have a stable population.

Although there is no necessary relationship between r and the current growth rate, there is a relationship between r and the Net Reproduction Ratio:

$$r \begin{cases} > 0 & \text{if and only if } NRR > 1 \\ = 0 & \text{if and only if } NRR = 1 \\ < 0 & \text{if and only if } NRR < 1 \end{cases}$$

The approximation for r in terms of $\log(NRR)$ suggests that this relationship ought to be true. A mathematical proof will be sketched later in this chapter. We shall see that there is an exact equation with a unique solution which r satisfies. But there is no direct way to solve this equation, so our approximation is the usual approach.

We sum up our discussion by listing the names and the roles of r. Little r goes by several names:

The intrinsic rate of natural increase. It is intrinsic because it is built into the rates of age specific fertility and mortality without reference to the accidents of age structure. It refers only to "natural" increase from an excess of births over deaths, taking no account of migration.

Lotka's parameter. Although it goes back to Euler, little r became familiar through the work of Alfred Lotka.

The Malthusian parameter. This name, popular in France, can be confusing. Malthus emphasized limits to population growth, whereas r is a rate assuming no Malthusian limits. The name comes from passages in which Malthus also discussed exponential growth without limits.

In evolutionary biology, r is prominent because Darwinian natural selection can often be described as favoring genes which promote vital rates implying higher values of r.

In this section we have emphasized three roles for little r:

- r is the exact growth rate of the stable population.
- r is the long-term growth rate when any initial population is projected forward in time with permanently unchanging rates.
- r is the parameter that appears in the e^{-rx} factor in the formula for the stable age pyramid.

Mathematical demographers also keep in mind two other roles defined and discussed in the next section:

- r is the unique real solution to the Euler–Lotka equation.
- r is the logarithm of the leading eigenvalue of the Leslie matrix divided by the length of the projection step.

* 10.6 The Euler–Lotka Equation

Our approach to Stable Population Theory in Sections 10.3 and 10.4 has been informal. We have observed from the outputs of projections that the proportions in age groups appear to settle down to fixed values when rates of fertility and survival remain constant, but we have not proved that they do. Most proofs require more advanced mathematics. But one fact can be established with elementary arguments. We can show that our formula for a stable age structure does indeed give a stable age structure. We do so in this section, because the demonstration gives extra insight into the nature of stable populations.

Consider, first, how we check whether a given vector of counts in age groups is or is not a stable age distribution for a particular Leslie matrix. For example, let A and K be the following stylized matrix and vector:

$$A = \begin{pmatrix} 0.9 & 0.8 & 0.7 \\ 0.6 & 0 & 0 \\ 0 & 0.5 & 0 \end{pmatrix}; \qquad K = \begin{pmatrix} 4 \\ 3 \\ 2 \end{pmatrix}$$

Is K a stable population vector for A?

For K to be stable, the proportions in the age groups have to stay the same when we project K forward using A, which means that every age group in K has to change by the same factor. Performing matrix multiplication, we find AK is the vector with elements 7.4, 2.4, and 1.5. The first age group increases by a factor of $7.4/4 = 1.85$. The second decreases by a factor of $2.4/3 = 0.8$, and the third by a factor of $1.5/2 = 0.75$. The factors are not the same, so K is not a stable vector.

The largest factor 1.85 is more than twice as big as the smallest factor 0.75. On a log scale, the range from smallest to largest amounts to $\log(1.85/0.75) = 0.90$. If K were a stable vector, the range on the log scale would be zero, since the factors would all come out to be the same.

We now perform the same test on our stable formula, working with symbols instead of with numbers. We apply our expression for the Leslie matrix A to our expression for the stable age vector K. We obtain an expression for the elements of the new vector, which we temporarily call N and which is given by the matrix product AK. We divide each element of the new vector N by the corresponding element of the starting vector K and ask whether the ratios come out to be the same.

We are interested in proportions, so constants like B and ℓ_0 do not matter, and we take $B = \ell_0 = 1$. For legibility, we take the age-group width n equal to 5, but the argument would be the same with any choice of n. The jth age group starts at age $x = jn - n$—in our case, at $x = 5j - 5$. Our stable formula for the jth element of K is a simple one:

$$K_j = {}_nL_x\, e^{-rx}$$

Our formula for the Leslie matrix A is cumbersome, and we only spell out one typical first-row element in full when we write down the product AK which gives our new vector N:

$$
\begin{pmatrix}
\cdots & \cdots & \cdots & (1/2\ell_0)({}_5L_0)({}_5F_{15} + {}_5F_{20}\frac{{}_5L_{20}}{{}_5L_{15}})f_{\text{fab}} \\
\frac{{}_5L_5}{{}_5L_0} & 0 & 0 & 0 \\
0 & \frac{{}_5L_{10}}{{}_5L_5} & 0 & 0 \\
0 & 0 & \frac{{}_5L_{15}}{{}_{10}L_5} & 0
\end{pmatrix}
\begin{pmatrix}
{}_5L_0 \\
{}_5L_5\, e^{-5r} \\
{}_5L_{10}\, e^{-10r} \\
{}_5L_{15}\, e^{-15r}
\end{pmatrix}
$$

The first row, which gives the first age group of our projected population, is the complicated one. We postpone dealing with it and begin with the second row. The second row generates the second element of our new vector N, the projected count of 5-to-10-year-olds after one projection step:

$$N_2 = A_{2\,1}\,K_1 = \frac{_5L_5}{_5L_0}\,{_5L_0} = {_5L_5} = e^{5r}({_5L_5}e^{-5r}) = e^{5r}\,K_2$$

Thus N_2 is obtained from K_2 by multiplying by a factor e^{5r}.

With the third row of A, we find that N_3 is obtained from K_3 by multiplying by the same factor e^{5r}. The quantity $_5L_5$ in the denominator of $A_{3\,2}$ cancels the $_5L_5$ in K_2, leaving $_5L_{10}\,e^{-5r}$ to compare against $K_3 = {_5L_{10}}\,e^{-10r}$. We see that similar cancellations occur in every later age group, yielding the same factor $N_j/K_j = e^{5r}$ for all $j > 1$. Because the factors all come out the same, our candidate formula for K is passing our test and looking promising. But the outcome of our test applied to the first age group is still in doubt.

In order for the first age group to increase by the same factor as the older age groups, we need $N_1 = e^{5r}\,K_1 = e^{5r}\,{_5L_0}$. But the expression we obtain by multiplying out the first row looks quite different at first sight. It is a sum over age groups:

$$N_1 = \sum (1/2\ell_0)({_5L_0})\left({_5F_x} + {_5F_{x+5}}\frac{_5L_{x+5}}{_5L_x}\right)(f_{fab})({_5L_x}\,e^{-rx})$$

We have no hope of turning this sum of terms into the single term $e^{5r}\,{_5L_0}$ by symbolic cancellation. Cancellation works for older age groups, but it does not work for this youngest group. However, all is not lost. When we divide the sum by $e^{5r}\,{_5L_0}$, we obtain the following equation:

$$1 = \sum (1/2\,\ell_0)\left({_5F_x}\,{_5L_x} + {_5F_{x+5}}\,{_5L_{x+5}}\right)(f_{fab})e^{-r(x+5)}$$

The right-hand side of this equation is a function of r. If r is a number that satisfies this equation, then the first age group will increase by the same factor e^{5r} as the other age groups, and the vector K will be a stable vector. We have arrived at an equation for r.

This equation is the Euler–Lotka equation (Lotka's equation for short), the equation we have been anticipating. For a general version, we replace 5 by n. As we shall see, this equation uniquely determines r. For any given set of schedules $_nF_x$, $_nL_x$, and f_{fab}, there turns out to be one and only one real number r which can be substituted for r in the equation to make the sum on the right-hand side add up to 1.

The condition on the first age group is deeper than the conditions on the older age groups which we studied first. With the older age groups, r could be any number. We could plug any value for r into e^{-rx} in the expression for K and symbolic cancellation would make the age-group factors all come out the same. It is only the condition on the new children, the first age group, that requires r to be a particular number, the solution to an equation. This makes sense. The projection of the higher age groups is just a matter of survival, and the fertility rates that help determine the growth rate do not affect it. The formulas for these rows satisfy the required condition for any choice of r. It is only when we require a particular ratio of new children to older people that we arrive at a condition pinning down r.

We have shown that our formula does give a stable age structure, one in which the proportions remain constant when projected forward in time. We have also shown that the factor by which each age group grows in one projection step spanning n years is e^{rn}. Thus the solution of the Euler–Lotka equation is indeed the growth rate of the stable population.

In our approach we have taken our stable population formula and used Leslie matrix multiplication to show it to be correct. We could, instead, have derived our formula by solving successively for each element of K in terms of the preceding one using the second, third, and higher rows of the Leslie matrix. Since the stable age pyramid is only defined up to the constant factor B which determines the total population size, with 10 age groups we would have 10 equations, 9 for determining K_2, K_3 up to K_{10} in terms of K_1 and the tenth for determining r.

In matrix theory, when the matrix product AK produces a vector, each of whose elements is the same multiple of the corresponding element of K, the vector K is called an "eigenvector" of A, and the multiple is called the "eigenvalue". Eigenvectors and eigenvalues may be complex numbers instead of real numbers. But the stable age distribution is a real-valued eigenvector of the Leslie matrix, and e^{rn} is a real-valued eigenvalue.

In the limit as $n \to 0$, we can write $f_x = \lim(_nF_x)(f_{\text{fab}})$ and $\ell_x = \lim {}_nL_x/n$. We obtain the continuous version of the Euler–Lotka equation:

$$1 = \int f_x(\ell_x/\ell_0)e^{-rx}\,dx$$

We can hunt for a solution to Lotka's equation by trying out various values of r. It is convenient to take logarithms, making the left-hand side 0 rather

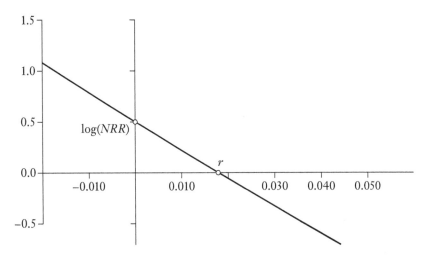

Figure 10.6   Logarithm of Lotka's integral for trial values of r

than 1. In logarithmic form, we are looking for a "root" or "zero" of the equation.

Let us define $Y(r)$ to be the logarithm of the right-hand side of Lotka's equation when we substitute a trial value of r. The true value of r is the value which makes $Y(r) = 0$. From here on in this section we set $\ell_0 = 1$. For the continuous version of Lotka's equation, Y has the form

$$Y(r) = \log \left(\int f_x \, \ell_x \, e^{-rx} \, dx \right)$$

Figure 10.6 shows a graph of $Y(r)$ versus trial values of r for our example with rates for Pakistani women from 2000. The curve is nearly, but not exactly, straight.

The first point to notice from the graph is that $Y(r)$ is a strictly decreasing function of r. We can prove this fact to be true.

$$r_1 \leq r_2 \text{ implies } f_x \, \ell_x \, e^{-r_1 x} \geq f_x \, \ell_x \, e^{-r_2 x}$$

We have weak inequality for all x, since f_x is zero at some ages. We have strong inequality whenever $f_x \, \ell_x$ is strictly positive. If the product is a continuous function of x, there is an interval on which it is positive, so the integral must be strictly decreasing in r. For large negative values of r, Y is large and positive. For large positive values of r, Y is negative— very negative, since the logarithm of zero is minus infinity. We see that the function $Y(r)$ decreases monotonically from positive to negative values. It is a continuous function of r, so it must cross the axis somewhere. The crossing point is the solution to Lotka's equation, the true value of r.

The point where Y passes through the vertical axis at $Y(0)$ is the logarithm of the NRR. If $Y(0)$ is positive, the NRR is greater than 1, implying that the true value of r must be found in positive territory to the right of the axis. If $Y(0)$ is negative and the NRR is less than 1, the true value of r already occurs in negative territory. If $Y(0) = 0$ and $NRR = 1$, then the true value of r is zero. Thus we confirm the relationships already mentioned between the NRR and the sign of r.

Knowledge of the slope of the function Y as it crosses the vertical axis facilitates approximations for the true value of r. In calculus, the slope is found by differentiation:

$$\frac{d}{dr} \log\left(\int \ell_x\, f_x\, e^{-rx}\, dx\right) = \frac{\int (\ell_x\, f_x)(-x)e^{-rx}\, dx}{\int \ell_x\, f_x\, e^{-rx}\, dx}$$

At a trial value $r = 0$, the denominator equals the NRR and the ratio of numerator over denominator is minus the cohort mean age at childbearing μ. In words, minus the slope of the logarithm of Lotka's integral (the right-hand side of Lotka's equation) at $r = 0$ is the cohort mean age at childbearing. A Taylor series like the series in Chapter 1 based on more derivatives has a third term which depends on the standard deviation σ (Greek lowercase *sigma*), the square root of the variance in ages of childbearing in the synthetic cohort:

$$0 = \log(NRR) - \mu r + \sigma^2 r^2 / 2 + \ldots$$

Solving this equation without the third term gives our usual approximation $r \approx (1/\mu) \log(NRR)$. Squaring this quantity, plugging it in for r^2 in the third term, and solving anew gives an approximation that takes variance in ages of childbearing into account:

$$r \approx \frac{\log(NRR)}{\mu} + \frac{\sigma^2}{2\mu}\left(\frac{\log(NRR)}{\mu}\right)^2$$

The Taylor series here is called a cumulant expansion and the solution method is called Reversion of Series, applied early to demographic analysis by Le Bras (1969).

Lotka's equation is the equation which determines little r. With discrete age groups and unit radix, it has the form

$$1 = \sum (1/2) \left({}_nF_x \, {}_nL_x + {}_nF_{x+n} \, {}_nL_{x+n} \right) (f_{\text{fab}}) e^{-r(x+n)}$$

The solution to this equation cannot be written out in symbols the way the solutions to a quadratic equation can. But for any trial value of r, we can find out if that trial value is too high or too low by plugging it into the right-hand side. If the answer is below 1, the trial value is too high. If the answer is above 1, the trial value is too low.

For example, consider our Leslie matrix for mares and fillies from Chapter 5. The ${}_5F_x$ values for $x = 0, 5, 10$ are $0, 0.40$, and 0.30, and the ${}_5L_x$ values are $4.75, 3.75$, and 1.50 with $\ell_0 = 1$. The first term in Lotka's equation is $(1/2) * (0 + 0.40 * 3.75)$, or 0.750 times e^{-5r}. Computing other terms in the same way, we have

$$1 = (0.750) \, e^{-5r} + (0.975) \, e^{-10r} + (0.225) \, e^{-15r}$$

Our approximation $\log(NRR)/\mu$ gives $r \approx 0.077$. Substituting 0.077 into the right-hand side of Lotka's equation, we obtain $0.750 * 0.680 + 0.975 * 0.463 + 0.225 * 0.315 = 1.032$ and $Y(r) = \log(1.032) = 0.032 > 0$, so this trial value is too low. What about a trial value $r = 0.082$? Plugging in gives $Y(r) = -0.007 < 0$, so this trial value is too high. With $r = 0.081$, $Y(r) = 0.0007$, so the true value is just a little below 0.081. At a long-term growth rate of 81 per thousand, our population of horses would be doubling every 8.5 years.

* 10.7 Life Left in Stable Populations

In life, individuals enter at birth and exit at death. They appear out of the womb and they disappear into the grave. If we imagine time running backward, as if we were playing a movie in reverse, individuals would appear out of the grave and disappear into the womb. The events of entrance and exit would look different, but the intervals between them would be the same. Why time does run forward in the world we know is a puzzle for physicists and philosophers.

In a stationary population, the flow of births is the same as the flow of deaths. A birth cohort, as we know, is a group of individuals sharing the same date of birth followed forward through time and increasing age. Age is time counted forward from birth. "Life left" is a name for time counted backward from death. A "death cohort" can be described as a group of individuals sharing the same date of death, followed backward through time and through increasing amounts of life left. Each member of a death cohort exits the cohort when time, running backward, reaches his or her date of birth. On a Lexis diagram, we could draw lifelines for death cohorts with slope -1 running back and up from time of death on the horizontal axis to the event of birth.

The assumption of stationarity makes the sizes of each starting birth cohort and each starting death cohort the same. The distributions of lengths of lifelines for the two kinds of cohorts are likewise the same. If we take our downsloping lifelines for death cohorts on a Lexis diagram and reverse time by flipping the time axis, we obtain ordinary upsloping lifelines with the same distributions of starting points and lengths, statistically indistinguishable from an ordinary Lexis diagram like Figure 2.4. At any point of time, the heights of downsloping lines for death cohorts represent life left, whereas the heights of upsloping lines for birth cohorts represent age. Thus we see that the distribution of life left in a stationary population is the same as the stationary age distribution.

This equivalence from Renewal Theory found in textbooks like Feller (1971, pp. 354–355 and 371) has a long history traced in special cases by Goldstein (2012). Demographers often call it "Carey's Identity". It is a valuable tool for studying populations of creatures in the wild. For example, Carey et al. (2008) study a population of Mediterranean fruit flies of unknown age captured in a season on samples of fruit and living on in the laboratory under controlled conditions. The distribution of life left after capture helps in the reconstruction of the unknown age distribution of free-flying flies in the wild.

In a population that is stable but not stationary, we can still imagine time running backward and still draw backward lifelines for death cohorts. But for any starting time, the size of the starting birth cohort is not the same as the size of the starting death cohort. Person by person, forward lifelines and backward lifelines are the same, but the mix of backward lifelines for individuals selected into the death cohort is not the same as the mix selected into the birth cohort. In a rapidly growing population, the backward lifelines for the death cohort are shorter on average, with more deaths coming from infants, since there are more infants on the scene to die.

Formulas for death cohorts in stable populations are messy but elementary. The ratio in sizes between death cohort and birth cohort at any time t is $d(r)/b(r)$, where $b(r)$ and $d(r)$ are the Crude Birth Rate and Death Rate, respectively, in the stable population for the given value of r. Setting $B(0) = 1$, deaths at age a at time t are given by $D(t, a) = e^{rt} e^{-ra} h_a \ell_a$. In the death cohort starting backward at time t, backward lifelines longer than z are given by $\int_z^\infty D(t, a)\, da$. The proportion of such lifelines is a death-cohort counterpart ℓ_z^b to the survivorship column of the ordinary lifetable. The distribution of life left in the stable population is proportional to $\ell_y^b e^{ry}$. Details are pursued in the exercises.

For questions involving lifelines in stable populations, like the distribution of life left, neither fertility rates nor Lotka's equation come into play. Individuals who are arriving by childbirth might just as well be arriving by magic. Entrances and exits are what matter, not how they come to happen. There is a mini-version of stable theory that dispenses with fertility rates and treats the intrinsic growth rate r and the lifetable ℓ_x values (with unit radix) as primary determinants. For any specified value of r, as long as survivorship actually reaches zero at some extreme age, there is a choice of Crude Birth Rate $b(r)$ which generates stable population proportions $b(r)\ell_x e^{-rx}$. This $b(r)$ is given by $1/\int \ell_x e^{-rx}\, dx$. In any stable population, the growth rate r is exactly equal to the CBR minus the CDR. That is, $b(r) - d(r) = r$. This equality is proved with calculus via the method of integration by parts introduced in Section 9.4 and included among the exercises.

The Stationary Population Identity from Chapter 2 tells us that with $r = 0$ we have $b(0) e_0 = 1$. In a stable population with $r \neq 0$, the product $b(r) e_0$ is not 1, but it does have an interpretation. Each member of the population aged x at time t has seen the population grow by a factor e^{+rx} since birth at time $t - x$. The average factor averaging over the stable population is the integral $\int b(r)\ell_x e^{-rx} e^{+rx}\, dx$ which equals $b(r)e_0$. Thus our product is the average factor of population growth experienced by members of the stable population.

10.8 Population Momentum

Stable Population Theory gives a complete account of the age structure and growth implied by a long period of unchanging vital rates. The next challenge is to understand effects of changes in vital rates. Rates can change in a variety of ways. A case of great interest is a one-time shift from one set of previously unchanging rates to a new set of henceforth unchanging rates. In particular, a rapid drop in fertility can take a rapidly growing more or less stable population into a slowly growing or eventually stationary population. China is a leading example. In its period of high growth up to the 1970s, China acquired an age structure heavily weighted toward younger people. Starting in 1971 with the "Later, Longer, Fewer" policy (later marriage, longer birth intervals, fewer births) and from 1979 onward with the "One Child Policy", birth rates fell rapidly. But the bulge of young people passing through childbearing ages, even with their lower rates of fertility, produced a new bulge of babies and further growth. In the wake of a shift from one demographic regime to another, actual growth rates do not settle down to the level of a new intrinsic growth rate for a considerable time.

The tendency for populations which have been growing to keep growing for many years, even when birth rates and intrinsic growth rates drop, is known as "Population Momentum". A population is like an aircraft carrier. The captain on the bridge, spotting a sandbar far ahead, reverses the propellers, but the carrier keeps moving forward, its momentum carrying it into the bar.

Stable Population Theory leads to formulas for population momentum. The stylized case of a sudden shift from a growing stable population to a stationary one was studied by Nathan Keyfitz and is called the "Keyfitz scenario". (See Keyfitz and Caswell (2005, pp. 196–198).) At time $t = 0$ a previously stable population with some nonzero value of Lotka's r experiences a sudden change in fertility with no change in lifetable. Fertility rates for all age groups rapidly change by the same factor, just enough to make the new NRR equal to 1. The new rates persist for a long time, ultimately creating a stationary age distribution.

The factor by which all the age-specific fertility rates are multiplied in order to achieve a new NRR of 1 is just 1 over the old NRR. If $_nF_x$ are the pre-drop rates, the pre-drop NRR is given by the usual formula: $NRR = \sum {_nF_x} \, {_nL_x} \, f_{\text{fab}}/\ell_0$. Dividing every $_nF_x$ by the NRR has the effect of dividing the sum by the NRR, producing a post-drop NRR of 1. From now on in this section, NRR stands for the pre-drop NRR.

We write $t = -\epsilon$ for a time just before the drop and $t = +\epsilon$ for a time just afterward. Here, ϵ (the Greek letter *epsilon*) stands for some tiny positive

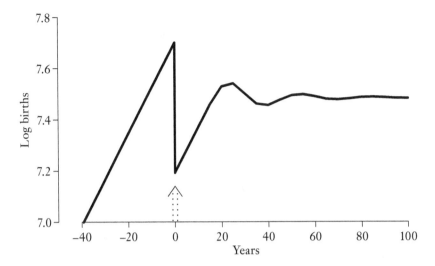

Figure 10.7   Logarithm of births in the Keyfitz scenario

number. Nearly the same women are at risk of childbearing just after the drop as before, but their post-drop rates of childbearing are only $1/NRR$ as high, so births $B(+\epsilon) = B(-\epsilon)/NRR$. On a logarithmic scale, $\log(B(+\epsilon))$ equals the difference $\log(B(-\epsilon)) - \log(NRR)$.

Ups and downs in the logarithm of births over time under the Keyfitz scenario are shown in Figure 10.7. The dotted arrow marks the instant of the drop. On the left, during the stable pre-drop years, births $B(t)$ are increasing exponentially, so $\log(B(t))$ follows an upward-sloping straight-line path. At the drop, $\log(B(t))$ falls by $\log(NRR)$. Afterward, $\log(B(t))$ begins increasing again, as ever-larger cohorts from the stable period reach childbearing ages. But the increase tapers off after half a generation or so, as smaller post-drop cohorts enter childbearing. We expect $\log(B(t))$ after the drop to be bigger than $\log(B(+\epsilon))$ but not to rise back as high as the maximum $\log(B(-\epsilon))$ under the old rates. An approximation recommended to Keyfitz by James Frauenthal supposes that $\log(B(t))$ ultimately settles down about halfway between $\log(B(+\epsilon))$ and $\log(B(-\epsilon))$. Writing U for a future time at which an ultimate stationary population is been achieved, we have $B(U) \approx B(-\epsilon)/\sqrt{NRR}$.

We can convert from births to population sizes. We divide births before the drop by the Crude Birth Rate before the drop $b(-\epsilon)$ to find

$K(-\epsilon) = B(-\epsilon)/b(-\epsilon)$. We multiply births in the ultimate stationary population by e_0 for $K(U) = B(U)e_0$. making use of the Stationary Population Identity which requires $1/b(U) = e_0$. These steps convert our approximation for births into an approximation for the effect of momentum on population size:

$$\frac{K(U)}{K(-\epsilon)} \approx \frac{b(-\epsilon)e_0}{\sqrt{NRR}}$$

An exact formula with age groups of width n is

$$\frac{K(U)}{K(-\epsilon)} = \frac{NRR - 1}{NRR} \frac{b(-\epsilon)e_0}{\mu(1 - e^{-rn})/n}$$

Let us apply the Keyfitz approximation to China. In 1980 the population of China was estimated at about 985 million, with a CBR of about $b(-\epsilon) = 0.024$ and an NRR close to 1.5. Had fertility rates dropped instantly to replacement levels by the same factor at all ages, the ultimate stationary population would have been on the order of $985 * 0.024 * e_0/\sqrt{1.5}$ million. In fact, contrary to the assumptions of the scenario, survival increased a good deal. The value of e_0 in the formula is used to convert from births to population in the ultimate stationary population, so a recent value like 70 years is sensible. The prediction for the ultimate stationary population driven by population momentum would be around 1.350 billion. Because fertility declines have been gradual and have not fully reached replacement levels, population in China has already exceeded even this high level.

The bumps in Figure 10.7 occur about a generation apart from each other. The period of growth before $t = 0$ resembles a baby boom that has echos in a little boom or boomlet among their children and again among their grandchildren. On a graph of $B(t)$ in place of $\log(B(t))$, these echos would show up as waves around the exponential trend. In advanced work, these waves are studied in terms of complex numbers with real and imaginary parts that satisfy Lotka's equation like the real number r. The waves are features of populations with unchanging vital rates during their approach to stability. Population waves have deep connections with the waves that physicists study—ocean waves, sound waves, light waves, radio waves, and particle waves.

The Keyfitz scenario starts with a stable population. Suppose instead that the starting population differs from the stable population determined by its age-specific vital rates. A further approximation by Espenshade et al. (2011)

makes allowance for such differences. The authors suggest projecting the starting population forward with its own vital rates till a stable age structure with intrinsic rate of natural increase r is established at time U. Dividing every age group in that stable population by $\exp(rU)$ gives a kind of stable equivalent to the starting population. The ratio of the size of this stable equivalent to the size of the starting population gives a factor by which to multiply the factor from the Keyfitz scenario for a more general overall measure of population momentum. (There is a formula for calculating this ratio directly from rates.) In this approach, overall momentum is displayed as a product of "nonstable momentum" (the new factor) and "stable momentum" (the Keyfitz factor). Nonstable momentum tends to dominate in more developed countries, and stable momentum in less developed countries.

Population momentum is one of the most important concepts that demographers bring to public policy. In government and among the press it is not widely appreciated that very substantial future increases in human numbers are already built into the present structure of world population. Momentum amplifies the challenges faced by any program for sustainable development.

HIGHLIGHTS OF CHAPTER 10

- Stable populations
- Lotka's r
- The Euler–Lotka equation
- Life Left in Stable Populations
- Population momentum

KEY FORMULAS

$$_n K_x^{\text{stable}} = B(_n L_x / \ell_0) e^{-rx}$$

$$r \approx (1/\mu) \log(NRR)$$

$$1 = \sum (1/2\ell_0) \left(_n F_x \,_n L_x + \,_n F_{x+n} \,_n L_{x+n}\right) (f_{\text{fab}}) e^{-r(x+n)}$$

$$1 = \int f_x (\ell_x / \ell_0) e^{-rx} dx$$

$$\frac{K(U)}{K(-\epsilon)} \approx \frac{b(-\epsilon) e_0}{\sqrt{NRR}}$$

FURTHER READING

A rich variety of applications of stable theory are found in Keyfitz and Caswell (2005), an expansion of the pathbreaking 1978 edition. Stable theory contributes to national transfer accounting in Lee and Mason (2011). More on population waves can be found in Wachter (1991) and more on their counterparts in physics in Georgi (1993).

EXERCISES FOR CHAPTER 10

1. Supplementing the demographic indices for populous countries in Table 2.1, the United Nations WPP (2012) shows Net Reproduction Ratios of 1.10 for Indonesia, 0.86 for Brazil, 1.39 for Pakistan, and 2.21 for Nigeria in 2012. Using values of the synthetic cohort mean age of childbearing of 29 for Indonesia and Brazil and 27 for Pakistan and Nigeria, calculate approximate values of Lotka's r.

2. Based on data for India in 2000 from Table 10.2 with a value for Lotka's r of 0.006, find the ratio of people over 85 to people 65 to 85 in a stable population.

3. Based on data for Togo in 1961 in Table 6.7, with Lotka's r of 0.027205, estimate what proportion of the group of women 15 to 50 are between ages 15 and 25 in a stable population.

4. If the *CBR* in the stable population for Togo in Exercise 3 is $b = 0.050360$, find the proportion aged 15 to 50 among all women in the stable population.

5. Suppose fertility rates in Indonesia, Pakistan, and Nigeria dropped abruptly to replacement levels in 2013 with no change in lifetable and remained at these levels for the foreseeable future as envisioned in the Keyfitz scenario. From information in Exercise 2 and Table 2.1, estimate the sizes of the ultimate stationary populations. Can you apply the Keyfitz formula to Brazil in 2013? If so, what would be the ultimate stationary population there?

6. Data for women in India in 2000 from Table 6.2 along with $_5L_0 = 4648$ are sufficient for writing down Lotka's equation. (These data are for women only and differ from data for both sexes in Tables 10.1 and 10.2.)

Find out whether the alleged value of 0.006 for Lotka's r is above or below the true value entailed by the data.

* 7. The synthetic cohort mean age at childbearing for Indian women in 2000 is estimated at $\mu = 25.730$, and the standard deviation in age at childbearing at $\sigma = 6.856$, with an NRR of 1.17712. How close do approximations based on the NRR and μ and on the NRR, μ, and σ come to the value of r calculated from Lotka's equation?

* 8. A formula for integration by parts is given in Section 9.4. Apply this formula with the functions $F(x) = h_x \ell_x$ and $G(x) = \exp(-rx)$ to prove that the Crude Birth Rate minus the Crude Death Rate is exactly equal to the growth rate r in a stable population.

* 9. Derive an expression for the proportion of those dying above age z among all those dying at time t in a stable population with growth rate r. Among all members of the stable population alive at time t, find an expression for the distribution of life left to them.

* 10. What is the average age of men in a stationary population equivalent to a synthetic cohort with age-specific mortality rates for U.S. men in 2010 from Table 7.1? What is the average length of life left for men to live in this population?

* 11. Let $p(x)$ and $c(x)$ be age-specific rates of production and consumption of goods and services. Let $\mu^P(r)$ and $\mu^C(r)$ be mean ages of production and consumption in a stable population with growth rate r. Show that the derivative with respect to r of the logarithm of the ratio of $\int p(x) \ell_x e^{-rx} dx$ to $\int p(x) \ell_x e^{-rx} dx$ equals $\mu^C(r) - \mu^P(r)$.

* 12. Given a survivorship function ℓ_x with unit radix, let $b(r)$ and $d(r)$ be the Crude Birth Rate and Crude Death Rate in a stable population with growth rate r. Find a Taylor series for the sum $b(r) + d(r)$ up to the term in r^2 expressed as functions of the quantities $\int x^k \ell_x e^{-rx} dx$ for $k = 0, 1, 2 \ldots$.

11

Migration and Location

11.1 Spatial Demography

People are found in places and move from place to place. All the processes we have been studying occur within space as well as across age and time. In this chapter we turn to methods of spatial demography. We leave behind the fiction of closed populations. In open populations, people enter and exit not just by being born and dying but also by crossing borders or changing categories of legal status. Migration across borders is a major component of population growth in many countries, especially the United States, influencing population composition, politics, economics, and social harmony. Great migrations are part of the drama of history, like the Exodus in the Bible, the trans-Atlantic flows of people to the Americas after 1500, refugees from Hitler, World War II, and other wars and famines, guest-worker entrants to the European Union or to the Gulf states. Movements within countries among regions, among places of different kinds, and especially from rural to urban areas likewise shape history and our own experience. Both movements between nations and movements within nations are treated in Section 11.2. In this era of globalization, however, the "space" that each of us inhabits is virtual as well as physical. We are positioned in networks, in social hierarchies, in structures of identity. Demographers, in partnership with geographers, have developed techniques to study such broader kinds of "locations". Section 11.3, by way of example, extends measures for the concentration of residents in cities to measures of concentration of wealth, information, and network connectivity.

Today, people can move from place to place by leaps and bounds, by airplane, ship, car, bus, or train. Prehistoric people moved by foot, step by step, here and there. Techniques for understanding haphazard movement, step by step, so-called "random walks", turn out to have applications throughout migration studies, public health, and forecasting. A few of them are presented in Section 11.4.

In earlier chapters the choice of topics is firmly fixed by tradition. Lifetables have been central to demography for hundreds of years; indices of fertility and marriage and stable theory for fifty. Migration and location are different. There is no standard accepted list of methods to be covered. Among many alternatives, the choice of topics in this chapter has been made with an eye to their importance for future studies, as new technology and new data open up new prospects for spatial demography.

11.2 Flows of People

When studying location, the leading distinction that all of us make is between rural places and urban places, between country life and city life. For most of history, most people were rural. During the last century migration from rural areas to cities accelerated and villages and countryside were transformed into towns, into cities, and eventually into metropolitan areas and so-called mega-cities. The United Nations keeps track of these changes and, using its own definition of "rural" and "urban", announced that urban residents became a majority of the population of the whole world late in 2006. Estimates of total rural and urban population from the United Nations since 1950 are shown as dotted and solid lines, respectively, in Figure 11.1. Around the crossing point in 2006 we see total urban population settling into exponential growth while total rural population continues to grow but at a diminishing rate.

Rural fertility is higher than urban fertility, but differences in birth rates are more than offset by people departing to cities. Much rural-to-urban migration occurs inside countries, like the streams of migrants that have turned Latin American centers like Sao Paulo and Rio de Janeiro into mega-cities. Other components of rural-to-urban migration involve

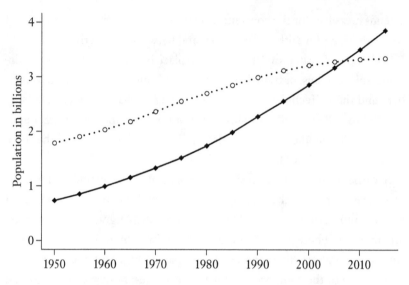

Figure 11.1 Rural and urban world populations

movements across national borders, like workers and families from north
Africa and southern and eastern Europe settling in the industrial centers
of western Europe. Migrants from Mexico to the United States, once
largely seeking agricultural employment, now increasingly head toward
urban areas. We must also bear in mind that people do not necessarily
have to move for the proportion urban to increase. As population grows,
sparse areas become densely settled areas, and places that were classified as
rural can be reclassified as urban. Defining rural and urban is itself a tricky
business (see Section 11.3).

Urbanization is a demographic process that brings opportunities along
with challenges. Economic innovation and development, cultural enrich-
ment, communication, and political engagement have often been stimulated by concentration of people in cities. But rapid urban growth may
strain the provision of basic services, exacerbate poverty, facilitate crime
or social dislocation, and raise what is at stake in the failure or success of
good governance. The nursery rhymes and folklore through which we as
children are introduced to the wider world are still grounded in our rural
past, contrasting with our increasingly urban present.

With regard to demographic methods for studying migration, we start
with a great advantage. Migration is a change of state, and the transition
matrices studied in Chapter 5 lend themselves to projections of rural and

urban subpopulations or to populations classifed by countries or areas of residence. The worldwide changes summarized in Figure 11.1 are made up of many cross-national and subnational components which in practice have to be separated out to be studied. However, the ideas involved can be illustrated by a simple three-state transition matrix A constructed to reproduce the trends seen in Figure 11.1:

$$A = \begin{array}{c} \\ D \\ S \\ U \end{array} \begin{array}{ccc} D & S & U \\ \left(\begin{array}{ccc} 0.950 & 0.032 & 0.000 \\ 0.228 & 0.898 & 0.001 \\ 0.035 & 0.097 & 1.029 \end{array} \right) \end{array}$$

Although we have only two states in our observed data, rural and urban, the projection separates out three states, "D" for deep rural, "S" for semi-rural, and "U" for urban. We discuss this setup in later paragraphs. First, note that we can use our matrix A to project a starting population through $n = 5$-year steps of time in the same way that we have used Leslie matrices in Chapter 5. Let $K(1950)$ be a population vector for 1950 with three elements 1.40, 0.38, and 0.73, giving populations in billions in states D, S, and U. Then the matrix product $A\,K(1950)$ is a vector $K(1955)$. Its elements turn out to be 1.34, 0.66, and 0.84. The projected total rural population $1.34 + 0.66 = 2.00$ billion is a little above the United Nations estimate for 1955 of 1.90 billion, but the projected urban population 0.84 billion is very close to the estimate of 0.85 billion. Further projections to compare with Figure 11.1 and projections into the future are included in the exercises.

Let us interpret the elements in the matrix A. For every person living in deep-rural areas at the start of a projection step, according to the first column of A, we expect 0.950 people at the end of the step still in deep-rural areas, 0.228 showing up in semi-rural areas, and a few, 0.035, in urban areas. In total, the deep-rural population has a high growth rate, allowing for a lot of migration over and above the 0.950 people per person who remain. In the second column, the interesting element is $A_{3,2} = 0.097$. This flow from semi-rural to urban areas is the dominant migration stream. In the third column of A, we see only a little migration back from urban areas to semi-rural areas, 0.001 per person, less in this simplified example than in the real world.

Our setup with two rural states D and S instead of one helps us illustrate two general facts about migration. First, much migration is stepwise migration. Instead of moving all the way from the remote countryside to urban centers in one big leap, for many people it takes several moves, sometimes several generations, to go from what geographers call the periphery to the urban core. In our case, the path from D to U is mostly made up of moves from D to S followed in later steps by moves from S to U.

Second, among all the residents lumped together in one big category like rural, some have higher probabilities of migrating than others. Migration rates are heterogeneous. Our data from the United Nations do not separate out people who tend to be movers from people who tend to be stayers, but splitting the rural category into two states D and S lets us do so. Our setup is an example of what is called a mover-stayer model. The unobserved states D and S are latent or hidden states which we invent to provide for heterogeneity. In our illustration, the latent states are estimated by searching for a best fit to the trends and they let us keep a single unchanging projection matrix A across 60 years or more. Real-world changes in the complicated rates going into our summary measures are absorbed into changes in the unobserved balance between deep-rural and semi-rural populations.

Projection methods can be adapted for studying more detailed migration flows. For instance, we can cross-classify people by age and country or province of residence. Our projection matrix then contains blocks, each block in the form of a Leslie matrix corresponding to a location. Here is an example B with three age groups and two locations, with m for entries for those who migrate and r for those who remain in their starting place:

$$
B = \begin{pmatrix}
r & r & r & m & m & m \\
r & 0 & 0 & m & 0 & 0 \\
0 & r & 0 & 0 & m & 0 \\
& & & & & \\
m & m & m & r & r & r \\
m & 0 & 0 & r & 0 & 0 \\
0 & m & 0 & 0 & r & 0
\end{pmatrix}
$$

When the step size n is small, the chances of being born and changing residence within one projection step is small, and the top-row elements in the off-diagonal blocks can be set to zero. Each subdiagonal element within a block combines probabilities of survival from an age group to the next with probabilities of keeping or changing residence. Reliable age-specific data on probabilities of residential change are rare, especially for country-to-country migration, so fully structured projection matrices like B are hard to estimate though simple to use.

If we label two areas X and Y, then the separate flows of people from X to Y and from Y to X are called *gross flows*. Gross flows are nonnegative numbers. Projection matrices like B estimate gross flows. When we take the flow from X to Y and subtract the flow back from Y to X, we obtain the *net flow*, which may be a negative, zero, or positive number.

For local short-term projections—for example, for counties or school districts making plans 5 or 10 years into the future—it is not practical to build matrices with gross flows between all the places where residents might come or go. Instead, a projection matrix providing for net migration flows can be used, for instance in the following form:

$$
C = \begin{pmatrix} f & f & f \\ s & m & 0 \\ 0 & s & m \end{pmatrix}
$$

In this matrix the entries labeled f represent fertility, and the entries s represent survival in the usual Leslie-matrix fashion. The diagonal entries m, positive or negative, add an allowance for net migration into each age group proportional to the starting population in the age group. There is no deep reason that net migration should be proportional to starting size, but for short time intervals this artificial device can give pretty good answers. The m entries are put along the diagonal so that they are clearly separated from the entries for survival on the subdiagonal that depend on the lifetable. When data on rates of flow are not readily available, a matrix like C can be constructed to reproduce as closely as possible a series of observed vectors of population counts using mathematical techniques of optimization, as indeed we have done to create our global urban–rural projection matrix A.

In more advanced work, demographers and geographers have also developed models for predicting migration flows. An influential approach goes back to a British civil servant Ernst Ravenstein, who in 1871 proposed a model for gross migration flows based on an analogy with Newton's Law of Gravitation. In a modern version of such a gravity model, the flow F_{ij} from location i to location j is given by a function

$$F_{ij} = \frac{G(M_i)^{\alpha}(M_j)^{\beta}}{d(i, j)^{\gamma}}$$

Here, G is a constant, M_i, the analogue of mass in Newton's Law, is the population of the sending location, M_j is the population of the receiving location, $d(i, j)$ is the distance between them, and α, β, and γ are parameters called elasticities which adjust the strength of the influences. In Newton's Law, $\gamma = 2$. The level of α registers the strength of "push factors", while β registers the strength of "pull factors". We shall not treat these models in detail here, but they have many applications and generalizations, not only to flows of people but to trade and influence.

11.3 Concentrations

The uneven distribution of people across the planet, shaped over epochs by resource availability, access, and historical accident, has been amplified over the last century by rural-to-urban migration and the pace of population growth. In this section we take up methods for studying patterns of concentration, beginning with the concentration of people in large urban centers, and then extending these methods to other kinds of concentrations, like the concentration of wealth among a country's citizens.

In 1900 the world's most populous metropolitan areas—London, New York, Paris, Berlin, Chicago, Vienna, and Tokyo—were fairly well defined by their official administrative boundaries. Today, built-up areas of high density sprawl out into each other, making it hard to decide how to draw boundaries or define urban entities. The United Nations has a category called "urban agglomerations". In 2010, the most populous were Tokyo, Delhi, Sao Paolo, Mumbai, Mexico City, New York, Shanghai, and Calcutta, all but two in the southern or eastern hemispheres. Different definitions lead to quite different lists. Medium-size cities, playing a large role

Table 11.1 The 10 most populous U.S. cities in 2010
(populations in millions for incorporated places)

1	New York	8.175	6	Phoenix	1.445
2	Los Angeles	3.792	7	San Antonio	1.327
3	Chicago	2.695	8	San Diego	1.307
4	Houston	2.099	9	Dallas	1.197
5	Philadelphia	1.526	10	San Jose	0.945

Source: 2010 U.S. Census (www.census.gov/popest/data/cities, accessed
26 Nov. 2013).

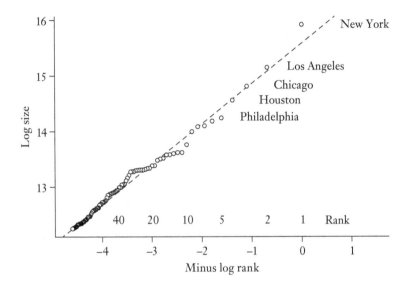

Figure 11.2 Rank-Size Plot for U.S. cities 2010

in urbanization, are likewise identified by varying criteria. At lower densi-
ties, distinctions between town and country have also become fuzzy. There
are administrative definitions, functional definitions with reference to economic networks, and statistical definitions based on density and clustering.

The U.S. Census Bureau publishes population counts for incorporated
places, using an administrative definition which is historical and sometimes
rather arbitrary, but which illustrates a suggestive demographic regularity.
The ten most populous places in the list are shown in Table 11.1.

A Rank-Size Plot for the 100 most populous places in the list is shown in
Figure 11.2. We construct this picture by plotting minus the logarithm of
the rank on the horizontal axis and the logarithm of the population count

on the vertical axis. We see a strong suggestion of a straight line. New York, at Rank 1, plotted at $-\log(1) = 0$ with log population of 15.91, lies above the line, a frequent occurrence for the largest city, called a primate city, in a country or region. But the smaller large cities, down to Spokane at Rank 100, plotted at $-\log(100) = -4.605$, hug the line closely. When ordered sizes of any kind give a straight line on a Rank-Size Plot, they are said to follow "Zipf's law", named after a Harvard linguist who wrote about cities in 1941.

Rank-Size Plots are useful because they give us a way of testing for what is called a power-law or scale-free distribution. Suppose sizes arise out of some random processes, like historical processes driving city growth. Suppose the probability of outcomes X larger than a level x is given by a power of x:

$$\text{Prob}(X > x) = (C/x)^{\alpha},$$

for some constant C, some positive exponent α, and all $x > C$. Then ordered sizes sampled from the probability distribution will tend to lie along a straight line of slope $1/\alpha$ on a Rank-Size Plot. Such a distribution is called "scale-free" because we can change the scale. We select the subset of values above some multiple of C, divide all values of x by the same factor, and find ourselves with the same distribution as we started with. In Figure 11.2, α is 1.378, not too far from $4/3$.

Examples of power laws are found in astronomy, when we replace cities by galaxies and populations by masses. They are found in linguistics, when we replace cities by words in a dictionary and populations by numbers of occurrences in a given body of literature. They are said to be found in the Internet, when we replace cities by websites and populations by numbers of links into the websites. They are found in demographic studies of peer influences, when we replace cities by college students and populations by numbers of acquaintances or Facebook friends. They are found in economics, when we replace cities by households and populations by dollars of household wealth.

With a power-law distribution, there tend to be a few sizes much larger than the bulk of the others, accounting for a large share of total size. When power laws apply to cities, a handful of the largest cities account for a high

Table 11.2   Rural and urban populations in 2010 for the United
Nations Major Areas, ordered by the rural-to-urban ratio

Location	N-Am	L-Am	Europe	Oceania	Asia	Africa
Population	351	589	733	36	4,167	1,033
Urban $U_{(j)}$	288	469	533	25	1,757	413
Rural $R_{(j)}$	63	120	199	11	2,409	620
Urban Y_J	0.083	0.217	0.370	0.377	0.881	1.000
Rural Z_J	0.018	0.053	0.112	0.115	0.819	1.000
Difference	0.064	0.164	0.259	0.262	0.063	0.000

Source: United Nations World Urbanization Prospects (2011), updated 26 April 2012
at esa.un.org/unup.

proportion of all city dwellers. When power laws apply to money, a small subset of all people own a large proportion of total wealth.

Demographers and economists have developed measures for quantifying the degree of concentration of population or wealth or other quantities, measures which take high values when power laws are in the picture. One way to understand these measures is to start with a more general question. When two kinds of people or objects are distributed across some set of locations, how separate are the locations at which each kind is to be found?

We illustrate this approach to concentration with a small example chosen to make calculations simple. The United Nations divides the globe into six "major areas", roughly corresponding to continents, whose urban and rural populations for 2010 are shown in Table 11.2. In the labels, "N-Am" stands for Northern America (not including Mexico), "L-Am" stands for Latin America and the Caribbean, "Oceania" includes Australia, New Zealand, and Polynesia, and "Europe" includes Siberian parts of Russia, making Europe more rural than expected. We examine these data to ask whether rural and urban people are mixed together or well-separated across these large-scale locations.

To quantify the separation between rural and urban populations, we calculate a measure D. In forming Table 11.2, we have already taken the first step in calculating D. That step consists in ordering our locations from least rural to most rural in terms of the ratio of rural to urban counts. The least rural area, N-Am, appears first in the table, with subscript $(j) = (1)$. The parentheses around these subscripts are a customary way of denoting ordered quantities.

The second step in calculating D consists in forming the cumulative proportion Y_J by adding up the first J sizes $U_{(1)} + \ldots U_{(J)}$ and dividing by total size, the sum of all the $U_{(j)}$—in this case 3,485 million. We take $Y_0 = 0$ and calculate $Y_1 = 288/3,485 = 0.083$, along with $Y_2 = (288 + 469)/3,485 = 0.217$, and so forth, up to $Y_6 = 1$. We do the same for cumulative proportions Z_J of the rural counts $R_{(j)}$. These cumulative proportions are shown in the lower middle rows of Table 11.2.

For the third step in our calculation, we subtract to find the differences $Y_J - Z_J$, shown in the bottom row of the table, and we pick out the maximum difference—in this case, 0.262 in the fourth column. This maximum difference is our measure of separation D.

The value $D = 0.262$ is not very high, indicating that rural and urban populations are mixed across all the continents. The measure could have been as high as 1.000, if, say, all urban people had been found in Europe and Asia and all rural people in the other continents. In this example, putting Siberia into Europe makes the urban–rural separation appear less than it would otherwise be. Our measure D is always sensitive to the choice of units of location, but it does not depend on totals for the groups U and R.

A visual sense of the separation measured by D can be gained from a graph like Figure 11.3. We form cumulative proportions of overall population X_J from the first row of Table 11.2. We have $X_1 = 351/6,907$, $X_2 = (351 + 589)/6,907$, and so on. We plot Y_J on the vertical axis against X_J on the horizontal axis and connect the points for the upper (urban) line on the graph. We plot Z_J against X_J and connect the points for the lower (rural) line. The line segments for Asia are much longer than the others, because Asia contains 60% of the world's population. The shading will be described shortly. On the graph, the length of the dashed vertical line is the maximum difference, equal to D. We see that the upper and lower lines are quite close to the diagonal line. The diagonal line would represent a case in which all continents had the same ratio of urban to rural population.

Our measure D is called "Duncan's Dissimilarity Index" after the sociologist Otis Dudley Duncan. An alternative formula for D is given in the

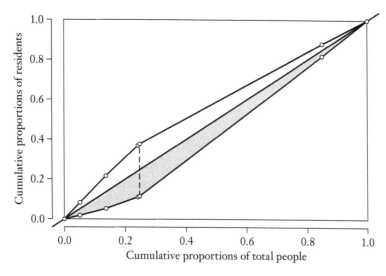

Figure 11.3   Computing indices of separation

exercises. The Dissimilarity Index can be interpreted as the proportion of
people of one kind (say, rural) who would have to move to create an even
spread. The Dissimilarity Index is particularly widely used for the study of
residential patterns by race. In place of rural and urban people, we might
have data on African Americans and other races. In place of continents, we
might look at neighborhoods or Census tracts within a community. High
values of D indicate a high degree of separation between racial groups,
which may be evidence of racial segregation.

We have been comparing the separation between two groups, between
the upper and lower curves on Figure 11.3. We can also compare either
one of the curves on its own to the diagonal. The diagonal represents
a group completely evenly distributed across locations in proportion to
population. Consider the lower (rural) curve. Instead of the maximum
difference between the curve and the diagonal, we can also compute the
area between the curve and the diagonal, the area shaded in Figure 11.3.
We multiply by 2 so that our new measure also falls between 0 and 1. This
measure is called the Gini coefficient G, and the curve being compared to
the diagonal is called a Lorenz curve, often applied to the study of wealth.
For this application, economic demographers treat each household as a
separate "location" and replace the count of rural people by a count of

dollars of household wealth. The Lorenz curve then tells us how much wealth is concentrated in how small a proportion of the whole population of households, and the Gini coefficient is a measure of inequality.

* 11.4 Random Walks

In the children's game of Blind Man's Buff, a child chosen to be "it" starts blindfolded in the center of a lawn and staggers around in random directions every whichway in small steps until he or she runs into another player. Blind Man's Buff gives us a picture of a kind of movement called a random walk with many applications.

In a random walk, the direction of each step is statistically independent of all the others. Knowing about previous steps does not help in predicting the next one. When we have many many tiny tiny steps in every time interval, stepwise motion starts to look like continuous motion, and a random walk is a close approximation to a process called a Brownian motion. The mathematics of Brownian motion is complicated, but one simple formula is easy and useful. We ask how far north or south of the starting point we find "it" after time t. The answer is that this random quantity has the kind of statistical distribution called a Normal or Gaussian distribution. The same is true of how far east or west we find "it". Furthermore, the difference or deviation in position north or south of the center after time t is independent of the deviation east or west.

Let us briefly review some material that may be familiar from courses in statistics. Concentrate on deviations north or south of the center. We play our game over and over (infinitely many times), each time writing down the position after the same elapsed time t. The formula for the resulting Normal distribution tells us that the proportion of games in which the deviation z comes out to be between x and $x + n$ equals the area between $z = x$ and $z = x + n$ under the bell-shaped curve

$$\frac{1}{\sigma \sqrt{t} \sqrt{2\pi}} \exp\left(\frac{-z^2}{2\sigma^2 t}\right).$$

The bell-shaped curve here is the probability density function. As before, the symbol σ is the Greek letter *"sigma"*, which for this Brownian motion is multiplied by the square root of the time t to give a typical value for the deviation from the center, a value called the "standard deviation". The standard deviation is defined to be the square root of the average squared value of the deviation. We expect to find about 95% of cases within two standard deviations on either side of the center.

What is noteworthy is the square root in the expression for the standard deviation. The standard deviation grows like $\sqrt{t}$, more slowly than t. This happens both for north–south and for east–west deviations, and so also for overall distance from the starting point. Since the dimensions north–south and east–west are statistically independent, we can study them separately and then combine them by multiplying probabilities, as one learns in courses in statistics. The constant σ depends on the sizes and rapidity of the underlying steps. If we have a number of individuals each independently taking a random walk from the same starting point, then the Normal distribution gives an idea of how spread out we expect to find them after time t.

For example, we imagine that the first members of our species *Homo sapiens* began spreading out from a starting point in eastern Africa perhaps 150,000 years ago in small individual bands each moving in something like a random walk. We do not know a good value for the constant σ, but, for the sake of illustration, suppose σ was around 3 miles per year. How spread out would we expect to find humans after 10,000 years?

We calculate a standard deviation north–south equal to $3 * \sqrt{10,000} = 300$ miles. Our formula would say that 95% of bands would be found between $2 * 300 = 600$ miles south and 600 miles north of the starting point, and similarly east and west. Ten thousand years is a long time, and 600 miles is not all that far. Random walks spread slowly.

This picture of human dispersion ignores mountains and deserts, food and water, plans and dreams. It also ignores something important to demographers, namely, population growth. Bands of humans did not just move. They died out or grew and split and grew. After what may have been an early burst of growth, reflecting advantages of evolutionary changes that turned *Homo erectus* into *Homo sapiens*, we imagine slow population growth, a little faster where density is modest and slower where human pressure on resources builds. The logistic model introduced briefly in Chapter 1 makes growth respond to density in such a way. It is possible to combine a random walk model for dispersion with a logistic model for growth. Near the center, high population size reins in growth, while locations far away are both receiving migrants and seeing populations swell. Together, these processes can make the highly settled area expand in a "wave of advance" both north–south and east–west not like the square root of t, but more rapidly, like t itself. An application of such a model to the demography of a later period after the beginnings of agriculture is famous from work of Ammerman and Cavalli-Sforza (1985).

Movements do not have to occur in physical space. We can consider quantities like demographic rates moving up and down on a graph in a random walk. In this way our formulas help with demographic forecasting. Randomness in the rate represents uncertainty in the forecast. The approach is called stochastic forecasting, after the Greek word for "dice". Steps in a random walk are added together, so any quantity that tends to change multiplicatively, like population size or a mortality rate, needs to have a logarithm in front of it to make it additive before we introduce a random walk.

Our example is taken from Lee–Carter models for lifetables described in Chapter 7. Consider the logarithm of an age-specific mortality rate like $_5m_{70}$ as it moves up and down on the vertical axis of a graph. If we plot the log-rate against time on the horizontal axis, we see a wiggly line, but a wiggly line with a trend. An ordinary random walk has no trend, but it is easy to insert a trend by adding a nonrandom step in one fixed direction in between every random step. The result is called a random walk with drift.

When a Lee–Carter model is fitted to historical U.S. female mortality rates from 1950 to 2007 and used for projection beyond 2007, as in Section 7.7, we have $\log(_5m_{70})$ starting at -3.8993 in 2007 and changing like a random walk with drift $\mu = -0.01165$ and sigma parameter $\sigma = 0.0125$. The drift equals the estimated Lee–Carter b_{70} constant times the mean of the year-to-year differences $k_{t+1} - k_t$ in the Lee–Carter time-specific parameters. The sigma parameter equals b_{70} times the standard deviation of these differences. Given these values, how uncertain is our forecast of $_5m_{70}$ in 2020?

We calculate as follows: In 13 years the drift brings the mean of the log-rate down to $-3.8993 + 13 * (-0.01165) = -4.0507$. The random walk formula gives a standard deviation for the log-rate of $\sqrt{13} * (0.0125) = 0.04494$. So then 95% of our predictions for the log-rate fall between

$-4.0507 - 2 * (0.0449)$ and $-4.0507 + 2 * (0.0449)$. Undoing the logarithm with an exponential function, some 95% of model predictions for $_5m_{70}$ in 2010 fall between 0.0159 and 0.0190. If the variability in model predictions reflects our subjective uncertainty about the future (something about which philosophers may argue), then there is something like 4 per thousand uncertainty in our guesses regarding $_5m_{70}$ in 2020.

Each rate $\log(_5m_x)$ has its own starting point, its own drift, and its own sigma. At one extreme, we could imagine each log-rate taking a random walk of its own. At the other extreme, we could imagine each log-rate moving in lockstep with the others, taking random steps always in the same directions. Lee–Carter models adopt this latter extreme. They assume perfect correlation between age-specific rates. The real world must lie between the extremes. However, for medium-term forecasts, the lockstep choice seems to work reasonably well. There are other sources of uncertainty not included in these stochastic forecasts, such as uncertainty about the validity of the model and about change-points in historical trends. Imperfect as they are, the systematic indications of uncertainty provided by Lee–Carter models and other stochastic forecasts are an antidote to overconfidence on the part of policy makers and the scientists who advise them.

11.5 GIS and Cartograms

A lot of activity in spatial demography has been stimulated by maps that can be made from computerized Geographical Information Systems or "GIS". From 1990 onward a system of files from the U.S. Census Bureau called TIGER let users plot boundaries of Census tracts and blocks. Satellite-based Global Positioning Systems went on to provide coordinates for locations and boundaries all over the globe, even in places in rural Africa without ground-based surveys. With Google Earth, Internet users can see recent views of almost any place in the world including their own backyards, and quantitative data of many kinds including population statistics can be linked to geographical positions. Such a system, with ever more sophisticated versions, is often called a "Digital Earth".

From the viewpoint of demographic methods, many uses of GIS depend on specific computer software for drawing maps and plotting variables, and there is not so much in the way of general principles to teach. However, one method is general, useful, and fun. It is the construction of cartograms, which can be based on the models of Section 11.4. A cartogram is a map in which boundaries have been moved so that each geographical unit, like a state, has an area on the new map proportional not to its physical area but to its population.

Figure 11.4 is a cartogram for the United States in 2009. States with lots of people like California, New York, and Florida have become bloated, and states with big physical areas but small populations like Montana have shrunk. In place of population, we can draw cartograms that make area proportional to other quantities like energy use or loss of old-growth forest across the globe. Cartograms are valuable not only for visual effect but for allowing demographers to adopt methods from spatial statistics that test for clustering. Cartograms control for the denominators of demographic rates. For example, if we plot the locations of cases of some special kind of cancer on a map, we will naturally see lots of cases where there are lots of people. Do cases also cluster around what might be sources of pollution? On an ordinary map, it is hard to tell. By plotting locations of cases on a cartogram, we control for the density of people, and then we can test for clustering that could reflect causal influences.

The method for constructing Figure 11.4 is an application of random walks. The idea is to sprinkle people over an ordinary map in proportion to their density in each state, that is, to the ratio of population to physical area, state by state. We then let each person move around in a random walk. People move in all directions, but there are more people in Ohio to be moving south to Kentucky than there are people in Kentucky to move north to Ohio. So there is net movement from high-density states to low-density states. As people move, we shift boundaries along with them just enough to keep net migration over the shifting boundary equal to zero. The people drag the boundaries with them. To keep people from spreading out forever, we sprinkle ghosts into the Atlantic, Pacific, Canada, and Mexico with density equal to the average density for the whole United States. The ghosts push back on the boundaries until we arrive at a new map with equal density everywhere. This new map is our cartogram, in which the ratio of population to area is constant. Details involve complicated computer programming, but the idea is easy to understand.

In our examples of random walks and Brownian motion, the drift and the sigma parameter have both been constants. In more advanced work, drift

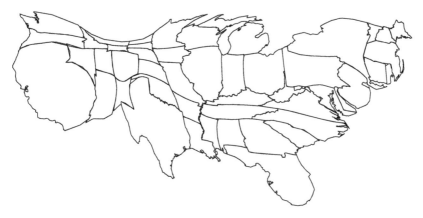

Figure 11.4 Equal density cartogram for the United States

and sigma can depend on location. Such processes are called diffusions. They have many applications throughout demography, including studies of the spread of knowledge, attitudes, and practices in contraception, fertility goals, marriage timing, health promoting behaviors, and a host of other topics, processes to which the nontechnical word "diffusion" is often applied.

HIGHLIGHTS OF CHAPTER 11

- Matrices for projection with migration
- Rank-Size Plots
- Dissimilarity Index
- Random walks
- Stochastic forecasting
- Cartograms

KEY FORMULAS

Power law $\quad\quad$ $\text{Prob}(X > x) = (C/x)^{\alpha}$

Dissimilarity Index $\quad$ $D = \max_{J} \left(\sum_{1}^{J} U_{(j)} / \sum U_{(i)} - \sum_{1}^{J} R_{(j)} / \sum R_{(i)} \right)$

Normal density $\quad$ $(1/(\sigma\sqrt{2\pi t}))\, \exp\left(-z^2/(2\sigma^2 t)\right)$
for random walks

FURTHER READING

Chapters 13 to 15 of Le Bras (2008) give a comprehensive guide to migration models and rank-size relationships. For human dimensions of urbanization, see Montgomery and Reed (2003). The Dissimilarity Index and its competitors are compared by Massey and Denton (1988). The Wave of Advance is presented by Ammerman and Cavalli-Sforza (1985). Construction of cartograms is based on Gastner and Newman (2004).

EXERCISES FOR CHAPTER 11

1. With the matrix A and vector $K(1950)$ from Section 11.2, find the projected counts of rural and urban people for 1980 and for 2010. The U.N. estimates are 2.698 and 1.737 billion for 1980 and 3.325 and 3.505 billion for 2010. How close do the projections come? Go on to project the rural to urban ratio for 2020.

2. A projection matrix C with $n = 15$-year-wide age groups for a certain northwestern U.S. county has entries 0.701, 1.013, and 0.314 in the first row, survivorships 0.968 and 0.943 down the subdiagonal, and allowances for net migration in the diagonal elements $C_{22} = -0.025$ and $C_{33} = +0.035$. With starting populations of women in the three age groups of 85,125 and 79,231 and 74,813, find the projected number of all children under 15 some 30 years from now. (Double the number of girls to allow for boys.) Is this child count greater or less than would be projected without the two diagonal elements allowing for net flows?

3. In preparation for a study of the influence on obesity of having thin friends, a sample of students in a class report how many "Facebook friends" each one has within the class. Here are the unordered responses: 11, 13, 12, 44, 10, 14, 14, 6, 6, 13, 8, 8, 9, 21, 13, 25, 7, 7, 95. Draw a rank size plot and determine whether the count of such friends (called the degree of the friendship network) appears to follow a scale-free distribution.

4. The proportions foreign born for the first five cities in Table 11.1 are 0.372, 0.391, 0.207, 0.287, and 0.116, and for the next five 0.249, 0.144, 0.261, 0.253, and 0.386. Compute the Dissimilarity Index D for the separation between foreign- and native-born across these ten cities.

Draw a plot like Figure 11.3 and estimate the area between the diagonal and the curve for native-born residents. The data on proportions come from the Census Bureau's American Factfinder system for 2010.

* 5. The difference between the upper and lower curves in Figure 11.3 grows for a while as we look from left to right and then declines. Use this feature to prove an alternative formula for D, namely,

$$D = (1/2) \sum \left| \frac{R_j}{\sum R_i} - \frac{U_j}{\sum U_i} \right|$$

In this formula the ordering of locations does not matter.

* 6. From the values of drift -0.011646 and sigma 0.012465 for $\log({}_5m_{70})$ for the Lee–Carter forecast described in Section 11.4, work back to estimates of drift and sigma for the $k(t)$ sequence. For $x = 70, 75, \ldots 90$, the b_x constants are 0.03998, 0.04453, 0.03991, 0.03398, and 0.02311. Furthermore, the 2007 values of ${}_5m_x$ are 0.020256, 0.032840, 0.054792, 0.092982, and 0.163512. Assume that e_{95} remains constant at 4 years. Generate Lee–Carter forecasts for corresponding ${}_5m_x$ values and suitably combine them for a forecast of e_{70} in 2020. Find an interval which you expect to contain 95% of the stochastic predictions from the model.

* 7. This problem explores a simplified version of a Wave of Advance as described in Section 11.4. We measure population size K as a proportion of a constant maximum size that can be sustained in the long term from available resources. At time zero, suppose $K = 10$, with all population members starting out in some one place. Consider some time t. For the first $t/2$ years, suppose total population size remains stationary, each person being replaced on average with one descendant, but suppose each person moves north or south (as in a long valley) in a random walk with $\sigma = 3$ miles per year. Write down a formula for $K(x, t/2)$, the density of people at location x at time $t/2$. For the next $t/2$ years, ignore migration but let population grow according to the logistic formula: $K(x, u + t/2) = 1/(1 + f(x)e^{-gu})$ with $f(x) = -1 + 1/K(x, t/2)$ and $g = 0.010$. Let $Z(t)$ be the location such that $K(x, t) = 1/2$ when $Z(t) = x$, that is, the location where popula-

tion size is reaching half its maximum sustainable level. By plugging in values of t or by studying the formulas, show that for large t the location $Z(t)$ moves outward from the starting point like a fixed multiple of t itself, not a multiple of $\sqrt{t}$.

Conclusion

In this book we have only been able to focus on the most essential demographic methods. What we have covered provides a foundation for studying other fascinating areas. Stable population theory has many further ramifications. Newer work in mathematical demography, not yet comprehensively treated in textbook form, includes random population models, population feedback and homeostatic control, and models with population, economy, and environment intertwined.

In the last few years, active collaboration between demographers, biologists, and geneticists has led to the new field of "Biodemography". Careful measurement and modeling of old-age mortality for nonhuman species as well as humans are leading to new demographic methods as well as new comparative understanding. The rich mathematical theories of population genetics are beginning to be appreciated and employed in demographic research. Genetic mapping may give demographers new tools for characterizing biological heterogeneity in populations.

Much of the day-by-day research that goes on in demography makes use of methods and models which come out of the field of statistics. These include refinements of proportional hazard models, log-linear contingency table models, structural equation models with what are called "identifying restrictions", logistic regression, splines, autoregressive and moving average models for demographic time series, Bayesian approaches to forecasting, and nonparametric likelihood-based models for unobserved heterogeneity. Even a summary would require a separate book.

Computer simulation has become a central tool for studying the demography of kinship. Most models in this book ignore the kinship ties that connect individuals in real populations. Computers can generate artificial populations with specified sets of vital rates and track the relationships of kinship among them. Behavioral responses on the part of individuals and dependencies between rates and the size, composition, and density of populations distributed over locations in physical and virtual space can all be incorporated into simulation modeling, now often called "agent-based modeling".

The excitement of demography comes not only out of the elegance and ingenuity of its methods but also out of the relevance of its subject matter. The future of our planet depends on bringing the growth of our population under control. Many of the methods presented in this book have direct application in monitoring progress toward that goal. Demographic forecasts are a key component of social planning and personal planning. Again, many of the methods have direct application to the difficult problems of prediction. Demographic prediction is so difficult because it depends on the values and choices of human actors—specifically, for example, on the readers of this book. The decisions each of us, and the rest of humans like us, make about marriage, parenthood, and survival-promoting behaviors will create the elements of the Leslie matrices of the future, write the script for the march of cohorts up the world's Lexis diagram, and empower the Renewal Equation to do its work.

Appendix A

Sources and Notes

All calculations are by the author unless otherwise stated. Data from Demographic and Health Surveys (DHS) were extracted by Romesh Silva for Tables 4.7 and 6.6 and by Tracy Brunette for Table 4.5 and data from the Health and Retirement Study (HRS) for Section 8.6 by Amal Harrati, replacing earlier hazard estimates computed by Sarah Zureick. Data for Berlin in Table 6.4 are a personal communication from Patrick Galloway from his studies of Prussian administrative sources. Tables in Chapter 4 for the cohort of U.S. women born in 1934 are taken from a reconstruction using the SOCSIM microsimulation program drawing on the sources and methods detailed in Wachter (1997). Projections for the figures in Chapter 10 rely on data from the United Nations WPP (2003). Futoshi Ishii pointed out the exact formula for population momentum in Section 10.8. Webb Sprague proposed the matrix formulation for net migration in Section 11.2. Kelsey Merriam gave advice about horses for Section 5.5. Andrew Noymer contributed many improvements. Sources of data from the Internet are cited with abbreviations as follows:

DHS   Demographic and Health Surveys, U.S. Agency for International
           Development portal
           www.measuredhs.com

HFD   Human Fertility Database
           www.humanfertility.org

HMD   Human Mortality Database
           www.mortality.org

HRS	Health and Retirement Study, National Institute on Aging
	hrsonline.isr.umich.edu
IDB	International Data Base of the U.S. Census Bureau
	www.census.gov/population/international/data/idb
PRB	World Population Data Sheet of the Population Reference Bureau
	www.prb.org
WPP	United Nations World Population Prospects
	esa.un.org/wpp

Appendix B

Useful Formulas

Growth Rate: $R = (1/T) \log(K(T)/K(0))$

Exponential growth: $K(t) = K(0)e^{Rt}$

Linear regression slope: $\dfrac{\text{mean}(X * Y) - \text{mean}(X) * \text{mean}(Y)}{\text{mean}(X * X) - \text{mean}(X) * \text{mean}(X)}$

Linear regression intercept: $\text{mean}(Y) - (\text{slope}) * \text{mean}(X)$

Exponential slope: $\dfrac{d}{dx}\alpha e^{\beta x} = \alpha \beta e^{\beta x}$

Exponential area: $\int_a^b \alpha e^{\beta x} dx = (\alpha/\beta)(e^{\beta b} - e^{\beta a})$

Survivorship: $\ell_{x+n} = \ell_x(1 - {}_nq_x) = \ell_x - {}_nd_x$

Interval conversions: $(1 - {}_1q_x)^n = 1 - {}_nq_x$

Person-Years Lived: ${}_nL_x = (n)(\ell_{x+n}) + ({}_na_x)({}_nd_x)$

Lifetable death rate: ${}_nm_x = {}_nd_x/{}_nL_x$

Remaining person-years: $T_x = {}_nL_x + {}_nL_{x+n} + {}_nL_{x+2n} + \cdots$

Expectation of further life: $e_x = T_x/\ell_x$

Annuity price: $\dfrac{B}{\ell_x}\left(\dfrac{{}_nL_x}{(1+i)^{n/2}} + \dfrac{{}_nL_{x+n}}{(1+i)^{n+n/2}} \cdots + \dfrac{{}_\infty L_{\text{xmax}}}{(1+i)^{\text{xmax}-x+e_{\text{xmax}}}}\right)$

Hazard rate: $h_x = -(1/n)\ \log(\ell_{x+n}/\ell_x)$

Survival from hazards: $\ell_{x+n} = \ell_x\, e^{-h_x\, n}$

Gompertz model: $h_x = \alpha e^{\beta x}\ ;\quad \ell_x = \exp\left((-\alpha/\beta)(e^{\beta x} - 1)\right)$

Age-Specific Death Rate: ${}_nM_x = {}_nD_x\ /\ ({}_nK_x\, T)$

Period lifetable: ${}_nq_x = \dfrac{(n)({}_nM_x)}{1 + (n - {}_na_x)({}_nM_x)}$

Age factors: ${}_1a_0 = 0.07 + 1.7({}_1M_0)\ ;\quad {}_4a_1 = 1.5\ ;\quad {}_\infty a_x = 1/({}_\infty M_x)$

Brass logit system: $\ell_x = \dfrac{1}{1 + \exp(-2\alpha - 2\beta Y_x)}$

Brass estimation: $\alpha + \beta Y_x = (1/2)\ \log(\ell_x/(1 - \ell_x))$

In the presence of other causes: ${}_nq_x^{\text{A}} = (s^{\text{A}})\, ({}_nq_x)$

In the absence of other causes: ${}_nq_x^{\text{A*}} = 1 - (1 - {}_nq_x)^{s^{\text{A}}}$

Coale-Trussell model: ${}_nF_x^{\text{marital}} = M\, n(x)\ \exp(-m\, v(x))$

Princeton Indices:

$$I_f \approx I_g I_m\ ;\quad I_f = \dfrac{B^{\text{overall}}}{\sum ({}_5K_x)({}_5F_x^{\text{Hutt}})}\ ;\quad I_g = \dfrac{B^{\text{marital}}}{\sum ({}_5K_x^{\text{married}})({}_5F_x^{\text{Hutt}})}$$

SMAFM: $\sum (n)\, (1 - PEM_x/PEM_{\text{ult}})$

Hernes model: $K(t) = 1/(1 + 1/(k\, a^{(b^t)}))$

Leslie matrix top row: $\dfrac{{}_nL_0}{2\ell_0}\left({}_nF_x + {}_nF_{x+n}\dfrac{{}_nL_{x+n}}{{}_nL_x}\right) f_{\text{fab}}$

Leslie matrix subdiagonal: $\quad \dfrac{_nL_{x+n}}{_nL_x}$

Lotka's Equation: $\quad 1 = \sum \dfrac{1}{2\ell_0} \left(_nF_x\,_nL_x + _nF_{x+n}\,_nL_{x+n}\right) (f_{\text{fab}})\, e^{-r(x+n)}$

Stable age pyramid: $\quad _nK_x^{\text{stable}} = B \left(_nL_x/\ell_0\right) e^{-rx}$

Stable proportions: $\quad _nK_x/_\infty K_0 = b \left(_nL_x/\ell_0\right) e^{-rx}$

Lotka's Parameter: $\quad r \approx \log(\text{NRR})/\mu$

Momentum: $\quad \dfrac{K(U)}{K(-\epsilon)} = \dfrac{\text{NRR} - 1}{\text{NRR}}\, \dfrac{b(-\epsilon)\, e_0}{\mu\,(1 - e^{-rn})\,/n} \approx \dfrac{b(-\epsilon) e_0}{\sqrt{\text{NRR}}}$

Duncan Dissimilarity Index: $\quad D = \max \left(\dfrac{\sum_1^J U_{(j)}}{\sum_1^n U_{(j)}} - \dfrac{\sum_1^J R_{(j)}}{\sum_1^n R_{(j)}} \right)$

Bibliography

Allard, M., Lebre, V., and Robine, J.-M. (1994). *Les 120 Ans De Jeanne Calment: Doyenne De L'Humanité*. Le cherche midi, Paris.

Ammerman, A. J., and Cavalli-Sforza, L. L. (1985). *The Neolithic Transition and the Genetics of Populations in Europe*. Princeton University Press, Princeton, NJ.

Arthur, W. B., and Vaupel, J. (1984). Some general relationships in population dynamics. *Population Index* **50**, 214–255.

Barbi, E., Bertino, S., and Sonnino, E., editors (2004). *Inverse Projection Techniques: Old and New Approaches*. Springer Verlag, Berlin.

Barbi, E., Bongaarts, J., and Vaupel, J. W., editors (2008). *How Long Do We Live?* Springer Verlag, Berlin.

Bennett, N. G., and S. Horiuchi (1981). Estimating the completeness of death registration in a closed population, *Population Index* **47**(2), 207–221.

Bongaarts, J., and Bulatao, R., editors (2000). *Beyond Six Billion*. National Academy Press, Washington, DC.

Bongaarts, J., and Feeney, G. (1998). On the quantum and tempo of fertility. *Population and Development Review* **24**, 271–291.

Bongaarts, J., and Feeney, G. (2002). How long do we live? *Population and Development Review* **28**(1), 13–29.

Bongaarts, J., and Potter, J. (1983). *Fertility, Biology, and Behavior*. Academic Press, New York.

Bongaarts, J., Burch, T., and Wachter, K. W., editors (1987). *Family Demography: Methods and Their Applications*. Clarendon Press, Oxford, England.

Brass, W. (1974). Perspectives in population projection. *Journal of the Royal Statistical Society, series A* **137**, 532–583.

Canudas-Romo, V., and Schoen, R. (2005). Age-specific contributions to changes in the period and cohort life expectancy. *Demographic Research* **13**(3), 63–82.

Carey, J. R., Papadopoulous, N. T., Müller, H.-G., Katsoyannos, B. I., Kouloussis, N. A., Wang, J.-L., Wachter, K., Yu, W., and Liedo, P. (2008). Age structure changes and extraordinary life span in wild medfly populations. *Aging Cell* **7**, 426–437.

Chiang, C. L. (1968). *Introduction to Stochastic Processes in Biostatistics*. John Wiley and Sons, New York.

Coale, A., and Demeny, P. (1983). *Regional Model Life Tables and Stable Populations*, second edition. Academic Press, New York.

Coale, A., and Trussell, J. (1974). Model fertility schedules. *Population Index* **40**, 185–258.

Coale, A., and Watkins, S., editors (1986). *The Decline of Fertility in Europe*. Princeton University Press, Princeton, NJ.

Cohen, J. (1995). *How Many People Can the Earth Support?* W.W. Norton and Company, New York.

David, P., Mroz, T., Sanderson, W., Wachter, K. W., and Weir, D. (1988). Cohort parity analysis: Statistical estimates of the extent of fertility control. *Demography* **25**, 163–188.

Demeny, P., and McNicoll, G., editors (2003). *The Macmillan Encyclopedia of Population*. Thompson-Gale, New York.

Edwards, R., and Tuljapurkar, S. (2005). Inequality in life spans and a new perspective on mortality convergence across industrialized countries. *Population and Development Review* **31**(4), 645–674.

Ellison, P. T. (2001). *On Fertile Ground: A Natural History of Human Reproduction*. Harvard University Press, Cambridge, MA.

Espenshade, T. J., Oligati, A. S., and Levin, S. A. (2011). On nonstable and stable population momentum. *Demography* **48**(4), 1581–1599.

Ewbank, D. C., de Leon, J. G., and Stoto, M. (1983). A reducible four-parameter system of model life tables. *Population Studies* **37**, 91–104.

Feller, W. (1971). *An Introduction to Probability and its Applications*, volume 2. John Wiley and Sons, New York.

Floud, R., Wachter, K., and Gregory, A. (1990). *Height, Health, and History: Nutritional Status in the United Kingdom, 1750–1980*. Cambridge University Press, Cambridge, England.

Floud, R., Fogel, R. W., Harris, B., and Hong, S. C. (2011). *The Changing Body: Health, Nutrition, and Human Development in the Western World since 1700*. Cambridge University Press, Cambridge, England.

Gastner, M. T., and Newman, M. E. J. (2004). Diffusion-based method for producing density-equalizing maps. *PNAS* **101**(20), 7499–7504.

Georgi, H. M. (1993). *The Physics of Waves*. Prentice Hall, Englewood Cliffs, NJ.

Glass, D., and Eversley, D. E. C., editors (1965). *Population in History*. Aldine Publishing Company, Chicago, IL.

Goldstein, J., and Wachter, K. W. (2006). Relationships between period and cohort life expectancy: Gaps and lags. *Population Studies* **60**, 257–269.

Goldstein, J. R. (2012). Historical addendum to 'life lived equals life left in stationary populations'. *Demographic Research* **26**(7), 167–172.

Goldstein, J. R., and Kenney, C. T. (2001). Marriage delayed or marriage forgone? New cohort forecasts of first marriage for U.S. women. *American Sociological Review* **66**(4), 506–519.

Guillot, M. (2003). The cross-sectional average length of life (CAL). *Population Studies* **57**, 41–54.

Hajnal, J. (1953). Age at marriage and proportions marrying. *Population Studies* **7**, 111–136.

Hill, M., Preston, S., and Rosenwaike, I. (2000). Age reporting among white Americans aged 85+. *Demography* **37**, 175–186.

Hummer, R. A., Rogers, R. G., Nam, C. B., and Ellison, C. G. (1999). Religious involvement and U.S. adult mortality. *Demography* **36**, 273–285.

Johnson-Hanks, J., Bachrach, C., Morgan, S. P., and Kohler, H.-P. (2011). *Understanding Family Change and Variation: Toward a Theory of Conjunctural Action.* Springer, New York.

Keyfitz, N., and Caswell, H. (2005). *Applied Mathematical Demography*, third edition. Springer, New York.

Keyfitz, N., and Flieger, W. (1968). *World Population: An Analysis of Vital Data.* University of Chicago Press, Chicago, IL.

Keyfitz, N., and Flieger, W. (1990). *World Population Growth and Aging.* University of Chicago Press, Chicago, IL.

Knodel, J. (1983). Natural fertility: Age patterns, levels, and trends. In R. Bulatao and R. D. Lee, editors, *Determinants of Fertility in Developing Countries*, volume 1. National Academy Press, Washington, DC.

Kohler, H.-P. (2001). *Fertility and Social Interaction: An Economic Perspective.* Oxford University Press, Oxford, England.

Laslett, P. (1971). *The World We Have Lost*, second edition. Methuen, London.

Laslett, P., editor (1973). *The Earliest Classics: Graunt and King.* Gregg International, London.

Laslett, P. (1977). *Family Life and Illicit Love in Earlier Generations.* Cambridge University Press, Cambridge, England.

Laslett, P., and Fishkin, J., editors (1992). *Justice between Age Groups and Generations.* Yale University Press, New Haven, CT.

Le Bras, H. (1969). Retour d'une population à l'état stable après une catastrophe. *Population* **24**, 861–896.

Le Bras, H. (2000). *Naissance de la Mortalité.* Gallimard Le Seuil, Paris.

Le Bras, H. (2008). *The Nature of Demography.* Princeton University Press, Princeton, NJ.

Lee, R. D. (1987). Population dynamics of humans and other animals. *Demography* **24**(4), 243–465.

Lee, R. D. (1994). The formal demography of population aging, transfers, and the economic life cycle. In L. Martin and S. Preston, editors, *Demography of Aging*, National Academy Press, Washington, DC.

Lee, R. D., and Carter, L. (1992). Modeling and forecasting the time series of U.S. mortality. *Journal of the American Statistical Association* **87**, 659–671.

Lee, R. D., and Mason, A., editors (2011). *Population Aging and the Generational Economy*. Edward Elgar, Cheltenham, England.

Livi-Bacci, M. (1971). *A Century of Portuguese Fertility*. Princeton University Press, Princeton, NJ.

Livi-Bacci, M. (2012). *A Concise History of World Population*, fifth edition. Wiley-Blackwell, New York.

Massey, D., and Denton, N. (1988). The dimensions of residential segregation. *Social Forces* **67**, 281–315.

McKendrick, A. G. (1926). Applications of mathematics to medical problems. *Proceedings of the Edinburgh Mathematical Society* **44**, 98–130.

Montgomery, M., and Reed, H., editors (2003). *Cities Transformed*. National Academies Press, Washington, DC.

Namboodiri, K., and Suchindran, C. M. (1987). *Life Table Techniques and Their Applications*. Academic Press, New York.

Oeppen, J., and Vaupel, J. W. (2002). Broken limits to life expectancy. *Science* **296**, 1029–1031.

Preston, S., and Coale, A. (1982). Age structure, growth, attrition, and accession: A new synthesis. *Population Index* **48**, 215–259.

Preston, S., Heuveline, P., and Guillot, M. (2001). *Demography: Measuring and Modeling Population Processes*. Blackwell Publishing, Oxford, England.

Robine, J.-M., and Vaupel, J. W. (2001). Supercentenarians, slower ageing individuals or senile elderly? *Experimental Gerontology* **36**, 915–930.

Rohde, D. L. T., Olson, S., and Chang, J. T. (2004). Recent common ancestors in structured populations. *Nature* **431**, 562–566.

Ryder, N. (1964). The process of demographic translation. *Demography* **1**(1), 74–82.

Schoen, R. (1988). *Modeling Multigroup Populations*. Plenum Press, New York.

Smith, D. P., and Keyfitz, N. (2013). *Mathematical Demography: Selected Papers*, second, revised edition, edited by Kenneth W. Wachter and Hervé Le Bras. Demographic Monographs. Springer, Berlin.

Strauss, W., and Howe, N. (1991). *Generations*. Quill Press, William Morrow, New York.

Tuljapurkar, S., Li, N., and Boe, C. (2000). A universal pattern of mortality decline in the G7 countries. *Nature* **405**, 789–792.

Vaupel, J. W., Manton, K. G., and Stallard, E. (1979). The impact of heterogeneity in individual frailty on the dynamics of mortality. *Demography* **16**, 439–54.

Wachter, K. W. (1980). Ancestors at the Norman conquest. In B. Dyke and W. Morrill, editors, *Genealogical Demography*, Academic Press, New York.

Wachter, K. W. (1986). Ergodicity and inverse projection. *Population Studies* **40**, 275–287.

Wachter, K. W. (1991). Elusive cycles: Are there dynamically possible Lee–Easterlin models for U.S. births? *Population Studies* **45**, 109–135.

Wachter, K. W. (1997). Kinship resources for the elderly. *Philosophical Transactions of the Royal Society of London, series B* **352**, 1811–1817.

Wachter, K. W. (2005). Tempo and its tribulations. *Demographic Research* **13**(9), 201–222.

Wachter, K. W. (2014). Population heterogeneity in the spotlight of biodemography. In P. Kreager, B. Winney, S. Ulijaszek, and C. Capelli, editors, *Population in the Human Sciences: Concepts, Models, Evidence*. Oxford University Press, Oxford, England.

Wrigley, E. A. (1977). Births and baptisms. *Population Studies* **31**, 281–312.

Wrigley, E. A., and Schofield, R. (1981). *The Population History of England*. Oxford University Press, Oxford, England.

Wrigley, E. A., Davis, R., Oeppen, J., and Schofiled, R. (1997). *English Population History from Family Reconstitution, 1580–1837*. Cambridge University Press, Cambridge, England.

Yashin, A. I., Iachine, I. A., and Begun, A. S. (2000). Mortality modeling: A review. *Mathematical Population Studies* **8**(4), 305–32.

Zhang, Z., and Vaupel, J. W. (2009). The age separating early deaths from late deaths. *Demographic Research* **20**(29), 721–730.

Index